EXPERIENTIAL PHILOSOPHICAL PRACTICE
Beyond Philosophical Posturing

José Barrientos Rastrojo

Experiential Philosophical Practice: beyond philosophical posturing
by José Barrientos-Rastrojo

This book first published in 2021

ISBN: 9798540805834
Translator: Thomas MacFarlane
Academic editor: Russian Association for Philosophical Practice, Russia

This book has been translated thanks to a grant awarded by the Vice-Rectorate for Research of the University of Seville in 2020 (Reference IV.11).2ª

For Ana and *my* Mexican friends:
"I remain in this land so beautiful and so calm because I have
found songs, caresses and solace."

However, whether someone is an intellectual or not is manifested above all in his relationship to his own work and to the societal totality of which it is a part. This relationship, not the work in specialized domains like epistemology, ethics, or even the history of philosophy, is what constitutes the essence of philosophy in the first place[1]

It might even transpire that by attempting to inject some health into a 'sick' society, philosophy itself would experience the beneficial effects of its own therapy[2]

---

[1] Theodor Adorno, (2005), *Critical Models: Interventions and Catchwords* (New York: Columbia University Press, 2005), 21–2.
[2] César Moreno Márquez, "De ida y por principio: no sin Fenomenología. Terapia filosófica y mundo de la vida," *Revista Internacional de Filosofía Aplicada HASER* 11 (2020): 168.

TABLE OF CONTENTS

FOREWORD

1. Zero *versus* Academia

Zero, a young vagrant with an invisible face, sensed our bodies rushing down the steps of the "Hidalgo" subway station in Mexico City. Some of us came from Reforma, others from the Alameda Central and the last were returning home for more roll sandwiches to sell on the street stalls. He had not eaten for days, but this time he had been unable to slake his hunger with Resistol:[3] the kid who sold it to him had believed that the human scum before his eyes did not deserve the ambrosia that he peddled. Fortunately, Crybaby had decided to be compassionate with Zero: her hand had drawn near and, with it, any appetite for life or food had disappeared. He had thus been transformed into a purely contemplative act: he perceived the urgency in the faces without the ability to judge. He thought that a fetus in its mother's womb must have felt the same way as he did: swimming in darkness and wishing that the amniotic fluid were infinite. For that reason, he knew that the cycle was drawing to a close: the sun had once risen for his eyes and now the time had come to extinguish them. He only hoped that on the other side they did not receive him with a ferocious thrashing, since he had already had his share.

A sudden shudder interrupted his last moments: some mad pedestrian had decided to cut short his superlative meditation by coming *too close*. Like a cornered animal, he sprang backwards and thus knew that he could still move his legs. He was terrified, for he recalled that light-haired young man in his reverie, perhaps a moment before he had walked down the stairs and was now walking back up them .... The light-haired young man offered him a double bun sandwich and a bottle of water, while he looked at his ankle and his heart, blackened by the vast city. Zero's pre-death trepidation prevented any dialogue. A second later, he recovered and made a gesture of thanks. The light-haired young man asked him his name, what he could do for him, if he could think of something else that he could bring him. He did not know how to reply. Without that food, he could have returned to the maternal womb sooner. However, his body and the light-haired young man had united to delay that step. Finally, the light-haired young man walked off

---

[3] The leading brand in the Mexican adhesives industry.

wondering whether Honneth's philosophy of disrespect or if Honneth himself would have stopped to "offer a smile" or "welcoming gesture" at that midday of the afflicted ankle. Some days afterwards, the light-haired young man returned to Spain, thinking that perhaps he should lay down a gauntlet on social media that really brought about a change or, at least, hindered the work of the grim reaper. Some weeks later, he continued to ponder on the possibility that philosophy might help the zeros to become ones or, at least, zeros with a decimal point. Several months later, he returned to Mexico, Brazil and Colombia where he discovered more zeros and wanted to be zero or nothing … or, at least, to spend some time among zeros, for he was tired of being someone and of a philosophy that had become mere *posturing*.

The ideas in this book emerged when, a few decades ago, José Ordóñez and Francisco Macera, two good friends of mine and better philosophers, introduced me to a way of philosophizing that deployed its essence in scarcely known contexts. It was philosophical orientation, as they called it, or philosophical guidance, consulting or counseling. With time, I opted for the term "philosophical practice" (*Filosofía Aplicada*), but that is neither here nor there.[4] My first contacts with the discipline were made through Peter Raabe, Tim Lebon and Lou Marinoff, but Ran Lahav, Lydia Amir and Schlomit Schuster, among others, also led me to a logical-argumentative and, in part, pragmatic approach to it. Slowly but surely, I discovered its constraints, which I began to set out at conferences and in papers.[5]

---

[4] I have explained the reasons behind this designation in previous works, for example, José Barrientos-Rastrojo, *Introducción al asesoramiento y la orientación filosófica* (Sevilla; X-XI, 2003), 197–200.

[5] Some examples of my work include the following: José Barrientos-Rastrojo, "Del pensar zambranista a la filosofía poiética en la consulta filosófica," in *Philosophers as Philosophical Counselors*, ed. José Barrientos-Rastrojo (Sevilla: X-XI, 2006), 207–21; "Philosophical Counseling as Poietic Philosophy," *Philosophical Practice* 3 (2006): 17–27; "El atardecer del Pensamiento Crítico. Disquisiciones poético-zambranistas sobre el *Critical Thinking*," *Proyectos de Vida* 3 (2007): 22–27; *Resolución de conflictos desde la Filosofía Aplicada y desde la Mediación* (Lisboa-Madrid: Universidad Católica Portuguesa – Visión

In contrast, the faculty remained unchanged. Except for the island that the ETOR group had created at my university, it still refused to except this facet of the discipline, displaying an incomprehensible and painful indifference. It should be noted that it was not that disdain which was saddening, but the belligerence with which the critics launched their attacks and their jaundiced inability to offer an informed justification for their tirades. Years later, I have had the joy of having companions, like José Antonio Marín Casanova, who have offered similar criticism, but so affectionately that they have stimulated dialogue, as their esteemed Richard Rorty proposed.

Notwithstanding this, the general posture of academia seemed implausible for two reasons. Firstly, because of the lack of acuity of their criticisms, often indulging in the straw man or *tu quoque* fallacy. On the other hand, the reading of Pierre Hadot or his Stoic

---

Libros, 2012); "La filosofía aplicada desde el pensamiento crítico y desde la racionalidad extendida. Del espíritu del cartesianismo y el hegelianismo al del unamunismo y el zambranismo," in *Temas de hoje. Temas de sempre. Educaçao, ética e filosofia prática*, coord. Eugénio Oliveira (Braga: APEFP, 2012), 152–77; "Fronteras analíticas de la racionalidad social contemporánea," *Sociología y tecnociencia* 3, no. 2 (2013): 71–88; "My involvement in Philosophical Practice," in *Philosophical Practice. Five Questions*, eds. Jeanette Bresson Ladegaard Knox and Jan Kyrre Olsen Friis (Copenhagen: Automatic Press – Vince INC, (2013), 15–32; "An *Experience* workshop with groups. Theory and practice," in *The Socratic Handbook*, ed. Michael Noah Weiss (Zürich: Lit Verlag, 2015), 375–83; "Experience and anagogic hermeneutic of symbol in Philosophical practice," *Journal of Humanities Therapy* 6, no. 1 (2015): 21–47; "L'orientamento esperienziale nella Filosofia Applicata como ampliamento della tendenza logico-argomentativa," *Rivista Italiana di Counseling Filosofico* 11 (2015): 9–31; "L'Educazione e la Filosofia Esperienziale Applicata come ricerca dell'originario. Da Maria Zambrano a Kitaro Nishida," in *La Pratica filosófica: una questione di dialogo. Teorie, proggeti ed esperienze*, eds. Elisabetta Zamarchi, Luca Nave and Giancarlo Marinelli (Turin: Carta e Penna, 2016), 21–9; "Philosophical practice as experience and travel," *Socium i vlast'* 4, no. 78 (2019): 29–44.

.

sources highlighted, as Ran Lahav has noted, that what was being put into practice was a new version of an old tradition. Moreover, Antón Pacheco has described, with his anagogic hermeneutics, how truths are accessed in an experiential fashion. Thus, philosophical practice could be an expression or incorporation of idealistic conditions in which philosophy is divided into classes, as will be explained throughout these pages. This being so, the objective of philosophical practice did not, or at least should not, deviate from the lines of authentic philosophy. Indeed, there were approaches that would not be to the taste of some theoreticians, just as Heidegger had difficulties in seeing eye to eye with Carnap, but to accept the outright rejection of the discipline involved falling into a new fallacy: undue overgeneralization. Obviously, it is necessary to promote change, to introduce the other, the disrespected, and, consequently, to surrender some of the power that philosophers have traditionally wielded. Nevertheless, would that have been the reason behind the dispute, namely, a quarrel based on the will-to-power?

Philosophical practice's criticism of university philosophy was also voiced: its advocates argued that university students were not taught to philosophize, but the history of philosophy. Some contended that they were trained after leaving university. Be that as it may, I continued to wonder why many of them persisted in writing PhD theses and in yearning after a university position, or how it was possible that practically all of us who devoted our time to philosophical practice had taken a degree course. If these philosophical practitioners were being trained outside faculties of philosophy, why did most of the practicing philosophers attending conferences in this regard hold a BA in philosophy? This also begs the following question: why did not the majority of philosophy workshops organized by non-philosophers, despite that fact of being on par with or better than those of philosophical practitioners, did not exude philosophy or confused basic philosophical notions, very much calling into question that it was the result of the history of thought? Lastly, I discovered that some philosophical practitioners were becoming gradually estranged from philosophical reading and study, dabbling in other disciplines, although that was not a matter of concern. Nonetheless, it was disturbing to note that they ultimately adopted practices that could hardly be understood as being philosophical or having originated from this discipline, taking into account the current canon and the horizon of possibilities that the history of thought offers.

This book does not intend to be controversial, but to describe the personal life course that has served as inspiration to write it, insofar as I have attempted to learn from all the criticisms that I have received which, despite the harm that they caused at the time, opened up avenues for gaining a deeper understanding of the discipline. The problem is that while the theoreticians persisted in their intellectual diatribes, Zero continued to clamor, as did No-one, the young woman in a Mexican prison who missed her husband, who she had murdered because, one fateful night of insomnia, he had wanted to kill their son because he could not sleep. Similarly, the invisible children of Morelia continued to whine, which they did every day during the four-hour car journey when accompanying their parents to sell souvenirs to the tourists who went to see the monarch butterflies. And the absent who slept and died on the streets of São Paulo, or their children who killed or were murdered on those of Rio de Janeiro and who continued to weep.

Excuse me for being bold, but when listening to the hundredth conference on the importance of the face in Levinas and the thousandth discussion on the relevance of philosophical hospitality, or when asked to reply to the millionth criticism of a scholar or student against the discipline, it seemed as if I were watching a performance more in consonance with the posturing of *Sálvame Deluxe*[6] or the painstakingly staged imposture of a photo posted on Instagram. That sensation increased when I asked the keynote

---

[6] A Spanish variety program broadcast on the commercial channel Tele 5.

speakers about the performance of their theories in relation to Zero, No-one or the invisible children. Thereupon, some held that neither was it possible to do anything about it, nor in fact should philosophy do anything, inasmuch as its purposes were internal to the discipline (a theory which will be debunked in this book by employing the objective/result dichotomy). Others advocated for organizing seminars with an eye to changing the economic political system. It sounded good but, after having attended those seminars for 20 years, arriving (perhaps owing to my short-sightedness) at the conclusion that they were futile, I preferred getting down to work over continuing to ponder on the new miraculous formula that would resolve everything on its own. Others proposed, as a first step, formulating and grounding a philosophical practice and then applying it. I have had close contact with three generations who have proposed this solution, but only those who have combined theory and practice from the beginning have ended up becoming philosophical practitioners; for the rest, philosophical practice continued to be an object of study of theoretical-practical philosophy, something that, by the way, is paradoxical.[7] I should not like to think that their *posturing* was down to the term's feigned root. However, their position was far too close to that of Horkheimer's and Adorno's who, when they were presented with an opportunity for revolution, drew in their horns. However that may be, I still trust that I am mistaken as to the members of the second and third groups.

---

[7] This is how I learnt that the study of philosophical practice should go hand in hand with research-action, as we have being doing for years in a research-action seminar at the University of Seville, with the participation of Nacho, Pablo, Nerea, José Antonio, Juan and Juan Diego, among others. This seminar has worked with groups from the poorest neighborhood in Spain and with elderly people without resources, thanks to the excellent work and mediation of Tiritas Creativas and to Concha Torres and Marciala.

2. Demarcation Criteria

At any rate, I am indebted to them since they have helped me to establish three demarcation criteria that underpin any vigorous attempt at implementing a philosophical practice and, therefore, to choose who I would like to work with in this field.

(1) *Deeds not words.* When theoretical debate is grounded in detailed studies (doubtless a highly worthwhile task), it is really an inquiry into the history of the spokesperson. If I consider that someone has created a philosophy for philosophers, I will employ it very rarely (although it is always a good idea to resort to theoretical sources to broaden the practical aspects). If, on the contrary, the discourse is the result of a philosophical life project with social and personal gains, that person and his or her writings will be worthy of my full attention and desire to implement joint projects.

(2) *Philosophical practice without theory-practice is meaningless.* To those who suggest that philosophical action consists of a defense of generic dialogue and who are unaware, for example, of the difference between instrumental reason and critical reasoning or who reduce reasoning to an argumentative act with a profound ignorance of poetical, symbolic, narrative and dramatic thought, I would recommend that they continue to read philosophy, as I do myself on a daily basis. Intensive study and frequent application would banish philosophical banality from workshops and counseling sessions and the blind imposition of theories of little significance, respectively.

(3) *Advocating for silence and work in a country of destructive and prepossessed belligerence.* When philosophy is understand from reductionist perspectives (within and without the discipline) or when someone attempts to impose his own perspective as the only valid one, instead of being open to the rest, I mentally recall the principle of *Hyperion*: "For stillness dwells in the land of the blissful."[8] The intention of this

---

[8] Friedrich Hölderlin, *Hyperion, or the Hermit in Greece* (Cambridge, UK: Open

stillness is to watch over Zero and No-one, rather than achieving the wherewithal for having the last word; namely, in the face of concern, occupation, and in the face of destructive and egocentric antagonism, constructive silence.

These are several of the main aspects that explain the spirit of this work and which have delayed its publication over the past few years.

3. Target Audience

As to its target audience, this book will be of use, first and foremost, to philosophical counselors/advisors/consultants, philosophical practitioners and people working in the field of philosophy for/with children and teenagers. It provides an approach that supplements those that already exist, much more closely related to rationalist, conceptual and, by and large, logical-argumentative tendencies.

Likewise, it will be useful for middle school teachers, for it encourages them to organize workshops for pupils in this educational stage and even for those participating in extracurricular education. It also offers teachers of other subjects tools that they can leverage in class and with which they can get started in this discipline, thus breaking with its idealist and Platonic image.

Furthermore, the book will also serve as a refresher course for lecturers in philosophy, teacher training and all those disciplines for which developing the capacity for reflective thought and experimentation is beneficial. Together with theoretical classes or lectures, the book proposes activities for approaching content experientially and anagogically. Thus, ethics classes or lectures can be supplemented by workshops in which communitarian dimensions or the implications of veganism can be experienced. The hermeneutics class does not only address Rorty, but also facilitates dialogues in which metaphysical imposition is evoked through ironic persuasion. While the metaphysics class combines

---

Book Publishers, 2019), 44.

Zambranian theory with a workshop project that encourages "the deciphering of the original sense" through knowledge of experience or the contemplation of the temporal forms necessary to bring this about.

Lastly, all those who are searching for a philosophy closer to existence and how to make it a reality, all those who sense that there is an urgent need for this discipline in our society, but have been disappointed by many books that do not connect with their reality, will find inspiration and a chance to catch their breath and vent their frustration in the following pages.

4. Content

This book contains three parts that describe different types of philosophical practice and analyze some of the criticism that they have received.

The first part addresses theoretical-practical philosophies, which are the usual subject matter of master classes, in opposition to philosophical practice. The latter supplements the former as, without a solid theoretical-practical basis, the structure of philosophical practice becomes blurred. Having said that, without the latter, the former become a solipsist project or, even worse, an imposture in which their incongruence ends up being their calling card, as occurred when Adorno, after defending revolutionary emancipation, used the political *system* to inhibit the liberating action of the young in 1968. This first part does not only dwell on theory, but also addresses the development of hermeneutic and metaphysical practice and Stoic workshops. Additionally, it explains some of the habitual formats of the discipline: from philosophical counseling sessions and philosophy workshops to philosophy in prisons.

The second part delves deeper into the constraints of logical-argumentative philosophical practice. Specifically, it proposes an action stemming from a more open rationality that includes symbolic, narrative, dramatic and poetical life or, in short, life experiences. Experiential philosophical practice is grounded in several premises: (1) our ideas, decisions and feelings are determined by what *we are*; (2) our identity (who we are) is based on the life *experiences* that have marked us; and (3) we pursue a philosophy that not only has to do with our ideas, but also transforms our existence. This part also expounds on the notion of experience and, above all, on the determinants necessary to achieve it (dispositions and scenarios): a conference can mark a turning point for a student and serve as a reason for a fellow student for surfing the Web. Dispositions and scenarios have an influence on whether the subject matter will transform one of them or become a deathly bore for the other.

Lastly, some of the criticisms that the discipline has received will be analyzed. These have served to broaden and improve it, insofar as they have allowed for discovering the errors of both those authors who defend different types of philosophical practice and those who lambast them. This itinerary will make it possible to understand that the discipline is not an adornment or just another contingency of philosophy, but a substantial condition of possibility that traverses it and which allows for the renewal of its corpus. Without it, only a constrained model for doing philosophy would be implemented, while neglecting all the other models. Similarly, without it, philosophy would disregard all those interlocutors who have nothing to do with it, for it has become a discipline employed *by* and *for* philosophers. This sort of philosophy would be represented by the classical exclusive model: a male, (1) Western, (2) heterosexual, (3) thinker (4) with a logical-argumentative rationality, (5) forming part of the normalizing system and (6) far removed from the ways of doing philosophy on the basis of any type of functional diversity. Even when new aspects are included in the philosophical discourse, as has occurred with indigenous philosophy, exclusion is not overcome until new subjects and agents come into play, for in the first case this would involve indulging in those philosophies of women formulated by men, instead of allowing the former to express their own views. Thus, philosophical practice opens up the possibility of conducting research and studies from the perspective of the excluded of both sexes: for instance, a PhD thesis on Sartre's concept of freedom from the viewpoint of a group of people who have spent 20 years in prison; or on the notion of future from the perspective of a group of elementary school children living in an indigenous community, whose income derives from their relationship with drug trafficking. Unlike other previous works, the intention of this book is not to offer a history of the discipline[9] or to contrast authors, for both aspects have already been covered. However, reference will be made to some of the relevant authors in the field, whenever necessary, and the footnotes will be useful for continuing to inquire into this subject. Together with these authors, it will also be necessary to resort to classical authors of philosophy, since philosophical practice is, first and foremost, philosophy, whereby it would be absurd to neglect or stray from it.

5. Acknowledgments

This book is the result of several years of work and endless courses and keynotes delivered in several countries, especially in Mexico, from which I have drawn inspiration and many of the virtues that have permeated my spirit over the past years. Those who know me and read my work on social media are aware of my attachment to Mexico, whose hospitality is surprising, for which reason I endorse the lyrics of the song, "I remain in this land, so beautiful and so calm, because I have found songs, caresses and solace". Accordingly, I would first like to express my thanks to all those people who have made it possible and who should be considered as co-authors of this book: the Dominicans of the convent of the University Cultural Center (Centro Universitario Cultural, CUC) who have hosted me for nigh on a decade and from whom I have

---

[9] The history of the discipline can be found in José Barrientos-Rastrojo, *Introducción al asesoramiento y la orientación filosófica* (Sevilla: X-XI, 2005).

learnt not only to contemplate life, but also to fight for it (Fathers Ángel, Miguel, Juan, Gonzalo, Alejandro, Laudelino, Didier, Leobardo, Javier and others who have come and gone during the past decade); Vicky Carrasco and Pedro Tello, the pillars of *Radiosofando* and close to my small Mexican heart; the members of the Educational Centre for Autonomous Creation in Philosophical Practice (Centro Educativo para la Creación Autónoma en Prácticas Filosóficas, CECAPFi) whose growth I have witnessed and who have dispelled my sloth by contending many of the theories contained in this book, thus allowing many of them to prosper (David Sumiacher, Paulina Ramírez, Óscar Valencia, Miguel Ángel Zapotitla, Soraya Tonsich, Ileana del Rey, Carlos Alberto Rodríguez, José Enrique Rendón, Siegfried Seedorf, Jesús Reyes and Jeannie Aiza, among many others, who have acquainted me with Mexican and Chilango affection and cuisine); the members of the Circle of Philosophical Practice, Art and Education (Círculo de Práctica Filosófica, Arte y Educación, CIPFAE) (Brenda Ludmila Sánchez, Yubia Medina and the rest of the team) who have known how to be close even when an ocean has separated us, plus many other Mexicans who have accompanied me and have placed their trust in my work in Mexico, including Gabriel Vargas, Aralia Valdés, Alexa Alfonsín and José Carlos Velasco, Miguel Mandujano, Gabriela Vallejo, Esther Charabati, Ángel Alonso, Marco Antonio López, Jorge Linares, Mauricio Beuchot, Paulina Rivero, José Luis Cisneros, Rolando Picos, Carlos Vargas, David Vico and Paola, to name but a few.

Further to the south, I have been rewarded with the friendship of two Brazilian teams, that of the Claretian University Centre in São Paulo, led by Renato Nardi, and that of the Federal University of Goias (Edmilson, Chrystian, Lorena, Diego, etc.), led by Wilson Paiva. Between Mexico and Brazil, I have received the kindness of the Marfil group in Colombia, run by Víctor Rojas, and in Argentina, in addition to the aforementioned, I am indebted to

Andrea Suárez, Federico Mana, Andrés Mattus, Jorgelina Russo, Carolina Monzón and Laura for their warmth.

Europe has given me inspiration and offered me the fraternity of the members of the Portuguese Association of Ethical and Philosophical Counseling (Associação Portuguesa de Aconselhamento Ético e Filosófico, APAEF), whose first generation was led by Humberto Dias and Leonor Viegas, those of the Portuguese Association of Ethics and Practical Philosophy (Associação Portuguesa de Ética e Filosofia Prática, APEFP), led by Eugénio Olivera, plus many other Portuguese friends such as Joana Sousa, Mendo Henriquez and Joaquim Pinto at the Catholic University of Portugal (UCP), plus María Teresa Santos, Magda Costa and their team at the University of the Azores (UAC). Lastly, Italy has attracted me through the Professional Philosophical Practice Society (Società Professionisti Pratiche Filosofiche, PRAGMA) and Luca Nave and Maddalena Bisollo, and through the Italian Association for Philosophical Counseling (Associazione Italiana per la Consulenza Filosofica, Phronesis) and Neri Pollastri.

Outside these contexts, philosophical practice has given me countless friends and colleagues to whom I would like to show my gratitude: Peter Raabe, Ran Lahav, Lou Marinoff, Lydia Amir, Zoran Kojcic, Michael Weiss, Leon de Haas, Ander Lindseth, Vaughana Feary, Sergey Borisov, Eduardo Vergara, Jorge Sánchez-Manjavacas, Shinji Kajitani, Félix García Moriyón, Walter Kohan, Trevor Curnow and many others who have accompanied me during these years and who, because of space constraints, cannot be mentioned here.

Likewise, my activities in Spain have been inspired by Pepe Ordóñez, Paco Macera, César Moreno, José Antonio Marín, Rafael Guardiola, Álvaro Rodríguez, Concha Roldán, María José Guerra, Javier Bustamante and many other students who have become enthused with philosophy and who, consequently, have encouraged me not to abandon the way (Víctor Hugo, Adria, Nerea, Pablo, José Antonio, Juan, JuanDi, Omar, Sara, Tania, Flor, Ramón, Diego,

Lamia, Fortunato, Virginia, Marina, Minerva, Edith, Coral, Marco, Rafael, Maricruz, Diego, Julio, Darío, Yamila, Sergio, Alejandro, Maru, Valentina, Federico, Miguel Eduardo, Brandon, Paula, Carmina, Maira, Buatu, Andrés, Fernando, Paola, Zuleika, Miguel, etc.).

Lastly, special mention should go to Ana, my companion in my adventures and misfortunes, and Leo, my indefatigable furry friend, who took me out for walks in the hills and mountains on both cloudy days and under the burning summer sun.

I. PHILOSOPHICAL PRACTICES

I believe that, to a considerable extent, philosophy has too often gone to alarming extremes of confusion, logomachy, erratic verbosity, when not sometimes dejection and procrastination, which have been favored, on the whole, among other reasons, by a sort of high-handedness in the awareness of a fundamentally crestfallen *return* and, on the other hand, a certain lack of *experiential and vital bedrock* with which reference is made not now to philosophical practices, which logically proliferate, but to the primordial pulse of a more theoretical philosophy[10]

---

[10] César Moreno Márquez, "De ida y por principio," 176, original emphasis.

CHAPTER 1
THEORETICAL AND PRACTICAL PHILOSOPHIES

1. A General Overview

In the main, a distinction can be drawn between two major universes in philosophy: the theoretical and the practical.

The former encompasses knowledge relating to philosophical reflection on the basis of reality. It covers disciplines like ontology or metaphysics, hermeneutics, epistemology, gnosiology and the theory of knowledge and argumentation, plus all the histories of philosophy from Antiquity down to the present day. This space has been broadened by inquiries into new spheres of reality, resulting in the emergence of feminine and/or feminist philosophy, a philosophy of mathematics, a philosophy of technology and a philosophy of indigenous communities. As regards this last case, the attention paid to new contexts has led to regional or regionalist philosophies, it now being possible to talk about a Japanese,[11] Chinese,[12] Aztec,[13] Yanomami,[14] Argentinian,[15] Pur'epecha[16] or Andalusian[17] philosophy. This taxonomy, which does not intend to be exhaustive but only illustrative, has been developed by thinkers who, on their own (habitually in their ivory towers or offices, and

---

[11] Jesús González Valles, *Historia de la filosofía japonesa* (Madrid: Tecnos, 2002).

[12] Wolfgang Bawer, *Historia de la filosofía china* (Barcelona: Herder, 2009).

[13] Miguel León Portilla, *La filosofía nahual estudiada en sus fuentes* (México DF: Instituto Indigenista Interamericano, 1956).

[14] Davi Kopenawa and Bruce Albert, *A queda do céu. Palavras dum xamã yanomami*, *A queda do ceu* (São Paulo: Schwarcz, 2015).

[15] Alberto Caturelli, *Historia de la filosofía en la Argentina 1600-2000* (Buenos Aires: Editorial de ciencia y cultura y Universidad del Salvador, 2001).

[16] Raúl Cruz Sebastián, "¿Habrá una filosofía p'urhépecha?" *Cultura P'urhépecha*, February 25, 2011, http://www.purepecha.mx/threads/4153-%C2%BFHabr%C3%A1-una-Filosof%C3%ADa-P-urh%C3%A9pecha.

[17] Juan Fernando Ortega, *Filosofía andaluza y filosofía en Andalucía. Delimitación conceptual* (Málaga: Universidad de Málaga, 2000).

without any commitment to interdisciplinarity), are devoted to opening the being and bodies, lifting veils concealing truths or dealing with generating new narratives and perspectives for fostering dialogue, to put it in Ortegian or Rortyian terms.

Together with theoretical philosophy, there is practical philosophy. This has traditionally encompassed ethics, political philosophy and similar disciplines such as bioethics and social philosophy. Although they share the same methodologies and way of doing philosophy, their objectives differ from those of the previous block. These would not be the being, knowledge, truth, the female identity or the essence of the technological condition, but the justification of individual and social ethical decisions. Despite the fact that some authors, especially American ones, imbue their writing with an oscillatory spirit, that is, their works seem to be directly applied to social reality, thus bringing about a change, there are many European authors who have become embroiled in lengthy disquisitions that all too frequently lose sight of the discursive thread or the subject's connection with the initial ethical question. For instance, Peter Singer explains the ethical aspects that should be borne in mind when making a donation in accordance with utilitarianism (for example, whether to donate 5 or 10 per cent of one's earning, depending on one's salary).[18] While, for his part, Thomas Pogge analyses the role of scholars in relation to world poverty.[19] However, Rawls takes the time, for instance, to define the basic characteristics of the theory of justice, according to the difference principle, among others. For all these reasons, it is improbable that their discourses will have a significant impact on a young man who, at a hospital, wonders about the legitimacy of the

---

[18] Peter Singer, *The Life You Can Save: Acting Now to End World Poverty* (New York: Picador, 2009); José Barrientos-Rastrojo, *Peter Singer. Sendas para un giro copernicano ético* (Ciudad de México: UNAM, 2020).

[19] Thomas Pogge and Luis Cabrera, "Académicos contra la pobreza: una idea para la que ha llegado su tiempo," *Revista Internacional de Filosofía Aplicada HASER* 3 (2012): 193–218.

assisted suicide of his elderly mother, condemned to vegetate on a ventilator. That son is not interested in listening to yet another laboriously erudite justification based on the argument's Kantian or Aristotelian nuances. Moreover, this explains why philosophy conferences and philosophy programs on television are unappealing, notwithstanding society's need for the discipline. This clearly evinces the dissonance between life and philosophy, which has been readily interpreted. Let us take a look at an example to which we will return when discussing another argument. It is the allegation of a character appearing in Irvin Yalom's novel *Quando Nietzsche chorou*: "Here is a truth with a supreme and irrefutable rationality. However, whenever I am really frightened, it does not calm my fears. This is the problem of philosophy: to teach it and to apply it in real life are two very different endeavors."[20]

This does not mean to say that such musings are not indispensable to the history of humanity. Nevertheless, our distressed young man would profit more from philosophy if, by attending philosophical practice workshops, he could obtain the philosophical tools necessary to tackle his ethical dilemma autonomously. Theory is necessary but insufficient on its own.

Over the centuries there have been authors who have glimpsed the need for a more practical philosophical approach. Here are two examples. In his *An Enquiry Concerning Human Understanding*, David Hume described two types of philosophy akin to those described here:

> The one considers man chiefly as born for action; and as influenced in his measures by taste and sentiment; pursuing one object, and avoiding another, according to the value which these objects seem to possess [...]. They make us feel the difference between vice and virtue; they excite and regulate our sentiments; and so they can but bend our hearts to the love of probity and true honour, they think, that they have fully attained the end of all their labours. The other species of philosophers

---

[20] Irvin Yalom, *Quando Nietzsche chorou* (Parede: Saída de Emergencia Parede, 2007), 220.

> considers man in the light of a reasonable rather than an active being, and endeavours to form his understanding more than cultivate his manners. They regard human nature as a subject of speculation; and with a narrow scrutiny examine it, in order to find those principles, which regulate our understanding, excite our sentiments, and make us approve or blame any particular object, action, or behaviour.[21]

Despite initially promising us philosophical practitioners connected with society, ultimately neither of the two are obliged to leave their studies to perform their work. The difference between practical and theoretical, or rational, philosophers, lies in their object of study, as already noted. Both strive to create a discourse, instead of helping others to do so.

On the other hand, even when "they make us feel the difference between vice and virtue; they excite and regulate our sentiments; and so they can but bend our hearts to the love of probity and true honour",[22] the frameworks spring from their peculiar, inherent and egocentric way of understanding reality. These philosophers do not abandon the comfort of their studies to listen to the discourses of indigenous people, but proclaim that their vision is superior, justifying their claim (at best) on the strength of the years of study that have equipped them with tools that are incommensurate with the "other", with all the Eurocentric disrespect[23] that this entails.

The hope of a philosophical dialogue returned when, centuries later, William James remarked, "The world to which your philosophy-professor introduces you is simple, clean and noble," before adding, "The contradictions of real life are absent from it."[24] When readers harbor the hope that the American's aim is to propose specific exercises for working with those who are new to

---

[21] David Hume, *An Enquiry Concerning Human Understanding* (New York: The Liberal Arts Press, Inc., 1955 [1748]), 15.

[22] Hume, *An Enquiry*, 15.

[23] Axel Honneth, *Disrespect: The Normative Foundations of Critical Theory* (Cambridge & Malden, MA: Polity Press, 2007), Kindle, 100–24.

[24] William James, *Pragmatism* (New York: Dover Publications, Inc., 1995), 8.

the subject, they will realize that his intention, as the good pragmatist he is, is to disassociate himself from metaphysical philosophies and to return to that superior habit of providing laypeople with the discourse. Thus, when criticizing rationalist and metaphysical philosophers for "dealing in shades", we disagree with James when he then contends that pragmatists who "live and feel, know the truth";[25] on the contrary, they access their own truth. The urge to construct the discourse in the suffocating, stale atmosphere of the dark and sometimes gloomy study of a scholar is repeated. Unfortunately, an unventilated space becomes full of carbon monoxide and it is unnecessary to consult a science textbook to understand the consequences that a lack of oxygen has for the brain. Furthermore, suffice it to read Martin Buber,[26] Levinas[27] or Nahua texts[28] to grasp the impact of the absence of social relationships on people.

Regrettably, the Kantian idea that fostered the coming of age of man through an autonomous thought has only been accepted as a personal obligation, but not as a responsibility that philosophers should have to others. It is important to recall the German's philosopher's classical work *What is Enlightenment?*

> Enlightenment is man's leaving his self-caused immaturity. Immaturity is the incapacity to use one's intelligence without the guidance of another. Such immaturity is self-caused if it is not caused by lack of intelligence, but by lack of determination and courage to use one's intelligence without being guided by another. *Sapere Aude!* Have the courage to use your own intelligence! is therefore the [heraldic] motto [*Wahlspruch*] of the enlightenment.[29]

---

[25] Ibid., 12.

[26] Martin Buber, *Yo y tú* (Madrid: Caparrós, 1995).

[27] Emmanuel Levinas, *Humanismo del otro hombre* (Madrid: Caparrós Editores, 1993).

[28] Miguel León Portilla, *La filosofía nahual.*

[29] Carl Friedrich, *The Philosophy of Kant* (New York: Modern Library, 1949), 132.

In should be noted that this section is not a critique of the more theoretical or academic approaches to philosophy, but of the reduction of its corpus and activity to the two aforementioned models of philosophy. It has nothing to do with contending, as I did in a keynote delivered in Portugal 15 years ago, that philosophical practice without a theory-practice is blind and that a theory-practice without a theory is pointless, but that, without either of them, it is easy to fall into a reductionism that is not only detrimental to them, but also to philosophy as a whole and its pursuit of limitless knowledge.

2. Characteristics of Theoretical and Practical Philosophies

Without wanting to be exhaustive, the following three characteristics of these philosophies stand out:

(1) Content. The pre-eminence of the topic over the subject.
(2) The role of the philosopher. Assuming the possession of truth and of philosophy and possessing the exclusive training that equips him with the tools to achieve it.
(3) Philosophical action. The primacy of saying over listening or of replying over asking.

2.1. Content. The Pre-eminence of the Topic over the Subject

The content of these philosophies is formed by a syllabus established according to the canon determined by tradition, which is broadened by circles of philosophical power. For instance, at nearly all faculties of philosophy the teaching of the module, "Prevailing Philosophical Currents", repeats a syllabus that usually includes phenomenology, hermeneutics, critical theory, postmodernity, structuralism and post-structuralism and existentialism, among others. The module "History of Ancient Philosophy" begins with the transition from the myth to the logos, before addressing the pre-Socratic philosophers, up until Plato and Aristotle, and covering the Hellenistic schools such as Stoicism, Epicureanism and Skepticism and currents like Gnosticism.

Students are taught this content which all too often does not manage to connect with their existence, thus establishing the classical distance between philosophy and life.

Fortunately, some professors manage to forestall this apathy. Even in these cases, however, the baseline is the syllabus, rather than the students, thus evincing the interlocutor's disrespect, employing the Honnethian[30] term.

The second way of avoiding this solipsism is through the assessment of philosophy students. In this respect, they can be asked to offer their *personal* reflections in essays and public presentations. Notwithstanding this, the external element of the canon is secondary and perceived as an adjectivization or predication (in the sense employed by Husserl in *Experience and Judgment*)[31] and never as a substantiality. Moreover, the proposal would be linked to a *personal* vision of the topic, whereby it does not enable students to listen to the other; namely, the subjective aspects are stressed, instead of drawing attention to the discourse of otherness (which requires philosophical practice workshops).

Explanatory masterfulness (which includes benefits that some new alternative pedagogies attempt to conceal) furthers this dynamic. Methodologically modifying its one-way nature to introduce a choral symphony, so as to overhaul theoretical explanations, would facilitate dialogue and chromaticism in the constitution of philosophy. The *logos* would not only derive from the professor's pulpit, but would be instituted as a symphonic dialogue. The danger posed by a masterful reductionism leads to the disregard of the other, to egocentricity, to blindness to difference and, ultimately, to the imperialism of a hegemonic class deaf to the polychromy of the real. In order that this colorfulness should emerge, it is not enough

---

[30] Axel Honneth, *The Struggle for Recognition: The Moral Grammar of Social Conflicts* (Cambridge, MA: Polity Press, 1995), 160ff.; Honneth, *Disrespect*, 101–24.

[31] Edmund Husserl, *Experience and Judgment: Investigations in a Genealogy of Logic* (Evanston: Nothwestern University Press, 1973), Kindle.

to think *about* it (an authentic onanistic game of mirrors), but *from* it, to wit, it should promote mechanisms that foster the word in the other. Firstly, dialogue, and only then debate.

2.2. The Role of Philosopher. Assuming the Possession of Truth and of Philosophy

Continuing with the imperialist menace, it can be observed *that theoretical-practical philosophers believe that they are in possession of the truth*. Their most extreme claim is that their years of study have placed them above laypeople. Some assert that only highbrow Hegelian study, the quaternary of being Heideggerian, daybreak in a clearing of the Zambranian forest and similar concepts are authentic philosophy. All other actions, like teaching conceptualization, problematization, argumentation and translating between oral and written languages, would not classify as such.

Several objections can be raised in this regard. For one, there is the progressivist argument: if it is assumed that only those who understand certain complexities of conceptual history are authentic philosophers, not only laypeople but also all those taking their first steps in the field should be prohibited from performing philosophical classifications. In this connection, there arises the problem of delimiting knowledge and philosophical action: when do we cross the threshold of philosophical knowledge? In point of fact, if the criteria were very strict, these would exclude most university students, including those taking master's degrees and those writing their PhD theses. If this is so, should it be claimed that most middle school teachers do not become involved in philosophical activities or that university freshmen philosophize? This would also beg the question of whether or not a university education is sufficient to do philosophy. Ultimately, it would first be necessary to determine what philosophy is and who is entitled to make that decision.

A second problem consists in determining whether or not the delimitation criterion depends on some or other tendency (analytical or continental, for example): what *lofty* truth is adequate for classifying someone as a philosopher? Assuming the aforementioned difference, philosophers themselves waver between the two. Franz Brentano, one of the precursors of analytical philosophy, criticized the fact that Wilhelm Dilthey's *Introduction to the Human Sciences*[32] was riddled with argumentative ambiguities, a lack of logical acuity and many errors of thought. Carnap censured Heidegger's *Was ist Metaphysik?*[33] for being replete with "crass errors", a "succession of meaningless words", before adding that neither did his philosophy serve as a "fable", "poetry", nor as a mere "working hypothesis". Searle sent Derrida an *affectionate* message: your words "parody" arguments. Nor did continental philosophers bite their tongues. According to Heidegger, Carnap's logic was "arid to the point desolation" and its one and only utility consisted in "that frankly despicable and fundamentally indignant preparation of the subject matter of an exam". In reply to Searle, Derrida claimed that the American philosopher's thought contained exiguous complexity, that is, he was criticizing its simplicity, *unworthy of true philosophy*. And, for his part, Adorno got his oar in, indicating that analytical philosophy was a specialist technique that could be understood and reproduced by automatons and which did not require persons.[34]

Besides this philosophical profoundness peppered with insults, pragmatic (like the aforementioned James) and postmodern thinkers deploy a dialectic theory that avoids the excesses of metaphysical univocity. Rorty is a paradigmatic case in this respect. The American philosopher presents philosophy as an immense conversation that fosters the democratic skills of

---

[32] Wilhelm Dilthey, *Introduction to the Human Sciences Volume 1* (Princeton, NJ: Princeton University Press, 1989).

[33] Martin Heidegger, *Was ist Metaphysik?* (Frankfurt am Main: Verlag Vittorio Klostermann, 2006).

[34] More on these disputes in Franca D'Agostini, *Analíticos y continentales. Guía de la filosofía de los últimos treinta años* (Madrid: Cátedra, 2000).

participants, aimed at generating far-reaching dialogue tending towards liberal solidarity.[35] The background music recalls the communicative action of Habermas, who was opposed to strategic determinations or those aimed at achieving ends.[36] Despite being well-disposed to democracy, both the American and the German reveal the mindset of theoretical-practical philosophers, whose objective is to prescribe how their readers should act, instead of offering them a chance to express their own opinions in order to foster in them skills that help them to achieve their ends (i.e., thinking for themselves). That attachment to the professor's pulpit, or that refusal to abandon it, hinders the emergence of the discourses of the disrespected. It should be stressed yet again that philosophers continue to think *about* and *for* them. Even Axel Honneth has explicitly described the architypes of disrespect, without it having occurred to him to approach the disrespected so as to ask them for their own opinion or to become involved, literally and effectively, in their misery.

The answer to this allegation may be that the disrespected are not even aware that they are being treated as such, owing to the manipulation of the system. Having said that, this leads to too many awkward questions: Is not this idea underpinned by a sort of imperialist paternalism? Is not the professor's pulpit also

---

[35] Richard Rorty, "Philosophy and the Future," in *Rorty & Pragmatism: The Philosopher Responds to his Critics*, ed. Herman J. Saatkamp, Jr. (Nashville & London: Vanderbilt University Press, 1995), 197–206; Richard Rorty, *Contingency, Irony and Solidarity* (Cambridge: Cambridge University Press, 1991), 73ff.

[36] "By 'work' or *purposive-rational action* I understand either instrumental action or rational choice or their conjunction. Instrumental action is governed by *technical rules* based on empirical knowledge. [...] By 'interaction,' on the other hand, I understand *communicative action*, symbolic interaction. It is governed by binding *consensual norms*, which define reciprocal expectations about behavior and which must be understood and recognized by at least two acting subjects," Jürgen Habermas, *Toward a Rational Society: Student Protest, Science and Politics* (Boston, MA: Beacon Press, 1970), 91–2, original emphasis.

determined by ideological intricacies of which philosophers are not, or do not want to be, aware? What authority do they have to determine that their ideology is sufficient to assess that of the disrespected? Are they not making the colonialist mistake of Westerners who send food to native people with the aim of assuaging their hunger, when they do not need it because their diet differs from that of their benefactors? Is there not a danger that the professor's pulpit may be a mechanism of the powerful for controlling the intelligentsia (Mannheim)[37] or that it intends to control minds by means of a banking pedagogy?[38]

A simple way of avoiding these dangers is to give the other a chance to speak, to abandon the professor's pulpit and the position of truth to become an advocate (friend) of wisdom or truth *together with the other* (was not that perchance the etymology of our term?): to follow the maxim that we are "standing on the shoulders of giants", without falling into the error of confusing ourselves with them, or that we should "'Cherish some man of high character, and keep him ever before your eyes, living as if he were watching you, and ordering all your actions as if he beheld them.'"[39]

A reply to the practical urgency suggested here is to be found in the forceful traditional assertion of philosophy that theory is the most practical of activities. Undoubtedly, philosophy has brought about paradigm shifts throughout history. However, does it not seem extravagant that the philosophers of schools of thought should profess to be the wellspring of these metamorphoses? Have not philosophers sometimes been mere chroniclers of a change due to phenomena outside their control? For instance, there is the Frankfurt School's critique of instrumental reason performed by

---

[37] Karl Mannheim, *Ideology and Utopia: An Introduction to the Sociology of Knowledge* (New York: Harcourt, Brace & World, Inc., 1936).

[38] Paulo Freire, *Pedagogia do oprimido* (Rio de Janeiro: Paz e Terra, 1970), 33ff.

[39] Lucius Annaeus Seneca, *The Complete Moral Letters to Lucilius* (Ottawa: Stoici Civitas Press, 2013), 27.

Horkheimer[40] and, subsequently, by Adorno.[41] Was the oeuvre of these thinkers sufficient to bring about change? A good criterion for determining whether or not a critical task is being performed adequately is perhaps to count the number of times an attempt has been made to silence, or to stab, philosophers in prison. It is uncanny how a philosophy that proclaims to be critical with the system does little to question or disturb it.

Accepting that this philosophy changes the system, is there not an abhorrent reality in which it is the philosophical hierarchy that provokes that change?

In short, when theoretical philosophy holds that the design of discourses is the best tool for developing critical thinking and the struggle against authoritarianism, this begs the question of whether critical activity should be the exclusive reserve of a chosen elite or should actually originate from society as a whole and, specifically, from those most in need of it.

A philosophy formulated by and for philosophers is doubtless bewildering. As is attending philosophy congresses at which interdisciplinarity is non-existent. Doubt is not being cast on the performance of philosophy in the context of a cultural elite. Nonetheless, it is bewildering to assert that it produces results for society when claiming that philosophy is a discipline that is only taught at university and in the final years.

2.3. Philosophical Action. The Primacy of Saying over Listening

The subject matter of this section can be inferred from the foregoing, for which reason suffice it to summarize it: theoretical-practical philosophy gives priority to saying over listening, to affirmations over questions. The master class is a clear example of

---

[40] Max Horkheimer, *Eclipse of Reason* (Eastford, CT: Martino Fine Books, 2013, Kindle).

[41] Max Horkheimer and Theodor Adorno, *Dialectic of Enlightenment: Philosophical Fragments* (Stanford: Stanford University Press, 2002).

this thesis. While teacher training or psychology lectures include theoretical and practical activities, *practicums* or real sessions at colleges or other public and private institutions, faculties of philosophy are still lagging behind.

Versus this master-class model, there is a need for philosophy workshops that update the discipline, as will be seen further on. Philosophical practice does not employ the philosophical canon as a pillar of education, but as a means, inasmuch as *the objective is not to learn content but to train in processes*. This does not mean to say that the role of practical thinkers is secondary because they do not focus exclusively on the history of philosophy. Quite to the contrary, they should ensure that philosophical processes are developed rigorously and according to the knowledge that conceptual history has bequeathed us. Thus, workshops are no less difficult than master classes, but more so, as to philosophical knowledge should be added skills like group management and encouraging listening and the emergence of philosophical action. Therefore, philosophical practitioners and university professors should enhance their listening and attention skills in order to foster community thought.

The resistance of some philosophers to integrating social actions is occasionally the result of a blinkered Adornian notion (as well as those of other authors) that it is the system that led to Auschwitz. Nevertheless, the second and third generations of the Frankfurt School have highlighted the fact that present-day society is sufficiently complex to classify it on the basis of the dearth of those combating it. Luciano Floridi cautions that, versus the idea that cars can lead to obesity by preventing the citizenry from walking as they did before, they can also be used to drive to a gym. The classification of a financial company as an institution that only pursues private gain overlooks the existence of ethical banks. The criticism of private companies for their greed fails to take into consideration the owner of a corner bar who, once he has earned enough to make ends meet, invests the rest in his clientele for social reasons or decides not to speculate because his business model has nothing to do with rampant capitalism. Honneth may have warned that the age of the social economy is currently impoverished with respect to its heyday in the 1960s, although this is not however a reason for denying its existence. The decline of this plurality in philosophy – a very unphilosophical attitude owing to its dogmatic connotations – may be due precisely to the lack of dialogue with other fields or to the comfortable position of some thinkers, whose arguments are hamstrung by their bourgeois status and who forget that their calling should encourage them to abandon the cave.

CHAPTER 2
PHILOSOPHICAL PRACTICES

1. A General Overview

If the agent of theoretical-practical philosophies is a subject who creates his own discourse which he imposes on, or proposes to, laypeople, that of philosophical practice helps the latter to exercise and deploy their own thought. The general outline of both is summarized below:

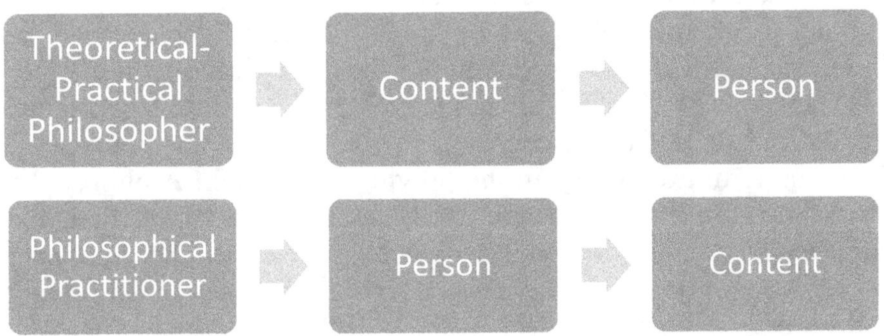

Source: own elaboration.
FIGURE 1.1. Theoretical-Practical Philosophy and Philosophical Practice.

While theoretical-practical philosophers teach or prescribe philosophical *content*, those engaged in philosophical practice facilitate, orchestrate or articulate the philosophical action (or *process*) of the people attending their workshops or counseling sessions. While the former think *for* people, the latter trust that they will achieve this *on their own accord*. Philosophical practitioners are aware that the people attending their sessions do not possess the skills to generate a thought process as complete as that of thinkers in the past. This is the essence of their work: to ensure that, during sessions, they train their still fledgling philosophical skills. At this point, there arises a question about which much has been written: what is to think? So as not to take off on digressions that lead nowhere, a simple Ortegian-type answer is proposed here: thought is to be found in the *content* and the *processes* that the history of thought has bequeathed humanity, specifically, that which is studied in philosophy courses at university.[42] This signifies that philosophical practice is not devoted exclusively to broaching the theory of Husserl, but would include workshops whose participants learn to discover the *eidos* of a concept through phenomenological reductions. Philosophical practice would not only explain Stoic theory, but would also include sessions whose participants would train in the *praemeditatio malorum*, the *parresia*, the *diakrisis* or the worldview. Philosophical practice would not only *exclusively* explain the theories of Paul Ricoeur or Friedrich Scheleiermacher, but would also include encounters whose objective would be to help students to discover their meaning, not only that which the author intended (Schleiermacher), but also from the text per se.

Note the term *exclusively* in the previous paragraph. A philosophy workshop worthy of its name has to be aware of its practical dimension, to wit, it should not be *reduced* to the masterful presentation of theoretical content. Having said that, it is important not to forget its philosophical grounds. If the purpose is reduced to "dialoguing" or to "thinking generically", it can hardly be claimed that what is involved is a "philosophy" workshop, as these actions are inherent to other professionals including educators and psychologists. On the other hand, if the workshop clearly develops a dialogue of *solidarity* that attempts to generate persuasive discourses and which shuns dogmatism – that is, grounded in the

---

[42] This is a point of departure and not of arrival, since to the legacy of the past should be added novel ways of thinking that have been gradually included in the canon: for example, poetical philosophy (Antonio Machado, María Zambrano, Nezahualcoyotl, etc.), hermeneutics based on new theories (such as the corporal, the symbolic or the analytical kind), the ways of reflecting of indigenous communities (the Purepecha, Yanomami, Zapotecos, Mexicas, etc.), those of oriental countries (Japan and China) and those deriving from new realities (like those of the philosophies of cyber existence of Floridi and Sadin).

theory of Rorty,[43] a conversation constructed in the *telling* word of Gadamer[44] or an analytical debate that strives to teach those participating to separate judgments made on the basis of an instrumental reason and critique, as explained by Horkheimer[45] – this can certainly be called philosophical work.

2. Characteristics of Philosophical Practice
2.1. Background
Analogously to the previous case, it is possible to describe five areas that summarize philosophical practice (or practices).

(1) Training. Rigor in the study of content and processes for designing and staging workshops.
(2) Paradigm shift. From content to processes.
(3) The role of the philosopher. From the throne of unequivocal truth to a choral symphony.
(4) Philosophical objectives and extra-philosophical results
(5) Baseline. From the pre-established syllabus to concern for fellow man.

2.2. Training. Rigor in the Study of Content and Processes
The first point deals with workshop models in which doubt is cast on their philosophical nature due to the fact that their procedures may be implemented by people without training in this field of knowledge. I have explained this point in previous works,[46] in which I have stressed that a philosophy workshop or counseling session is not specifically so because it introduces dialogues or addresses (allegedly philosophical) concepts like freedom, justice, love and existence. Educational, psychological, psychoanalytical or

---

[43] Richard Rorty, "Philosophy and the Future," 197–206.

[44] Hans-Georg Gadamer, "Gadamer's Philosophical Legacy", *Symposium* 6, no. 2 (2002): 115–34, esp. 118, original emphasis.

[45] Max Horkheimer, *Eclipse of Reason*, 8–44.

[46] José Barrientos Rastrojo, "Philosophical practice as experience and travel," 29–44.

conversational sessions over a pleasant glass of orange wine from Seville can also revolve around the aforementioned. Although both elements (neither the wine nor the Seville setting, but dialogue and concepts) are relevant to achieving the established objectives, philosophical rigor would call for qualifying the type of dialogue around which the session revolves and how these concepts are philosophically addressed. I have offered examples of such encounters above (which will be examined in greater detail further on) whose philosophical nature would not be called into question, for which reason there is no need to recap on them here.

When this approach to philosophical practice is proposed in training courses replete with students taking pedagogy, teacher training or psychology degrees, it leads to a certain amount of frustration among them, for they compare it with other courses. In the latter, a thorough knowledge of the history of philosophy is not essential for learning how to organize workshops, whereby this proposal begs the following question: how can someone without a philosophy degree possibly undertake the organization of a philosophy workshop?

The first thing that I do with these groups is to encourage them to begin reading and studying philosophy, because they are being trained to be *philosophers* (philosophical practitioners). Secondly, I remind them that to take a master's degree in medicine they are usually required to hold a bachelor's degree in the same discipline, which is also the case with other degree courses like engineering and mathematics. After all, a master's degree is tantamount to *specializing* in a previously studied area of knowledge.

However, this requirement does not mean to say that those professionals who have not studied philosophy cannot *stage* philosophy workshops without this entailing the discredit of the philosophy that they propose. This is due to three reasons.

Firstly, there are many master's degrees in philosophy (and in other disciplines such as history, philology, etc.) that accept postgraduate students holding degrees in other subjects. This circumstance gives a philosophical sheen to previous studies. For instance, every year the master's degree course in philosophy of the University of Seville includes postgraduate students holding a bachelor's degree in East Asian studies, journalism or fine arts, among others. If this occurs in theoretical-practical philosophy, it should also make sense in philosophical practice.

The problem is that since students lack a solid knowledge of the fundamentals of philosophy, lecturers are obliged to limit the amount of theory that they teach them or to repeat basic content. Thus, I believe that the alternative of certain master's degree courses in philosophical practice would best respond to this circumstance: to create preparation or foundation courses for those without any previous knowledge of philosophy. This second option would continue to hinder or limit training, philosophically speaking, by attempting to summarize the subject matter of four-year degree courses or 2,400 hours of lectures (in Spain) or three-year degree courses or 1,800 hours of lectures (in Europe) in courses with less than 100 hours of lectures.

Accordingly, there is a third option that I consider to be more satisfactory and rigorous than the first two. In some subjects like psychology, extension courses on specific subjects for people who have not taken the degree have been proposed. This is the case of courses on assertiveness, conflict resolution between parents and their children or teachers and their pupils, and relaxation techniques. These courses do not intend to convert students into psychologists, but to provide them with specific knowledge and tools for any eventuality. They probably will not be able to open a psychology consultancy to help people to deal with their personal traumas, but will indeed be able to employ assertiveness with their work colleagues and even to organize small workshops with them, once they have become accustomed to practicing it assiduously.

The training model of philosophical practice for non-philosophers could be imbued with such a spirit without compromising the philosophical rigor required. Instead of a philosophical practice training course, which would require a profound knowledge of most of the history of thought, they could design courses for training, for instance, prison officers or inmates to organize Stoic philosophy workshops (something which is already being done in Brazilian prisons in the framework of the BOECIO project).[47] Such training courses would last a few months and would involve three content blocks: (1) the theoretical principles of the Stoics, their philosophical position and their connection with others lines of thought; (2) the basic techniques of authors including Chrysippus, Seneca, Marcus Aurelius, Epictetus and Musonius Rufus; and (3) skills for fostering creativity and managing groups and individuals during encounters. Although those taking this course would not obtain a degree in philosophical practice, they would be empowered to apply these techniques in their daily lives or for proposing such workshops, for they would be trained not only in practical aspects, but would also possess a comprehensive knowledge of the subject matter underpinning their actions.

The difference between these trainees and those taking a master's degree in philosophical practice is that the latter would study the application of theoretical knowledge, namely, focusing on the aforementioned points (2) and (3), and would employ it for any current. Philosophical practitioners would not only be able to organize and lead Stoic workshops, but also those addressing the philosophy of any other author in the history of thought. Thus, they would not only organize workshops, but would also design them and, by extension, would be able to offer training in each one of them. As in the case of psychologists, not all philosophy would be taught, but indeed the philosophical mechanisms that serve to undertake a particular philosophical work. We could say that philosophical practitioners are empowered not only to stage workshops, but also to design them.

---

[47] The BOECIO's Facebook profile can be found at https://www.facebook.com/ProyectoBoecio (accessed January 15, 2020).

2.3. Paradigm Shift. From Content to Processes

Inasmuch as academic philosophy is accustomed to teaching content in a one-way fashion, it is not always a simple task to understand philosophical practice because it has a different objective. The father of world philosophy congresses has the following to say in this regard: "Our aim is to encourage ordinary people to reflect philosophically for themselves, not to give them finished philosophical solutions, to accompany them in the open-ended process of philosophical reflection, not to supply them with philosophical products."[48]

Instead of providing them with content to be memorized, the intention is to enable participants or counselees to think for themselves. Philosophical practitioners would not construct (or remember) content (although this is a laudable and very necessary task for the activity in question), but would cultivate sessions in order that group members should generate it themselves. Philosophical practitioners do not profess to be plants that grow on their own accord, but gardeners who provide the necessary nutrients, water and protection so as to allow the discourse to emerge from the other.

In a nutshell, philosophical practice deals with *cultivating processes and not with generating content.*[49] Thus, although the works of Nietzsche can be read in a session, they do not have to be taken at face value, but serve (1) as a staff on which group members can lean to take their own steps or (2) as a cudgel against which they should think. If a philosophy whose mission is to

---

[48] Ran Lahav, "The Philosophical Gardener: A New Paradigm for Philosophical Practice," in *New Frontiers in Philosophical Practice*, ed. Lydia Amir (Cambridge, Cambridge Scholar Press, 2017), 36.

[49] Needless to say, it is possible to do a philosophy of philosophical practice, as can be observed in the papers appearing in the *Revista Internacional de Filosofía Aplicada HASER* (https://editorial.us.es/es/revistas/haser, accessed January 17, 2020), or any other journal pertaining to the discipline (*American Philosophical Practitioners Association, Journal of Humanities Therapy, Pragma, Phronesis, Practical Philosophy, Childhood & Philosophy*, etc.).

encourage others to dispense with that support is not generated, would not this be tantamount to condemning them to persist in their Kantian immaturity? Would not this imply fostering a philosophy as an ideology?

Before concluding, it is important to stress yet again that this is not an argument against content, for the reasons mentioned above, but against the reductionism of restricting philosophy to theoretical books and refusing to experience the pulse of its theses; in other words, in addition to being familiar with the thought of María Zambrano, *living from* it.

2.4. The Role of the Philosopher. From the Throne of Unequivocal Truth to a Choral Symphony

The foregoing is linked to the third distinctive aspect: the philosopher's abandonment of his claim of being in possession of the truth, which places him above all other subjects and discourses. This democratizing aspiration brings us back to Rorty and Habermas who, even though they never tried to put their own theories into practice, paved the way for us to do just that.

The purpose of these philosophies is not to win battles by using skills to conquer, persuade and, ultimately, impose truths on others. On the contrary, specialists help people to acquire skills for the autonomous creation of truths. This is not a simple task because it does not involve fostering an open dialogue in which any discourse is valid, to wit, in which the criterion of legitimacy would depend on the act per se of pronouncing predicative judgments. On the contrary, if their aim is to train people to think critically, they should pay special attention to conceptualization, questioning arguments or the profoundness of definitions. Yet, if the group develops a dogmatic posture which leads its members to a poor classification system, specialists have the obligation to "thump the table" to activate them in order that their descriptions should be more profound and critical. In the main, a session of this type obliges the philosopher to "sow discord". For instance, if the participants consider that men are superior to women, they should reduce this idea to the absurd and introduce contradictions that make it untenable, and also vice versa.

As to other types of workshops, if their intention is to train those participating in them in phenomenological thought, philosophers should make an effort to ensure that reductions are performed correctly. And if the purpose of the session is to help group members to decipher the original sense, as in the case of Zambranian thought, or if they desire to act as a mirror that helps others to acquire their own face, as in the case of Nahuatl thought, they should not ignore inquiry.[50]

Their task is not to proclaim from their pulpits what should be thought according to the established ethical, ontological or epistemological notions, but to inquire into the position of the other. Lipovetsky has noted that the history of humanity has had three moments: firstly, when priests established what was acceptable behavior, secondly, when this was up to philosophers and, thirdly, when it became the responsibility of the citizenry.[51] In this last ongoing stage, it is up to philosophers to provide the citizenry with the necessary tools to allow them to do so.

The resulting models of truth differ from the classical ones: the objective pursued is to create musical symphonies in which, obviously, not everything goes. The community of inquiry models for philosophy for/with children, which recuperate a social truth without this in any way detracting from the process' rigorousness, are paradigmatic. The presence of different interlocutors makes one's own position harder to defend, since it can be contested by others, provided that at least one of them is well-versed in the history of philosophy.

---

[50] Miguel León Portilla, *La filosofía nahual*; Miguel León Portilla, *Los antiguos mexicanos a través de sus crónicas y cantares* (México DF: Fondo de Cultura Económica, 1994), 114–80.

[51] Gilles Lipovetsky, *El crepúsculo del deber. La ética indolora de los nuevos tiempos democráticos* (Barcelona: Anagrama, 1994), 9–20.

This symphony does not imply that all should play the same instrument, but does indeed mean that they should all listen and strive to be compatible so as to create a common symphony. This case is analogous to a society in which minorities should enter into the debate to the same extent as majorities. From this it should not be inferred that the music has to be harmonious, but that, as in the 12-tone system, there can be discordant sounds which, paradoxically, can make the argument evolve along unexplored avenues. As a result, the discourse ceases to be inert to become a living organism that depends on those breathing life into it. Certainly, it is a challenge because the dialogue does not only have to address new content, but also different forms of expression and thought. This is even more of a challenge when there is a need to establish criteria of validity. Nonetheless, as in the case of philosophy for/with children, they have to be designed by those who deploy the discourse. This task is as complex as listening to Schoenberg's "Prelude" from Suite for Piano, Op. 25 … but just as enthralling.

2.5. Philosophical Objectives and Extra-philosophical Results

The purpose of philosophical practice is to help others to do *philosophy*, although this may yield non-philosophical results. This circumstance can be equated with the role of the artist: his purpose is driven by his desire to remain faithful to the required aesthetics, to wit, he is inspired by the muses to paint a landscape, to produce a sculpture or to write a book. However, the reading of that book or the contemplation of that landscape or sculpture often brings about radical changes in the subject by taking him beyond pathological perspectives. Nonetheless, this does not convert the author into a clinical psychologist.

The role of the philosopher is not to offer therapy; nonetheless, as Peter Raabe observes, philosophy can indeed be therapeutic.[52]

---

[52] Peter Raabe, *Philosophical Counseling. Theory and Practice* (Westport: Praeger, 2001), 205.

Philosophical practice enhances argumentation skills, deciphers the original sense, develops analytical skills for studying a problem[53] and the body's powers of understanding,[54] and motivates the deciphering of the content of a text from within it.[55] This learning process can lead to unexpected results, which has prompted some authors to claim that philosophy can be a therapy.[56] To my mind, these are the *results* of the empowerment offered by philosophy workshops, but never their objective. María Zambrano was aware of this potential when remarking, "Those who keep company with me … benefit from it admirably so, as they themselves and others have admitted, but, however, it is evident that they have not learnt anything from me, but have discovered many a beautiful thing which they already possessed in themselves."[57]

---

[53] Frederic Schick, *Making Choices: A Recasting of Decision Theory* (Cambridge: Cambridge University Press, 1997); Jesús Mosterín, *Racionalidad y acción humana* (Madrid: Alianza, 1987).

[54] Maurice Merleau-Ponty, *Phenomenology of Perception* (New York: The Humanities Press, 1962).

[55] Thus, the content and the world deployed in the text "is not immediately supported by psychological structures, but mediately by the structures of the work," Paul Ricoeur, *Del texto a la acción* (México DF: Fondo de Cultura Económica, 2002), 118. On the other hand, Chladenius "sees that to understand an author perfectly is not the same thing as to understand speech or writing perfectly. The norm for the understanding of a book is not the author's meaning. For, 'since men cannot be aware of everything, their words, speech and writing can mean something that they themselves did not intend to say or write', and consequently, 'when trying to understand their writings, one can rightly think that had not occurred to the writers'. Even if the reverse is the case, 'that an author meant more than one has been able to understand', the real task of hermeneutics is not, for him, to understand these extra things, but the books themselves in their true, ie objective meaning. [...] 'unfruitful passages can become fruitful for us', as they 'encourage many thoughts,'" Hans-Georg Gadamer, *Truth and Method* (New York: The Cross Road Publishing Company, 1982), 161–2.

[56] An objective that has been pursued by some philosophical counselors.

[57] María Zambrano cited by Juan Fernando Ortega, "Prologue," in María Zambrano, *Filosofía y educación* (Málaga: Ágora, 2007), 16.

Therefore, it seems odd that philosophy workshops worthy of their name should pursue purposes that having nothing to do with philosophy. In this regard, it could provocatively be held that the purpose of philosophical practice is not to lessen anguish; on the contrary, it may sometimes be necessary to exacerbate it in order to provoke a crisis. This assertion may clash with the ideology of Western societies, occupied with curing, reducing stress and normalization. Nevertheless, authors such as Ortega y Gasset, Sartre and Heidegger have taught us that anxiety and crises are precisely the first step towards accessing an authentic subject and that flight or symptomatic treatment makes it impossible to approach this philosophical headland. Ontological growth requires constant breaks, or exiles in Zambranian terms, so as to return with a more mature and profound countenance, less dependent on the structures that establish how we should be.

2.6. Baseline. From the Pre-established Syllabus to Concern for Fellow Man

The last aspect involves the need to develop attentive listening skills. As their work forms part of the choral circle that promotes questioning, philosophical practitioners should cultivate skills that allow them to connect with the spirit (the *Geist*) of a group or individual.

When critical thinking workshops are organized at unearthly hours, drowsiness and habit pose a challenge to philosophical counselors or practitioners. Participants become withdrawn and avoid answering questions and interacting with those posing them. Here, it is essential to listen so as to stretch individuals without snapping the thread.

Philosophical practitioners should make people shake off their indolence and, at the same time, prevent the most active members from robbing them of the opportunity to make a contribution to the group. For this purpose, some or other technique should be implemented, but, above all, it is essential to connect with the spirit of the group members and encourage them to take action. Firstly, philosophical practitioners feel that they are entering them; then they glimpse the ball and chain that they are dragging behind them, thus preventing them from going beyond their cave, and, consequently, begin to provide them with towlines which, although they have always possessed them in their inner beings, they have not noticed until now. Some group members, who are more prepared, will want to lend a helping hand. If they are allowed to do so, neither will those member with problems leverage their own resources, nor will they have developed thanks to them. For this reason, philosophical practitioners will silence the group, turn on the light so as to allow them to discover their own resources and support their small steps forward, constantly encouraging them while they take each step, even the most minute ones that they are incapable of perceiving.

Once the ball and chain has been removed, the exercise has to become harder for the training to be effective. At this moment, philosophical practitioners cease to be helpers to become hindrances. The thread is becoming dangerously taught and attentive listening is decisive. The thread is subtle but, with each impulse, it increases in size and becomes stronger like a muscle. The art of philosophy manages to increase its thickness by inches without snapping it. That volume increases when group members begin to walk on their own, offering reasons and replies that before they were incapable of coming up with, and when their apathy becomes satisfaction with having performed a task that was previously a burden.

If the activity has involved successive questions and encouragement, beginners will start to wonder where the limits lie. The answer is obvious: while the thread withstands the tension, without snapping. Ridiculing people in front of the rest of the group, asking them for replies that they do not want to offer or are incapable of formulating or implying that they are not answering for themselves but according to what the philosophical practitioner wants to hear is tantamount to snapping the cord. Good results are obtained when group members become confident (or recuperate their confidence) in their capabilities and, ultimately, in the help that the rest of the participants and the philosophical practitioner offer them.

This is an example of the model in which philosophical practice works with processes and not with content. The action does not depend on memorizing a syllabus that has nothing to do with the group, but on a philosophical dance between the philosopher and its members for the purpose of enhancing their thinking skills.

Before concluding, it is important to stress that this does not signify that we become philosophers by training in techniques. It is not a question of avoiding the narrative of the concept of *eidos* so as to focus solely on the phases (reductions) with which it is obtained, but of vitalizing sessions in which phenomenological reductions are updated with the consequences that this Husserlian training has for people. This evinces the analogical and evidential approach inherent to a experiential philosophical practice, which will be covered further on. In sum, this proposal implies talking about the ontology of weights, lifting them so as to strengthen the philosophical muscle, thus resulting in a greater ability to cope with existential dilemmas or a greater capacity for understanding reality.

Chapter 3
Philosophical Practice workshops

1. Lipman&Sharp's Philosophy for Children

A number of philosophical applications will now be briefly described in order to illustrate the foregoing explanations. The first to be formulated and now the most widespread is Matthew Lipman's philosophy for/with children. It consists in a training process (or life project, in the words of Juan Carlos Lago)[58] that begins in the pre-school education stage and ends in the high school stage (3/6-18 years) and which serves to foster and improve critical, creative and careful thinking. It is based on dialogue and reflection on personal and group experiences in a community of research or inquiry. Critical thinking develops research, analytical or conceptualization, reasoning and translating skills. Each one encompasses a specific skills set. Carla Carreras has summarized them as shown (see Table 1.1)[59].

Creative thinking hones the skills of children and teenagers for finding novel questions and answers and an opening to the world that surpasses traditional canons. There are three models of creative thinking:[60]

(1) Amplificative thinking. It broadens the problem and, thus, our capacity for thinking in more distended ways. For instance, it includes metaphysical reflection, which allows us to fly from the metonymic to the transcendental.

---

[58] Juan Carlos Lago, *Redescribiendo la comunidad de investigación. Pensamiento complejo y exclusión social* (Madrid: Ediciones de la Torre, 2006), 23.

[59] Carla Carreras, "Filosofía para Niños: el desarrollo global de las habilidades de pensamiento," in *Filosofía para niños y capacitación democrática freiriana*, ed. José Barrientos Rastrojo (Madrid: Liber Factory, 2013), 99.

[60] Matthew Lipman, *Thinking in Education* (Cambridge: Cambridge University Press, 2003), 243–7.

(2) Defiant thinking. It challenges that which is established, including epistemological, social and ideological norms.
(3) Maieutic thinking. It allows for discovering previously possessed knowledge which hitherto has not been noticed.

THINKING SKILLS			
Research skills	Analytical or conceptualization skills	Reasoning skills	Translating skills
They inform about the world	They organize information	They broaden knowledge by only using reason	They explain, apply or formulate the result of knowledge
Formulating hypotheses Discovering Observing Searching for alternatives Anticipating consequences Selecting possibilities Imagining, etc.	Formulating precise concepts Offering examples and counter-example Discovering similarities and differences Comparing and contrasting Defining Grouping and classifying Serializing, etc.	Looking for and offering reasons Making inferences Reasoning conditionally Reasoning analogically Establishing cause-effect relationships Establishing part-whole relationships Establishing relationships between means and ends Evaluating, etc.	Explaining: narrating and describing Interpreting Improvising Translating from oral to sign language and vice versa Translating from oral to visual language and vice versa Translating different languages Summarizing, etc.

TABLE 1.1. Thinking skills in Philosophy for childre.

As to the criteria for good creative thinking, Lipman includes originality, productivity, imagination, independence or the capacity to think for oneself, experimentation or the ability to bring ideas to life, breaking with the habitual channels, holism which unifies the parts and the whole, expression (which links the being of the creator with his work), self-transcendence, surprise (which gives the final product freshness), synergy ("generativity") or the ability to encourage positive attitudes towards the creativity of others, maieuticity and inventiveness.[61]

Lastly, careful thinking, whether social or ethical, fosters (1) paying attention to the other, (2) raises awareness of the thought mechanisms with which content is presented and (3) qualifies the content per se in a profound way. If two young people were asked to draw a tree, the most *careful* rendering would be that which has more nuanced colors for each leaf, that which contains more elements or that which faithfully depicts the grooves of its trunk, instead of drawing them as mere vertical lines. Careful thinking would do the same in relation to reflection and argumentation. This thinking encompasses the following modes:

(1) Affective thinking. It does not only access the content of judgments, but also reflects on the forms that it takes.

   The description of how children are obliged to multitask in class can be expressed as a complaint, as the satisfaction of seeing that the pupils are, at last, motivated to act, or as a statement that studies the pros and cons of such a determination. Drawing from the premise that "emotion is a type of thought", an awareness of the affectivity attached to ideas reveals part of the content presented.[62]

(2) Active thinking. Continuing with the idea that there is thought in actions, it is essential to learn how to decipher the messages that these convey. These range from simple non-verbal language to complex actions integrated into a global attitude. The latter should be understood on the basis of the "projects" of the actions and of the "scenarios" that they create.[63]

(3) Normative thinking. It allows for raising awareness of the normative thinking that shapes the ideas of the subject and is revealed by analyzing the relationships between what is thought and what should be thought, according to those norms.

---

[61] Ibid., 245–7.
[62] Ibid., 266–7.
[63] Ibid., 267–8.

(4) Empathic thinking. It involves accessing the emotions that are generated and exchanged in a dialogue or when attempting to understand reality communally.

(5) Appreciative thinking. Its evaluations being qualitative, rather than quantitative, it distinguishes between analytical evaluating and the more poetic and vital valuing, and between analytical estimating and esteeming.

Sessions are divided into the following stages:

(1) Introduction. The children form a circle and are explained the basic rules so as to make dialogue and argumentation possible.

(2) Listening. In turn, the children read aloud a passage from one of the program's novels.

(3) Questions. Questions are posed which link the passage to the lives of the children and one is chosen consensually.

(4) Discussion. A dialogue is opened to answer the question, employing the three types of thinking listed above.

(5) Conclusions. The children can end the session with a final conclusion.

(6) Evaluation. The session is evaluated according to the criteria established by the children themselves.

The subject matter of Lipman's methodology combines the main topics and skills covered in the history of philosophy, from logic (*Harry Stottlemeier's Discovery*) to political philosophy (*Mark*), through ethics (*Lisa*) and aesthetics (*Suki*), among others. The stories revolve around the pupils of a school who are of the same age as those reading the novels, thus encouraging them to identify with the characters. The profiles of the main characters are varied but very specific in order that children may explore the different ways of approaching problems. Subsequent programs have employed similar methodologies, such as Angélica Sátiro's *La mariquita Juanita*,[64] or have innovated, like the visual philosophy of Ellen Duthie. Nevertheless, all identify the philosophical act

---

[64] Angélica Sátiro, *La mariquita Juanita*, 2nd ed. (Barcelona: Editorial Octaedro, 2017).

with analytical skills such as those listed above. We will return to this issue further on.

The Lipmanian link between philosophy and critical thinking stems from the American tradition that observes the need to improve critical thinking skills for making good citizens. A well-known example is John Dewey's *How We Think*.[65]

2. Stoic Workshop Processes

The Stoics were also aware of the importance of performing philosophical exercises, for they considered the discipline to be an art of life. To attain peace of spirit, autarchy and ataraxia, they believed that efforts should be made to (1) control one's passions (*ethos*), (2) to be critical in one's assertions (*logos*) and (3) to devote oneself to the study of nature (*physis*) as a mechanism contributing to the first two aspects and for occupying one's rightful place in the world.

These different exercises form the basis of a philosophical practice program that we are currently running in prisons in the framework of the BOECIO project (the subject of another book in the process of being written). The project's main objective is to design and implement a training program for confined people that fosters their critical thinking, self-knowledge and emotional control through a number of philosophical exercises. Its specific objectives are as follows:

> (1) To improve critical thinking, dialogic and analytical skills.
>
> (2) To achieve greater emotional control and to channel violence with critical mechanisms that lead to a greater capacity for social and structural critique with real effects.
>
> (3) To enhance the capacity of reflection, profoundness and subtlety in relation to issues and problems arising in

---

[65] John Dewey, *How We think* (New York: Dover Publications, 2003).

daily life and to have the ability to establish connections with complex systems of thought.

(4) To evaluate the development of the workshops and the performance of the educators.

Each one of the 22 sessions making up the program, which lasts nearly six months, is structured as follows:

(1) Initial contact and analyzing the activity performed during the previous week (15 minutes).
(2) Explaining how the exercise should be performed during the following week (35 minutes).
(3) Weekly reading (10 minutes).
(4) Leave-taking and individual meetings with the participants (10 minutes).

Specifically, the workshop devoted to acceptance and humility begins with fairly complex tasks which bring impotence and perplexity to the surface; for example, threading a needle. Feelings and how they could be expressed with a greater peace of mind are also analyzed.

A chaotic image can also be employed to encourage those participating in the workshop to feel and accept the harmony or internal order of the work. For instance, we have used Jackson Pollock's *Autumn Rhythm*[66], in the visual dimension, and Schoenberg's Three Piano Pieces, Op. 11, No. 3, an example of 12-tone music, in the aural dimension.

This aim of this training is to accept the absurd or the meaningless from an aesthetic angle, without becoming frustrated.

Following this, group members are explained how the Stoics achieved this acceptance using the writings of Epictetus and Seneca, such as the following two passages:[67] "For this is the

---

[66] The picture can be downloaded at https://www.metmuseum.org/es/art/collection/search/488978 , last access June, 4th, 2021

[67] A full description of the development of each one of these workshops will be included in a book on the BOECIO project, which is about to be concluded.

strongest proof of trouble and misfortune. I want something to happen, and it does not happen; and what creature it more wretched than I? I do not want something, and it does happen; and what creature is more wretched than I?"[68]

> All life is slavery: let each man therefore reconcile himself with his lot, complain of it as little as possible [...]. Call good sense to your aid against difficulties: it is possible to soften what is harsh, to widen what is too narrow, and to make heavy burdens press less severely upon one who bears them skilfully. [...] Neither let us envy those who are in high places: the heights which look lofty to us are steep and rugged. Again, those whom unkind fate has placed in critical situations will be safer if they show us little pride in their proud positions [...].[69]

Since the exercise is performed in two sessions, tasks are proposed for each one of the two weeks. The first week is devoted to studying the participants' personal limitations, their reactions to others or the reality that they refuse to accept, which lead to violence, frustration and anger. First, their characteristics are analyzed from the perspective of an external agent, that is, as if the reaction belonged to another person. Afterwards, they will think about it as something inherent to them. The reflections emerging in each situation are noted down. During the second week, the situation described before will have become something appealing and desirable, to wit, it will have been re-semanticized on the basis of their incomprehension of and their frustration towards their acceptance of and coexistence with the absurd. Importantly, that that appeal does not intend to bring about a positive transformation of the unbearable, but an aesthetic contemplation of the absurdity assumed as part of existence.

---

[68] Epictetus, *The Discourses as Reported by Arrian, The Manual, and Fragments, Vol. I* (Cambridge, MA, London: Harvard University Press, William Heinemann Ltd., 1956), 343.
[69] Lucius Anneo Seneca, *Minor Dialogues: Together with the Dialogue on Clemency* (London: George Bell and Sons, 1889), 272.

3. Zambranian Workshop Processes

María Zambrano understood philosophy as a way towards her own personal salvation and that of the rest of humanity. Juan Carlos Marset observes that the Andalusian thinker decided to study philosophy to save her father: in him she saw the Galdosian characters of nineteenth-century Spain, victims of "dispersion" and perplexity in the face of the adverse reality that had been their lot in life.[70] "This expressive difficulty of her father coincides in part with the definition of philosophy that María Zambrano formulated years later: 'To think is to decipher what one feels.' It was precisely in those years that María Zambrano decided to study philosophy 'to save' her father."[71]

When her friend Lezama Lima died, she began to exchange correspondence with his wife, María Luisa Bautista, who underscored the value of her letters: "My dear María, you are incapable of imagining the company that you offer me with your letters, you, so alone, and how I feel your company each time that I receive them and see how sweet sorrow tastes when you tell me with very beautiful words, 'Know that knife, that ice, those embers, that grief, that emptiness and, for an instant, address it as if it were by your side.'"[72]

She even tells the story of how they prevented a young man from committing suicide. Working with descending into the abyss, knowledge of experience and the discovery of evidential truths helped them to achieve this:

> In Rome, I became acquainted with a girl, whose papers I have in my possession, who took her life in a terrible manner, because she had never received a word of love, because she believed that she would never hear one, for she felt ugly. And that was not true. How she would

---

[70] Juan Carlos Marset, *María Zambrano. I. Los años de formación* (Sevilla: Fundación José Manuel Lara, 2004), 32.

[71] Ibid., 257.

[72] José Lezama Lima, María Zambrano Alarcón, and María Luisa Bautista, *Correspondencia* (Espuela de Plata, Madrid, 2006), 231.

have become beautiful if some man had found her so. But no; and she thought that her brother did not love her – a brother who was going to wed [...]. And in order to prevent her brother from following suit, we kept him at home – in the Lungotevere – for two months, after which he got married and now has two daughters who, after another Christian name, are called María and Araceli, for they say that they are indebted to us for having been born because we saved their father. Camilla de Jogu, which was her name, was highly intelligent and sensitive, with splendid eyes. And there was someone who loved her, a young and courageous friar who died a year after her, and a friend of her brother's, a strange character from the Piazza del Popolo.[73]

These example and others, which cannot be mentioned here because of space constraints, evince the power of the Andalusian authoress in relation to philosophy. A Zambranian workshop program would seek the general purpose inherent to her definition of philosophy: to decipher the original sense. It should be stressed that this does not mean that it is obligatory to obtain therapeutic results, although this is usually the case, as has been seen in the aforementioned passage from Zambrano's oeuvre.

Obtaining results depends on the staging of a series of sessions focusing on categories of philosophy, to wit:

(1) Descending into the abyss.
(2) Circumambulation.
(3) Rebirth from a constant *incipit vita nuova*.
(4) Evidential epistemology.
(5) Knowledge gained from experience.
(6) Hermeneutics and access to different temporal and timeless modalities.
(7) Hermeneutics and access to time according to its expressions, distinguishing, for example, between the time of love and that of boredom or hope.
(8) Awareness of the different modes of speech (stammering, auroral, transmitting, melodious, etc.) and silence.

---

[73] María Zambrano, *Cartas de la Pièce (correspondencia con Agustín Andreu)* (Valencia: Pretextos-Universidad Politécnica de Valencia, 2002), 129.

We will not dwell here on exemplifying each one of the workshops, because close to 100 Zambranian sessions and exercises can be found in *Vectores zambranianos para una teoría de la filosofía aplicada a la persona*, which can be downloaded free from the Internet.[74] Nonetheless, it should be stressed that all of them obtain *results* as regards skills pertaining to (phenomenological) vision and insight and understanding the profound (hermeneutics) and the other, as well as one's own nature and the original sense.

4. Hermeneutic Practice Workshop Processes

Hermeneutics is the discipline that deals with human understanding. Its history has offered us different modes that go beyond mere individualistic or social psychological comprehension. In theoretical-practical philosophy lectures, its theory provides students with speculative tools, without this necessarily improving their practical skills.

The intention of hermeneutic practice workshop programs is to trace those modes on the basis of the experience of each one of them. To achieve this, the accent is placed on the theories of Claidenius, Schleiermacher, Ricoeur and the Stoics so as to experience different forms of understanding and to open up different ways of approaching, in this case, a text. The exercise subsequently shifts from the written word to life, consolidating the hermeneutic openings of others, events or reality in general. Each session is summarized below.

The aim of the first workshop is to access the different meanings of a text maintaining the same words, but changing the subtext or expression of the spirit in which it was written. It starts with the reading of a passage, for instance, the first lines of Letter No. 37 from Seneca's *The Complete Moral Letters to Lucilius*: "You have promised to be a good man; you have enlisted under oath [...]."[75]

---

[74] José Barrientos Rastrojo, *Vectores zambranianos para una teoría de la Filosofía Aplicada a la Persona* (Sevilla: Universidad de Sevilla, 2010).

[75] Lucio Anneo Seneca, *The Complete Moral Letters*, 100.

As the most timid member of the group is requested to read this, he or she will do so in an expressionless tone. Then, he or she is asked to draw a line on the blackboard that expresses the level of emotionality. After drawing a straight line, another with ups and downs is drawn so that someone can interpret it as if he or she were under the orders of a conductor. A more dramatic reading of the passage, with greater intensity, is then requested. Once a reading that differs greatly from the initial one has been achieved, the participants are asked to explain the differences between the first and last readings. Most of them focus on formal issues, namely, a louder reading or one with more pauses; however, they soon focus on its performative character. This happens when they start to make comments like "Mary was not convinced by the text" or "Peter seemed to be demanding something". This is when the hermeneutic work begins, since those perceptions do not derive from the content, but from its vocal and, sometimes, gestural appropriation. Henceforth, these interpretations are encouraged by asking in what part of the passage and even what word "demand" or "confidence" has appeared.

The second workshop is aimed at training hearing and hermeneutic skills of group members as regards acuity or subtlety. One of their number is then offered a key with which to understand the text, while the rest are expected to guess what that key is. Possible keys include "read the text as if you were in love", "read the text as if you were angry" or "read the text as it you were selling lottery tickets". The activity becomes progressively more complex with the introduction of keys such as "read the text as if you were in the midst of a storm" or "read the text as if you were a cat whose tail has been trodden on". If the key is not discovered, another person is requested to give his or her interpretation and so forth, until the key is deciphered. The participants analyze how the meaning-key has been deciphered, chiefly through the use of words and their link to the meaning. For instance, if the key is "read the text as if you were angry", the interpreter will "strike" or "assail" the group members by means of intonation, while if the key is "read the text seductively", the words should "allure" the others, converting them, in the first case, into a projectile and, in the second, into a net that entraps them. It should be noted that in this session the aim is to sing the text. María Zambrano observed that the "notes" of her book *Notas de un método*[76] should be understood as musical notes. Thus, the comprehension of the work depends on a musical hermeneutics. The history of philosophy is full of texts that were written to be listened to and not read. As a matter of fact, works like *The Complete Moral Letters to Lucilius* are Epictetus' class notes and not a text written by the philosopher. As were the courses written by Ortega y Gasset, Heidegger and Foucault. This workshop recuperates that oral spirit of philosophy and oral philosophical comprehension skills, viz., that the aforementioned subtlety be found in listening or in the pronunciation or vocal percussion.

The first two sessions[77] confirm the loss of the original sense of the text due to the imposition of the subject. This was explained by Heidegger on the basis of the modern loss of senses. According to the German philosopher, entities have forfeited their authentic meaning due to the utilitarian dictatorship that, for example, converts ore into coins or gears. Ore, which was open to an infinite number of meanings (as explained by Husserl with his eidetic variation)[78] has enclosed this plurality in the pragmatic restriction.

---

[76] María Zambrano, *Notas de un método* (Madrid: Editorial Mondadori, 1989).

[77] Although here a session is devoted to each workshop, usually two are devoted to each one.

[78] Edmind Husserl, *Experience and Judgment*, 322–30; Dieter Lohmar, "The Phenomenological Method of Eidetic Intuition and Its Clarifications as Eidetic Variation," in *Husserl: German Perspectives*, eds. John J. Drummond and Otfried Höffe (New York, Fordham University Press, 2019), 120; César Moreno Márquez, "Break/Freak: Fenómeno (Notas para una geneidética: Eidos y monstrum)," *Daimon. Revista de Filosofía* 32 (2004): 55–75; César Moreno Márquez, "Tentativas Sobre el Rostro. Eidos y Punctum," *Er: Revista de Filosofía* 19, no. 19 (1995): 103–29.

Consequently, "Does ore feel trapped/in coins and gears?/In the petty life/ imposed on it/does it feel homesick for earth?"[79] Additionally, the pragmatic meaning is reduced to the object of a reality that is not the same, but is an external construct created by the modern subject. This circumstance is exacerbated because when that meaning abandons the entity, it become nothing, namely, its present and future being becomes dependent on external imposition. A paradigmatic example of this is illustrated by the shoes of the peasant woman from her own interpretive perspective: "The peasant woman wears her shoes in the field. Only here are they what they are. They are all the more genuinely so, the less the peasant woman thinks about the shoes while she is at work, or looks at them at all, or is even aware of them."[80]

The only way of escaping from this vicarious experience is to change the hermeneutic practice, but this forms part of a subsequent session. If the meaning cannot derive from equivocal postures in which everything goes, at attempt should be made to find a more adequate key so as to pronounce the text first, before arriving at understandings through its canto.

Schleiermacher claimed that "every act of understanding is the reverse of an act of speaking, and one must grasp the thought [of the interpreter] that underlies a given utterance";[81] consequently, "the hermeneutic task consists in perfectly reconstructing the author's whole internal compositional labor".[82] To achieve this, the interpreter should immerse himself "as much as possible in the whole constitution of the writer".[83]

Group members are encouraged to discover who the author of the proposed text is, in this case, Seneca. They can employ all the

---

[79] Rainer Maria Rilke, *Rilke's Book of Hours: Love Poems to God* (New York: Riverhead Books, 1996), 100.

[80] Martin Heidegger, *Basic Writings* (New York: HarperCollins, 2008), 159.

[81] Friedrich D. E. Scheleiermacher, *Los discursos sobre hermenéutica* (Navarra: Universidad de Navarra, 1991), 79.

[82] Idem.

[83] Ibid., 67.

means available, including their mobile devices. Guessing the author's name is not enough, for they should also understand his frame of mind when writing the passage, which is an essential key to its interpretation. This text could be read on the basis of "the will to become committed to the truth", "freedom of speech despite the consequences" or "the dual relationship between physical pain and greatness of spirit". Once a consensus has been reached, the text is individually recited with that key and an attempt is made to improve progressively, in light of the knowledge gained in the previous sessions. This leads to the appearance of diverse meanings to be explored and perfected in different oral presentations. At the end of the session, the participants opt for one of them which is first read individually, taking turns, and then by the group as a whole.

The next workshops begin by challenging the idea that the meaning of the text is the author's, as noted by Schleiermacher. Gadamer resorts to Chladenius to explain this:

> Chladenius reaches a highly interesting conclusion. He sees that to understand an author perfectly is not the same thing as to understand speech or writing perfectly. The norm for the understanding of a book is not the author's meaning. For, "since men cannot be aware of everything, their words, speech and writing can mean something that they themselves did not intend to say or write", and consequently, "when trying to understand their writings, one can rightly think that had not occurred to the writers". Even if the reverse is the case, "that an author meant more than one has been able to understand", the real task of hermeneutics is not, for him, to understand these extra things, but the books themselves in their true, ie objective meaning. [...] "unfruitful passages can become fruitful for us", as they "encourage many thoughts".[84]

Other meanings that the text might contain, without the author being aware of them, are discussed. Likewise, the image of Van Gogh's shoes is recuperated to pose the question of how the

---

[84] Hans Georg Gadamer, *Truth and Method*, 161–2.

meaning of the text can be discovered beyond the reader's or the author's impositions. Heidegger's answer is based on the fact that when Van Gogh painted those shoes, he did not require any meaning, but remained subject to attentive listening, allowed their light to traverse him, became the shoes and only at that moment painted them. The difference with the previous hermeneutics is that the evident meaning of the shoes in the work of art did not derive from the painter but from themselves. The shoes used Van Gogh, his hands and his art to lay themselves open or to extract their meaning. Van Gogh did not paint, but it was the shoes that possessed the artist in order to generate a self-portrait.

The example of Van Gogh is repeated in aesthetics as a whole: it occurs when a writer narrates the next chapter of his novel according *to what his characters require of him*, never according to his own subjective caprice. Obviously, the author could kill off a character on a personal whim. But if this contradicts the life of the character in question, an ontological-aesthetic gap will be created, thus diminishing its *plausibility*.

Based on this theory, a Ricoeurian session is designed in which the meaning of the text does not derive from the imposition of its author or from that of readers, but from the text per se. As the French philosopher notes, "Writing is not simply a matter of the material fixation of discourse; for fixation is the condition of a much more fundamental phenomenon, that of the autonomy of the text. A threefold autonomy: with respect to the intention of the author; with respect to the cultural situation and all the sociological conditions of the production of the text; and finally, with respect to the original addressee."[85]

What must be done so that the text speaks for itself and its meaning imposes itself even on the interpretation of the reader? What must be done so that something that does not have a mouth, brain or

---

[85] Paul Ricoeur, *Hermeneutics & the Human Sciences* (Cambridge: Cambridge University Press, 1981), 91.

conscience expresses its intentionality? The answer is to modify the reader, in line with Van Gogh.

This concretion is inspired by several sources: the *lectio divina*, a section of Ran Lahav's deep philosophy groups, Husserl's eidetic variation, the reading of a mantra, the *telling* word of Gadamer and the music of words in Zambrano. All have their differences. For example, the mantra seeks to liberate the mind, while in this case the intention is to fill the ambience or atmosphere with the text, but ensuring that someone who sees it from without can find similarities in the procedure.

Firstly, the philosopher reads the initial phrase, following a previous silence that extracts the instrumental value of the words. The idea is that the text should take shape, to wit, that it should acquire the value of the *telling* word of Gadamer.[86] The reading should seek the rhythm of the text, even with the philosopher marking the beat with his foot. The members of the group are then invited to take turns to read the same text. Those who do not want to participate only have to say "pass". The relationship with the text becomes that which is established with the sacred, for which reason the philosopher expresses his respect for it and the different readings. He should then say "thank you" to each one of them, after their reading. If there are less than 10 members in the group, the same phrase should be read in at least three rounds.

Following this, the text is deployed. Some words or complete phrases, with impressions inspired by the text, are added to it. If the phrase is "you have promised to establish the strongest chain to wisdom and you have enlisted under oath. Any man will be but mocking you if he declares that this is an effeminate and easy kind of soldiering", the philosopher says the following: "You have promised, *you have obliged yourself by giving your word*, to establish the closest, *strongest* chain to wisdom, *to the highest philosophy*, and you have enlisted under oath. Any man will be but

---

[86] Hans Georg Gadamer, "Gadamer's Philosophical Legacy," 115–34, esp. 118, original emphasis.

mocking you if he declares that this is an effeminate and easy kind of soldiering, *because he does not know what he says*." The next member of the group continues with a similar phrase, but allowing the text to speak for itself: "You have promised to establish the strongest chain to wisdom, *supreme excellence*, and they have obliged you under oath, *there is no going back*. Any man will be but mocking you, *with both sarcasm and fear*, if he declares that this is an effeminate and easy kind of soldiering."

It should be observed that the intention is that the text should speak for itself and not that the participants should offer their subjective interpretations. Long presentations are a sign that they are putting too much of themselves into it, thus concealing the text. In such an event, the philosopher should encourage them to make more concise presentations by using himself as an example when the second round begins.

After concluding with a phrase, work begins on the next one until at least the first paragraph has been read.

Then, echoes based on the two phrases are performed. First, all the members of the group should read a phrase that has caught their attention. The philosopher repeats it with the same sacral care (and slowness and in a high tone of voice), as with the previous phrases. When all of them have made their contribution, each one of them reads only one word or paraphrase with a maximum of three words. This should be done without a predefined order and the philosopher should repeat each one of the words or paraphrases. Since at least five minutes should be devoted to this task, the atmosphere becomes increasingly more impregnated with the text.

The session ends with homework: noting down the phrase that has had the greatest impact on the participants on small piece of paper. They should carry this on them for the rest of the day, copy the text in the notebook of their mobile phones or, if possible, memorize it. Every morning (and, if possible, every night) they should read out the phrase aloud, before briefly reflecting on how it has become linked to their past experiences or to what they expect in the near future. Subsequently, they are asked to note down another phrase below it.

The homework, on whose content the participants will reflect in the following session, serves to cover the last mode of hermeneutics: the anagogic mode. This stems from a subjective hermeneutics in which the interpreter plays the role of the interpreted. The daily reading of their phrases brings them closer to the text, until it becomes an interpretation of or a way of developing it. They take different approaches according to their ontological constitution or the experiences through which they live the text, but the interpretive baseline and result is the fragment. This leads to a new form of interpretation in which the subject and object become inverted and, consequently, in which they understand due to the fact that the interpreted are they themselves.

The foregoing is a general overview of this series of workshops that, if they were organized fortnightly, would cover a term. To sum up, the aim of the project's four blocks is to access meaning by:

(1) Imposing the meanings of the participants.
(2) Imposing the meanings of the author.
(3) Listening to the meaning of the text per se.
(4) Listening to the meanings on the basis of life experience.
(5) The participants' appropriation on the basis of the text's hegemony.

5. Eidetic Variation Workshop Processes

In order to receive a good training, those participating in workshops of this type should develop their perceptive skills, based on the five (or the 11 that Zubiri listed) senses. Moreover, thought constitutes another mode of perception as there is content that requires argumentative processes of synthesis: a complex philosophical theory cannot be seen, heard or touched, although, after months of study, it will be understood by means of synthesis and synergic reflections on its elements.

Phenomenology has been the principal discipline devoted to the study of what appears. It has prevented deceptions and has made us aware of the invisible filters characteristic of perspectives (such as science) that were claimed to be neutral and objective.

Edmund Husserl, its father, pursued the direct experience of the world of life, of that which we live. Phenomenology tells us that far too often we understand on the basis of scientific categories that construct the world relying on their neutrality and objectiveness. However, as with any perspective, science derives from particular conclusions that encourage us to treat its alleged objectiveness and neutrality with caution. The same occurs with developmentalism: its ideological structure has been neutrally imposed on many, to the point that many do not understand why criticism is directed at certain policies that "by any reckoning" are not only for the benefit of poor countries, but are also implemented in a neutral and non-colonial manner.

The ability of phenomenology to bracket blinding interpretations is useful for philosophical counseling, pornographically bent on its task, that is, to help to strip reality naked, as already noted in relation to Ortega y Gasset. This skill is evidenced by Peter Raabe, one of the most internationally renowned philosophy educators: "A common expression I often hear from my clients is, 'I can see so many more options now where I thought I only had two choices before.' There is a joy of anticipation from not knowing where the path will lead, and it is not unusual for the client at this stage to actually take pleasure in the process of discovery and in the power of the experience of a greater autonomous agency."[87]

We have developed a workshop that trains phenomenological vision (and understanding) based on Husserl's eidetic variation. Its objective is to connect us with the *eidos*, the form, or, if you wish, with the naked reality of a concept, namely, that which is not

---

[87] Peter Raabe, *Philosophical Counseling*, 162.

influenced by particular visions. César Moreno explains this in the following terms: "Eidetics is the knowledge of the *eidos*, this being, in its *immediate (abstract) facet*, the set of essential features *of whatever could not lack something susceptible to the eidos* to *be and become what it is* and to make it thinkable in the course of its spontaneous or methodical conception. The *eidos* connects that 'something' with an *internal horizon* (Husserl, 1980: 34) or inherent to possibilities."[88]

The *eidos* is the essence that determines the being and appearance of something. It would be the "bookness" of a "book" or, in other words, whatever a book does that makes it such, regardless of cultural, historical or subjectivist determinations, namely, irrespective of whether it is understood as a printed or electronic book, whether its content is narrative or philosophical or whether it has a physical weight or is a mere idea in our minds. Another example of *eidos* would be the color red. Its *eidos* would encompass all its varieties, provided that it did not become orange or violet. Eidetic variation could also inquire into the *eidos* of "color", which implies both the difference with what it is not (sound, texture) and the opening to its full chromatic *horizon*.[89] The same can be said about the study of the "human being" in which, as Moreno notes, "a Muslim and a bushman, a carpenter and a surgeon, a Kurdish peasant and a Portuguese fisherman can coexist perfectly,"[90] before adding, "If, for example, an attempt were made to capture the *eidos* of 'human being', we should avoid becoming blocked or hindered by the mere *inductive community* of the 'universality' of 'man' ethnocentrically (unconsciously) restricted to *us-men*, so that the other men, the *dissimilar*, may be ejected from the *eidos* of 'man' to become 'barbarians' or 'non-men'."[91]

---

[88] César Moreno Márquez, "Eidos y periferia. rutina y trascendencia in extremis en el horizonte de una humanidad proteica e híbrida," *Recerca* 12 (2012): 24.
[89] Ibid., 37.
[90] Ibid., 35.
[91] Ibid., 36.

Eidetic variation trains our gaze and understanding and helps us to be aware that the elements that we believed to be inherent to a concept only constitute one of its facets. This occurs with "poverty" which has more than economic connotations. This concept serves to describe the phases of eidetic variation:

(1) To consider and explain an arbitrary case of *eidos*

The example does not have to be chosen conscientiously. It is phenomenologically deployed by different means, such as an explanation, the account of a case or even a song. These means begin to attune us to the *eidos*.

After noting them down, the participants directly narrate the experience of the poverty of a mother who cannot feed her children or that of a father who feels that he lacks the affection of his children, the surprise of finding one's current account empty, the lack of whiteness of the color black or the appearance of a wall that should have been painted long ago.

(2) Empirical example

The initial example of each member and the group as a whole is completed with others that have been directly experienced. They then continue to relive the experience of "poverty" through new faces, thus achieving a "productive activity which consists in running through the multiplicity of variations".[92]

(3) Cases of imagination

(3a) Examples of phantasy

Familiar examples are supplemented by other imagined ones that have not been experienced. These open up the *eidos* to new meanings that, albeit far removed from the participants' own experiences, provide it with a broader horizon. They are thus capable of surpassing the experienced spatiotemporal constraints, it now being possible to ponder on the poverty of a sixteenth-century character or that of a Mapuche currently living in Chile, "[…] for the acquisition of pure concepts or concepts of essences, an empirical comparison cannot suffice but that, by special

---

[92] Edumund Husserl, *Experience and Judgment*, 329.

arrangements, the universal which first comes to prominence in the empirically given must from the outset be freed from its character of contingency."[93]

Eidetic variation allows for fertilizing, making pregnant, the *eidos* so as to witness a polyphonic birth. Husserl encourages us to resort to history and fiction, but his words urge us to think about the possibilities of spawning examples using non-discursive means.

> [...] naturally, it is necessary to exercise one's phantasy abundantly in the required activity of perfect clarification and in the free reshaping of phantasy-data, it is also necessary, before doing that, to fertilize one's phantasy by observations in originary intuition which are as abundant and excellent as possible: whereby this is not to say that experience as experience has here a function in grounding validity. Extraordinary profit can be drawn from the offerings of history, in even more abundant measure from those of art, and especially from poetry, which are, to be sure, imaginary but which, in the originality of their invention of forms [*Neugestaltungen*], the abundance of their single features and the unbrokenness of their motivation, tower high above the products of out phantasy and, in addition, when they are approached understandingly, become converted into perfectly clear phantasies with particular ease owing to the suggestive power exerted by artistic means of presentation.
>
> Thus, if one is fond of paradoxical phrases, one can actually say, and if one means the ambiguous phrase in the right sense, one can say in strict truth, that "feigning" [*Fiktion"*] *makes up the vital element of phenomenology as of every other eidetic science*, that feigning is the source from which cognition of "eternal truths" is fed.[94]

---

[93] Ibid., 323. Further on, he remarks, "For a pure *eidos*, the factual actuality of the particular cases by means of which we progress in the variation is completely irrelevant. And this must be taken literally. The actualities must be treated as possibilities among other possibilities, in fact as arbitrary possibilities of the imagination" (Ibid., 332).

[94] Edmund Husserl, *Ideas Pertaining to a Pure Phenomenology and to a Phenomenological Philosophy* (The Hague/Boston/Lancaster: Martinus Nijhoff Publishers, 1983), 159–60, original emphasis.

This progress brings into focus the horizon of "poverty" eliminating its patterns dependent on the aforementioned contexts. This focusing should not lead to its disfiguration, at least not to the point of confusing it with another *eidos*, for, as Moreno declares, its "sameness must be preserved".[95]

(3b) Aberrant examples

Moreno introduces a play on variations that takes them to the limit: monstrous or aberrant examples. The professor from Huelva explains an exercise that he asks his students to perform: "For instance, for *teaching* purposes I often ask my students to imagine a face … and that they should *definitely* not focus merely on a known, familiar, vicinal one, but should try to imagine (and think about!) the strangest, most anomalous and (apparently) ex-centric or extra-vagant, 'foreign' or exotic (in the strongest sense of the word) face."[96]

Basing himself on artistic avant-gardes, Moreno proposes possible and impossible eidetic variation to his students. As to the latter, Man Ray's *Cadeau* stands out: an iron with spikes on its base, which makes them wonder whether or not it continues to be an iron, despite the fact that it is impossible to eliminate creases with it.[97]

Moreno qualifies the distinction between variation and alteration: alternation implies a succession of images in which when one appears, the last one disappears; however, variation involves maintaining all the faces, "one on top of the other". The image of variation is akin to an *eidos* painted on top of a transparent sheet and the progressive superposition of new variations that respect and shape the horizon of meaning of the pursued *eidos*.

> We now have a better understanding of the eidetic path which, as Husserl held, should be of *variations*, not of *alternations* of the given-

---

[95] César Moreno Márquez, "Eidos y periferia," 37.
[96] Ibid., 28.
[97] Ibid., 28–9.

> imagined, variations that, as a whole and in their full diversity, should be able to cohabit or coexist "in" the *eidos* – and, above all, with those that are most far removed from our prejudices, routines and understanding.[98]
>
> Alterations imply that each altered example would be seen successively, but the *eidos* is not achieved in succession but in variations, namely, seeing all the object or face *eidos* one on top of the other. The *eidos* would be the synchronic variation of all the empirical and phantasized examples.[99]

From a musical perspective, action is akin to listening to several instruments interpreting the same symphony. The *eidos* is not the interpretation of a violin, a guitar or a drum, but the form that occurs in each one of them without being any of them.

There is a less perfect analogy in writing: it would be like reading dozens of books by the same author, until managing to capture the *style* with which he is identified. The ability to distil this eidetic style would be essential, for example, for a literary expert who had to decide if the newly discovered work of a dead author had really been written by him. Similarly, this would be the case of an art expert who had to clarify whether a newly discovered painting attributed to Murillo was really his. This is possible because the methodology is not only based on *existing* empirical variations, but also on training in possibilities of imagination. In this sense, the strategy is strengthened by the flight of fancy of the variations: "Imagination/fancy is decisive the further away it "sends" us, that it, to the extent that we could, with its help, go beyond trivial or routine examples."[100]

In sum, this phase allows us to make epoché and to free ourselves from the particular determination and empirics of the *eidos*. "Only

---

[98] César Moreno Márquez, "De los objetos impelentes. ¿Quién iba a imaginarlos? Contribución a una fenomenología de la imaginación como configuración de escenas," *Anuario filosófico* 51, no. 2 (2018): 299–300, original emphasis.

[99] César Moreno Márquez, "Tentativas sobre el rostro," 109ff.

[100] César Moreno Márquez, "De los objetos impelentes," 281.

if we become conscious of this bond, putting it consciously out of play, and so also free this broadest surrounding horizon of variants from all connection to experience and all experiential validity, do we achieve perfect purity. Then we find ourselves, so to speak, in a pure world of imagination, a world of absolutely pure possibility."[101]

(4) First decantation or the first "unitary link in continuous coincidence"

The *eidos* of poverty is progressively distilled. This does not only depend on explanatory or discursive materializations, for the variations are sensitive to other explanatory modes, to wit, formats that put out (ex-hibit) the *eidos*. The participants should be constantly reminded about the meaning of what is being sought, since the task is not consistent with the usual activity. To help them, the following passages from Husserl can be used:

> It then becomes evident that a unity runs through this multiplicity of successive figures, that in such free variations of an original image, e.g., of a thing, *an invariant is necessarily retained* as the *necessary general form*, without which an object such as this thing, as an example of its kind, would not be thinkable at all. While what differentiates the variants remains indifferent to us, this form stands out in the practice of voluntary variation, and as an absolutely identical content, *an invariable what, according to which all the variants coincide*: a general essence. [...] This general essence is the *eidos* [...].[102]
>
> It then becomes evident that *a unity runs through* this multiplicity of successive figures, that in such free variations of an original image, e.g., of a thing, an invariant is necessarily retained as the necessary general form, *without which an object such as this thing*, as an example of its kind, *would not be thinkable at all*. While what differentiates the variants remains indifferent to us, this form stands out in the practice of voluntary variation, and as an absolutely identical content, an invariable what, according to which all the variants coincide: a general essence. [...] This general essence is the *eidos* [...].[103]

---

[101] Edmund Husserl, *Experience and Judgment*, 333.
[102] Ibid., 323–4, emphasis added.
[103] Idem., emphasis added.

(5) The invoking word on the basis of "and so forth" ("*und so weiter*")

The *eidos* could be categorially explained, namely, with words. However, Lohmar highlights that what appears in the definition of *eidos* would not merely be *sensitive content but appeals*, "intentional components" or "givennesses that can arise only in the transition between intentional acts".[104]

The concepts employed in the definition or explanation should be charged in such a way that, we could say, the words cease to inform to conjure up realities, as with a magic spell or enchantment.

Thus, what is proposed is to transform the previous definition into a poem or song. This can be achieved by detaining the workshop in the previous phase and by giving the participants enough time to bring about this transformation.

The question as to the number of variations (or cases) necessary to achieve the first decantation depends on a second regulatory criterion that Husserl calls "*und so weiter*" ("and so forth"). The participants will have sufficient material to perform the first valid decantation when they feel that they have no need for any more variations to understand the *eidos*: as they have started to become aware of the author's style, they do not need to read further works of his, insofar as those that they have already read are sufficient to understand it. Alternatively, they could gain further practice by continuing the song or by offering additional general examples respecting the *eidos*, as they have understood his style.

The full process up until this point is summarized by Husserl:

> Starting from an arbitrary red and continuing in a series of variations, we obtain the *eidos* red. If we had taken another red as our exemplary point of departure, we would certainly have obtained by intuition another multiplicity of variations; but it immediately becomes apparent

---

[104] Lohman, "The Phenomenological Method," 120.

that this new multiplicity belongs in the open horizon of the and-so-forth of the first, just as the first belongs in the horizon of the latter; the *eidos* is one and the same.[105]

(6) Critical and *epoché* phase

This phase dwells on the critique of the *eidos* obtained, that is, noting down missing or superfluous elements in the first decantation. Likewise, the activity of epoché is increased by bracketing biases that have gone unnoticed.

This is practiced (1) by emphasizing the realm of phantasy, (2) introducing new agents with modes of phantasy differing from those of the initial group and (3) fostering epochés that have been overlooked.

Epoché consists of bracketing or deactivating frames or categories that limit the meaning of an event. The frames often function with the concealing potential of an ideology, that is, they offer an allegedly naked definition of the *eidos*, but, however, without a *modality* of the concept based on its own realm. This has occurred when differentiating between the rich and the poor world, as if it were a natural dichotomy in view of their gross domestic products (GDPs). Notwithstanding this, critique has shown us that the terms "rich" and "poor" are established on the basis of monetary criteria. An analytical (and destructive) vision of that dichotomy reveals that we can also be *poor* in affection and *rich* in intelligence.

Since the objective of this workshop is to connect with the *eidos* of poverty, it is important to stress that this phase detects and transforms into epoché supposedly neutral frames which would prevent us from seeing poverty in its nakedness and, in this case, accessing those non-economic meanings.

(7) Eidetic intuition

The completion of these phases results in an eidetic intuition of poverty or, at least, contributes to discover and deactivate empirical biases based on ideological filters and to approach the concept from

---

[105] Edmund Husserl, *Experience and Judgment*, 338.

a transcendental perspective, to wit, one that is not limited to those spatial, temporal or ideological filters.

Ultimately, the program serves to gain a subtle vision that helps to strip reality of the spheres that color it and of which we are usually unaware.

6. Introductory Metaphysics Workshop Processes

There can be many philosophy projects and sessions due to the diversity of the discipline. Their *objectives* depend directly on the philosophical currents involved and, in all cases, facilitate the expression of philosophical concepts, which increases the participants' experiential knowledge of them and helps them to develop their hermeneutic skills. Thus, children will be hard pressed to understand the typology of the being and teenagers will be bored by it, if it is explained to them without bearing in mind their level of comprehension. However, they will remember it if stereograms are employed, inviting them to explore the *disposition* that should be acquired to achieve these 3D representations.

Similarly, it is difficult to explain the being as a place in which the entity is concealed without performing some or other exercise in order to perceive the tension between its visibility and invisibility. This case is used to explain a philosophy project *inhabited* by the nature of metaphysics.

Firstly, groups of no less than 20 members are asked to answer a question, which allows for at least two types of replies, in a text containing between 300 and 600 words. Are sentiments necessary for gaining an understanding of reality? Should abortion be defended? Is democracy the best political system? Is Christmas an invention of El Corte Inglés,[106] the Church, the Romans or some or other institution? Does the Internet help people to develop? Is our society advancing or languishing? Does beauty depend on the eyes of the beholder or the object?

---

[106] A Spanish department store chain.

Secondly, they then publically present their texts without the possibility of rebuttal. Nor are they permitted to modify their own stances after listening to the rest of the presentations, but should stick to their guns.

Following this, physical or printed picture frames are created. These frames contain images with colors, drawings (flowers, animals or specific people) or situations based on faces (for instance, anguish through the repetition of Munch's *The Scream*), while there is always a white one among their number. The group members are then divided into teams of three or four who, to the extent possible, are strangers. They have to decide on how they will present their reply in that frame, unfamiliar to the rest. Once the presentation format has been decided on, each team should adapt it to the frame that they have received. Therefore, this stage requires clearly delimited phases which should be completed in depth.

The following session begins with the presentations, one member of each team being chosen to this end. The rest should focus on the format and not on the content, as this holds the key that the rest of the teams should decipher. Once the presentation has been made by one of the members of a team, the rest of the teams should attempt to decipher the key, qualifying their choice. A second person chosen from each team then gives or represents the answer with the aim of helping the other teams to discover the key or to confirm it with a second representation. The previous discussion is repeated. Finally, a third member of each team repeats the action. If the key or frame of some or other team is not discovered, it is given to the team that has made the best attempt to present it to the rest. As the frames are discovered, all the teams are asked to reflect on how each one of them has been depicted in the representation of the text. The session finishes when all the teams have become familiar with the frames. This is followed by group reflection on the nature of the frame per se (not on each one of the frames) and its influence on the content. Likewise, they also consider the differences between the frame and the replies (the being and the entity in the metaphysical dimension).

The third session is a repetition of the previous one, but this time substituting the frames with music. To this end, a different type of music (classical, rock, jazz, pop, country, Gregorian chants, etc.) is sent to the mobile devices of each team (whose members are not the same as before), who are then expected to offer individual replies to the previous question. First, they listen without writing. Subsequently, they are allowed to write for five minutes while listening to the music or merely remain in silence. As before, the teams should discover the musical key on the basis of the presentation, before reflecting on the nature of the frame and its invisibility.

The fourth session is devoted to analyzing other frames that surround not only our own discourse, but also existence as a whole. In each case, it is important to shift from more specific categories towards more abstract ones and from the most visible (entity) to the most invisible (being or *apeiron*), albeit with an essential influence on our lives. One of the abstract and invisible categories that can be understood and inhabited by all, like, for example, thought, music, beauty, etc., is chosen. From the most invisible, the opposite transition is made, attempting to inhabit specific realities. Imagine that the most invisible is thought. The group members are asked to look at a pencil, without abandoning that contemplation, in order that they should perceive how thought constructs them. Following five minutes of contemplation, they will gaze upwards and inhabit the first object on which their eyes come to rest. This is repeated with whatever is below it and to its right and left. Finally, they are asked to inhabit the air on the basis of the category of thought. As homework, they are given the task of searching for something that integrates more realities, with an eye to repeating the exercise after the session.

The following day, they will inhabit things *from* other fundamental realities and will search for an ultimate one that serves to integrate all those that have been presented.

We will not dwell here on the metaphysical notions of these workshops, although we will indeed list a few of them in order that readers so inclined can search for them in the history of philosophy: being, entity, habitation, attentive listening, stepping back, categories, concepts, contrasts, relationships, content and form, quality, phenomena, noumenon, essence and modes of production.

CHAPTER 4
LOCATIONS FOR PHILOSOPHICAL PRACTICE

1. Foreword. Objectives and Results (or Performances)

Before commencing this section, it should be stressed that what is understood here as objectives of philosophy are its own internal purposes. For instance, since María Zambrano attempts have been made to decipher the original sense; since Rorty, to foster a supportive dialogue through persuasion, to combat metaphysical dogmatism and to accept the creation of philosophical lexicons and systems only as a personal, rather than imposed, activity; since Husserl, to attain a profound vision of that which appears through phenomenological reductions or actions, such as eidetic variation; since Adorno, to create the right conditions so that Auschwitz should never repeat itself; since Horkheimer, to combat instrumentality using a critical questioning;[107] since Chrysippus, Seneca and Marcus Aurelius, to attain a more critical life (*logos*) in which passions are mastered and prudent decisions are made (*ethos*) and there is a deeper knowledge of reality (*physis*); since Foucault, to create an archaeology of knowledge that frees it from constituent or constituted power. There are more purposes if to these are added other authors or an inquiry is made into how philosophers have even searched for several purposes during their lives.

This task can be made more tolerable by grouping together philosophers according to specific criteria. Thus, the continental philosophers would be more inclined to deploy the being and their analytical counterparts to resort to argumentative problem-solving, normally of an epistemological character. On the other hand, the Frankfurt School would focus on emancipation from oppressive

---

[107] Edmund Husserl, *Experience and Judgment*, 322–30; Lohmar, "The Phenomenological Method," 110–32; César Moreno Márquez, "Break/Freak," 55–75; César Moreno Márquez, "Tentativas Sobre el Rostro," 103–29.

powers (classified in different ways in each age), versus the hermeneutic tendencies that pursue understanding (on the basis of the subject, the text, the being, etc.) or the phenomenological ones that strive to deploy phenomena (on the basis of intentionality, the *nous*, the body, the event, etc.).

If the areas of common philosophical knowledge were used as a criterion, epistemology would analyze and generate theories of knowledge, ethics would deal with the legitimacy of moral actions, aesthetics would involve reflection on questions associated with art and the philosophy of technology would be devoted to pondering on technical and technological notions.

As has been seen, philosophical practice would give shape to all this knowledge, allowing for inhabiting in philosophical theories or from those of their authors. It respects the purposes of philosophy, owing to the fact that it forms part of its body, whereby we do not concur with those who (1) defend purposes that have nothing to do with philosophy per se, (2) do not properly justify the actions performed in counseling sessions or workshops, (3) assume in a reductionist manner that this discipline only has one purpose and (4) end up confusing the discipline itself with others, in spite of the fact that it cannot be denied that there are possible synergies with them.

One of the reasons why the philosophical nature of our field is all too frequently transgressed or confused with others is, as already observed, the neglect of philosophical training. Taking a degree in philosophy is not enough, for it is also necessary to maintain the philosophical tension in our own work throughout our life course. This is achieved by reading works on philosophy on a daily basis that (1) improve our own philosophical training and (2) put us on a firmer footing in the discipline. After a career lasting more than two decades, I have witnessed how many philosophy undergraduates and graduates have gone over to the field of philosophical practice or have started to study psychology, pedagogy, psychoanalysis, meditation, coaching or other disciplines. They have become enthused by these areas of study that under no circumstances should be regarded as inferior. Nonetheless, they have maintained the label of philosophical practitioners even when (1) their practice has been far removed from the literature on philosophy or (2) they have not managed to identify in depth the philosophical nature of their actions, for they appeal exclusively to "argumentation and the use of philosophical concepts".[108]

Unlike objectives, results or performances are those elements that are achieved through philosophical action and which are not pursued. In this sense, philosophy can be therapeutic without being a therapy, namely, rehab results can be obtained, even though this has not been the aim. If it were not justified, this statement could become a desideratum, for which reason three examples of the potential of philosophical practice and philosophy for/with children are described below.

First and foremost, reference should be made to the dozens of empirical studies of philosophy for/with children which substantiate this. The first was performed by its founder, Matthew Lipman, who in 1970 analyzed the performance of the discipline with one experimental and one control group. The group participating in philosophy workshops during four months mentally matured two years versus the other which maintained a normal progression, according to the results of the California Test of Mental Maturity (CTMM). Félix García Moriyón also obtained positive results in a philosophical study performed on teenagers,[109] with those participating in philosophy sessions improving in sciences and mathematics[110] versus those who did not. Similar

---

[108] José Barrientos Rastrojo, "Philosophical practice as experience and travel," 29–44.

[109] Félix García Moriyón (coord.), *La estimulación de la inteligencia racional y la inteligencia emocional* (Madrid: Ediciones de la Torre, 2002).

[110] John F. Martin and Mark L. Wenstein, "Thinking Skills and Philosophy for Children: The Bethlehem Program, 1982-1983," *Analytic Teaching* 5, no. 2 (1985): 28–31.

results have been obtained in other studies, with an improvement in social relationships and self-esteem,[111] mental flexibility and creativity,[112] and cognitive skills.[113] A hundred of these studies have been compiled by the aforementioned García Moriyón on the website of the Institute for Advancement of Philosophy for Children, founded by Mathew Lipman himself.[114]

The second case endorsing the performance of philosophy (philosophical practice) has to do with a research project of ours financed by the John Templeton Foundation in the United States, through the University of Chicago, in 2016. Entitled, "Can wisdom be learned in several contexts?", also known as the "Wisdom Philosophical Practice Project" or "W3P", its objective was to analyze the efficiency of Stoic workshops held in Mexico, Croatia, Norway and Spain. The project coordinators were David Sumiacher (Mexico), Michael Weiss (Norway), Zoran Kojcic (Croatia) and yours truly (Spain). Furthermore, the team also included the experimental consultant and data analyst Jesús Gómez Bujedo and, later on, Guro Hansen joined Weiss in Norway. The findings, which were published in South Korea[115] in 2019, brought to light ways of demonstrating the efficiency of Stoic workshops (see Figure 1.4).

---

[111] Susan Gardner, "Participation in a Community of Inquiry Nourishes Participants' Perspective-taking Capacity: A Report of a Two Year Empirical Study. Philosophy for Children on Top of the World," *Educational and Child Psychology* 20, no. 2 (1999): 65–79.

[112] Daniela G. Camhy and Gunter Iberer, "Philosophy for Children: A Research Project for further mental and personality development of primary and secondary school pupils," *Thinking* 7, no. 4 (1988): 18–25.

[113] Félix García Moriyón, Roberto Colom, Santos Lora, María Rivas, and Vicente Traver, "Valoración de 'Filosofía para Niños': un programa de enseñar a pensar," *Psicothema* 12, no. 2 (2000): 207–11.

[114] Further information at: https://www.montclair.edu/iapc/research-in-philosophy-for-children/ (accessed December 24, 2019).

[115] José Barrientos and Jesús Gómez, "Can wisdom be taught by philosophical practice? An experimental research," *Journal of Humanities Therapy* 10, no. 3 (2019): 35–61.

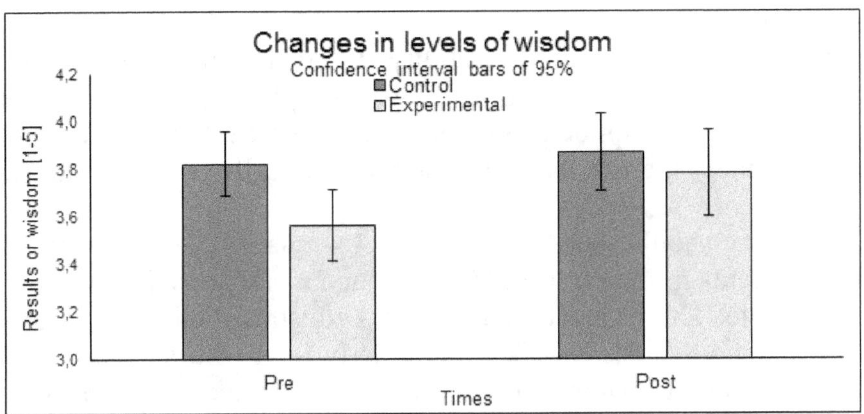

Source: José Barrientos and Jesús Gómez, "Can wisdom be taught by philosophical practice? An Experimental Research," *Journal of Humanities Therapy* 10, no. 3 (2019): 35–61.
FIGURE 1.2. Changes in leves of wisdom in philosophical workshops.

The control groups only improved by four hundredths of a decimal, while the experimental group improved fourfold.

The affective level of the control group increased by two hundredths of a decimal, while that of the experimental group did so by seven hundredths of a decimal. In the cognitive dimension, the control group improved by only a few hundredths of a decimal, whereas the experimental group's improvement was fivefold. Lastly, in the reflective dimension, the control group improved by 10 hundredths of a decimal, while the experimental group's improvement was twofold.

As to the conclusions of the experiment, it was observed that the control group had developed some skills that we mediated because the activities included group reflections and other mechanisms that should have only been implemented in the experimental group. For this reason, the following project (BOECIO) takes into account these aspects so as to fine tune the results.

The aim of the ongoing philosophical practice project in prisons is to analyze the efficiency of philosophy workshops in relation to specific data. Its first phase, implemented between 2018 and 2019, yielded promising results: increases of 15.2 and 23.4 per cent in emotional control and the ability to take problems lightly, respectively, in the experimental group, plus a 14.3 per cent increase in open-mindedness versus 2.6 per cent in the control group, namely the results of the former practically multiplied those of the latter by seven.

These data should be supplemented by qualitative evidence or developments in the philosophical practice workshops that we have held to date. The increase in autarchy is illustrated by the case of a shy girl who decides to talk to an elderly man who she sees on a daily basis and to whom no one dares to talk, since some prisoners decide to get in contact with their parents after not having spoken to them for years or even because of their decision to kick their drug habits. The results obtained at the prison of Santa Martha Acatitla (Mexico) thanks to the philosophy workshops are a good example of this.

> Noteworthy among the results obtained in those workshops is the fact that they contributed to decrease the drug consumption and addiction of certain people deprived of their freedom; many of the inmates of both sexes assumed and put into practice the workshop content (Greek philosophy, existentialism and poetry); some people abandoned the idea of committing suicide; it managed to generate a genuine interest in philosophical content, to the point that after the workshops had concluded, the students from both prisons requested that they be continued.[116]

Their improved reflective capacity is evidenced by the fact that, after pondering on existentialist topics, some of the prisoners participating in our workshops have decided to abandon drug trafficking or the idea of committing suicide. Lastly, there have been cases in which very violent people (or groups) have resolved

---

[116] Ángel Alonso, "La soledad de las guerreras de Santa Martha," *Revista Internacional de Filosofía Aplicada HASER* 10 (2019): 15.

to reconsider their actions and opt for a more strategic approach or have improved their capacity to understand others and, as a result, have become more patient, after attending the workshops. It should be noted that these cases do not prove that philosophy has a normalizing or reintegrating capacity, but have yielded results that highlight that those participating in them control themselves, to wit, acquire skills that prevent them from being manipulated by the ideology of the system. Moreover, they acquire lateral thinking skills for problem-solving and for mastering their passions.

All these results underscore the ability of philosophical practice to modify groups and individuals in a critical way. Therefore, it should come as no surprise that the discipline has already become, or is on its way to becoming, established at different universities with the introduction of counseling sessions and workshops, as will be seen below.

2. Philosophical Counseling

Philosophical counseling is understood as an activity developed by practitioners who offer their services to people with problems that can usually be treated with philosophy.

There are counseling sessions that leverage philosophy for resolving conflicts, without calling into question the frame in which they are generated. Seen from the perspective of the first generation of the Frankfurt School or on the basis of Foucauldian notions, this option casts serious doubt on the critical capacity of the work performed. Having said that, most of the sessions allow for developing a critique of that which has been lived, which ends up resolving conflicts[117] or helping people to learn to live with the problematic status of existence.

Versus the problem-solving lines of some therapies or tendencies that urge people to search for happiness without questioning the term, that is, without being fully aware of the distinction between capitalist happiness and that defended by Seneca in *De vita beata,*

---

[117] José Barrientos Rastrojo, *Resolución de conflictos*, 157–8.

we usually caution that the aim of philosophical consulting should not be to achieve happiness, but frequently to calm (to cope with) anxiety. The reasons for this have been noted above, but suffice it to appeal to authenticity on the basis of Sartre or Heidegger to understand it.

Based on the foregoing, the first action that a philosopher should perform in a counseling session does not usually involve helping people to cope with personal dissatisfaction, but is to inquire into the reasons why their situation is painful for them. In doing so, the reason behind their suffering is challenged.

Imagine that a young woman attending a counseling session has a problem with the recent divorce of her parents and asks us for advice on how to reunite them or, at least, to alleviate her pain. The philosopher's action is not based of providing people with personal calming techniques, at least in the initial stages, but to challenge the system causing unhappiness. On the one hand, that feeling may be motivated by the social structure that determines what we should suffer in each circumstance. With his sensology, Mario Perniola has explained how the system is currently determining not only how we should think, but also the type of reaction that we should have to life events.[118] The divorce of someone's parents would, at any rate, lead to sadness. That feeling is challenged in sessions by offering examples of other societies or historical circumstances in which divorce did not have negative connotations. On the other, bringing eidetic variation into play can help to analyze the different facets of divorce, including profiles.[119] This could also be achieved by performing an analysis on the concept of divorce from an Ortegian perspective.[120]

---

[118] Mario Perniola, *Del Sentir* (Valencia: Pretextos, 2008).

[119] Lohmar, "The Phenomenological Method," 110–32.

[120] "Reality, precisely for being so and for being found outside our individual minds, can only achieve those multiplications in a thousand facets and beams [...]. Truth, reality, the universe, life—whatever you wish to call it—breaks into innumerable facets, into countless vertices, each one of which gives on to an individual. If he has known how to be faithful to his point of view, if he has

If we were to take a step back, questioning suffering and pain as negative aspects of life, this would fine tune the approach to the problem. A society of spectacle and immediate satisfaction provides pain with an unhealthy semic fabric. However, it is important not to forget that this has positive aspects, for instance, as a mechanism for personal development. This circumstance is not only repeated in the works of mystical authors, but also forms the basis of María Zambrano's interior exiles. Working with these authors does not re-semanticize suffering, but can be used as a resource for discovering truths which, otherwise, would have gone unnoticed.

It should be stressed that the aim of this type of counseling is not to rehabilitate or cure people; it simply philosophizes on their sorrow. Nevertheless, the results allows for accessing deeper levels that are often therapeutic.

3. Philosophical Practice for/with Children and Teenagers

In addition to the excellent work that philosophy for/with children has performed, philosophical practice implements methodologies for children in different contexts: from formal education and extracurricular activities to communities at risk of social exclusion. The ability to make progress in critical thinking, the deep analysis skills of the Oxonian school, the advances in formal logic from Aristotle to Perelman,[121] Descartes' conception of analysis,[122] the

---

resisted the eternal temptation of changing his retina for another imaginary, what he sees will be a real aspect of the world. And vice versa: each man has a mission of truth. Wherever my pupil is, another is not there; whatever my pupil sees of reality is not seen by another. We are irreplaceable, we are necessary […]. Within humanity each race, within each race each individual is an organ of perception differing from all the rest and like a tentacle that reaches bits of the universe inaccessible to the rest. So, reality is offered in individual perspectives," José Ortega y Gasset, *Obras completas 2* (Madrid: Alianza, 1998), 19.

[121] Chaïm Perelman and Lucie Olbrechts-Tyteca, *Tratado de la Argumentación. La Nueva Retórica* (Madrid: Gredos, 1989).

[122] Rene Descartes, *The Discourse on the Method* (New York: The Liberal Arts

informal logic of Gutteridge,[123] Johnson-Blair[124] and Diestler,[125] the Marxian analysis with children that Benjamin showed us in *Radio Benjamin*[126] and the critical thinking of Ennis,[127] Richard Paul and Linda Elder[128] all serve as necessary tools for children at risk of social exclusion.

Children's homes in Mexico and Spain and youngsters living in marginalized communities who attend philosophy workshops do not always possess adequate tools for coping with the ideology of the systems that manipulate them. For instance, we have accompanied children and teenagers belonging to indigenous communities, like the Raramuri, who consume Resistol (a glue used as a drug in Mexico), a habit shared by other youngsters with whom we have become acquainted on the streets of Mexico City. Both they and their families were unaware of the consequences that Resistol could have for their lives. As in the case of Freire's culture circles, it is not a question of changing an ideology for another, stressing that the drug is dangerous for their physical health and their existential life, depending on mafias, but to equip them with skills that allow them to question the ideology of the system that has converted them into the pawns of vested interests that do not take them into account.

A Habermasian session could also help them to change their vision aimed at achieving ends for communication actions in their

---

Press, 1950).

[123] Moira Gutteridge, *Constructive Critical Thinking* (Toronto: Hartcourt Brace, 1995).

[124] Ralph H. Johnson and Anthony A. Blair, *Logical Self-defense* (Toronto: McGraw Hill, 1977).

[125] Sherry Diestler, *Becoming a Critical Thinker: A User-friendly Manual* (New York: MacMillan, 1994).

[126] Walter Benjamin, *Radio Benjamin* (Tres Cantos: Akal, 2015).

[127] Robert H. Ennis, *Critical thinking* (New Jersey: Prentice Hall, 1996).

[128] Richard W. Paul and Linda Elder, *Critical Thinking. Tools for Taking Charge of Your Professional and Personal Life* (New Jersey: Pearson FT Press, 2013).

environment, that is, to challenge the idea that, in all facets of life, all actions should be driven by personal interests.

Through our work with children living in the poorest neighborhood in Spain, we have noticed a high level of conflict for several reasons. One has to do with the mechanisms of social exclusion employed by children of diverse ethnic groups, for example, Gypsies against Jews or Muslims. The Rortyian workshops aimed at fostering solidarity and persuasive understanding are tools that yield swift results in these circumstances.

Obviously, philosophical work is also necessary with the so-called "socially normal", namely, at education centers that in class teach the ideal of a generation of responsible citizens. This is from where the Lipmanian idea stems, but it should be recalled that this was also endorsed by previous philosophers, such as John Dewey in his *How We Think*, Giner de los Ríos[129] as a pioneer of Krausism in Spain and even by committed teachers like Blas Zambrano,[130] María Zambrano's father.

4. Philosophical Practice in Prisons

Eduardo Vergara started to organize workshops in Seville prisons in 2007, as with Vaughana Feary[131] and Horst Gronke,[132] among others.

Grounded in the theory of the ETOR group, Vergara's working methodology is based on training in critical thinking and analyzing ideas. Leveraging philosophy, he helps inmates to "open their field of vision".[133] His methodology is usually based on the analysis of

---

[129] Francisco Giner de los Ríos, *Obras selectas* (Madrid: Espasa Calpe, 2004).

[130] Blas Zambrano, *Artículos, relatos y otros escritos* (Badajoz: Diputación de Badajoz, 1998).

[131] Vaughana Feary, "Philosophical Practice in correctional facilities. Theory and practice," *Journal of Humanities Therapy* 4, no. 19 (2013).

[132] Horst Gronke and Uwe Nitsch, "Moving through Dialogue – Free Thinking in a Confined Space. Socratic Dialogue in Tegal Penal Institution," *Practical Philosophy* 5, no. 2 (2003): 13–25.

[133] A video of his work is available at:

eloquent philosophical phrases, like Nietzsche's "What does not kill me makes me stronger". On the basis of a conscientious study of their elements and the history of philosophy, he opens a group reflection in which the inmates offer their perspectives and obtain, in addition to content, a philosophical gym session aimed at mental training. Vergara is aware of the need for the history of thought during sessions, since philosophers allow us to go beyond our limited reflections. However, it takes into consideration that theory should not hinder the inmates' reflections, which is the workshop's authentic objective.

In Mexico, Ángel Alonso has worked at several prisons through the initiative of Marco Antonio López Cortes, one of his students, and the aforementioned BOECIO project: "The project's main objective is to equip those deprived of their freedom with philosophical tools and content that allow them to reflect on their lives, the meaning and significance that imprisonment may have by putting notions into practice, thus making their time in prison more 'tolerable', with an eye to contributing to their social reintegration."[134]

The Marfil group, run by Víctor Rojas, a professor at the Minuto de Dios University Corporation (Corporación Universitaria Minuto de Dios, UNIMINUTO), has worked with juvenile delinquents: "The Marfil group started to conduct research on juvenile delinquents at the Centro de Educación Amigoniano (CEA) and Redentor y Hogar Femenino Luis Amigó (HOFLA) in order to understand, among other matters of interest, the multiple ways in which the youngsters build their identities."[135]

This identity-building process involves recognizing and deconstructing the stigmatization endured by those participating in

---

https://www.youtube.com/watch?v=hFMNuHb6kXw (accessed January 25, 2020).

[134] Alonso, "La soledad," 15.

[135] Víctor Rojas (ed.), *Filosofía para niños: diálogos con menores infractores* (Bogotá: UNIMINUTO, 2015), 143.

the workshop. The sessions "have allowed the research team, and the students who are completing their social service and professional internships there, to de-normalize and denaturalize prior conceptions and value judgments that have historically, socially and culturally been constructed as regards marginalized and socially excluded minors."[136]
In England, Peter Garrett commenced his philosophical work at HMP Whithemoor, a maximum security prison for men in Cambridgeshire. The project grew until giving rise to Prison Dialogue, a non-profit association that has been functioning for more than 25 years now.

> In the part called "What was learnt from prison dialogue?" he concluded that dialogue groups contribute to making the prison community more human. They create a community of joint investigation, in which the point isn't being in favour of something or being against it. The point rather is mutual listening and consideration. Seeking mutual understanding also inspires the participants to respect each other. They learn to think about their viewpoints, and to alter or revise them. The participants gain in self-confidence, because their opinions are viewed as relevant, even if they are different from others' viewpoints.[137]

Although recently created in 2018, the founders of the institution Philosophy in Prison have a long track record. Its main members include Mary Margaret McCabe, Bill Brewer and Tom Harrison. Special mention should go to McCabe, a professor emeritus of Ancient Philosophy at King's College (London) who has published many works on authors such as Socrates, Plato and Aristotle. Philosophy in Prison's objectives are "to promote philosophical education in prisons and to explore the practical and philosophical principles that this involves" and "to set up stand-alone philosophy courses in prisons in the UK, accessible to a broad range of those in custody". Its achievement are noteworthy:

---

[136] Ibid., 93.
[137] Horst Gronke and Uwe Nitsch, "Moving through Dialogue," 13–25.

> In the doing of philosophy – in facing the questions of an insistent interlocutor, in learning to hear others and to see the value of different points of view, in reaching for coherence and consistency and shaping well-formed argument, and in thinking about how what we do may – or may not – be governed by principle – in all of these ways philosophy gets us to think about how we think. [...] Philosophical conversation works by question and answer, by speaking and by listening. So it works through accountability: both parties to the conversation are accountable for what they say. In the process, therefore, each learns to listen to the other, to hear the other, to seek to understand and even respect that account, different as it is.[138]

Although the philosophical connection of some actions is not that clear, it serves to highlight the work of philosophy in the English-speaking world. There are many other examples that cannot be included here because of space restraints.

Philosophical work is not only performed with prisoners, for the BOECIO project has recently begun to design workshops for prison officers and management teams, with the aim of developing self-control and critical thinking. Nonetheless, the rest of the philosophical returns from the different workshops described here are useful for achieving epistemological, comprehensive, ethical and even identity-related and ontological improvements.

5. Philo-Cafés.

Philo-cafés usually have a dual purpose: to promote democratic societies by creating spaces of well-informed dialogue and to enhance critical thinking. Both are fairly close to the ideas of Lipman and, before him, to those of the American democratic philosophers. In the contemporary age, they would be associated with the spirit of Rorty and his followers.

There are various formats that can be classified according to several criteria; an illustrative example is the importance of and

---

[138] VV. AA., "Why Are We Needed?" *Philosophy in Prison*, accessed February 1, 2020, https://www.philosophyinprison.com/why-we-are-needed.

time devoted to theory. There are philosophy cafés that include philosophical presentations that take up half of the sessions, namely, approximately one hour. Afterwards, there is a coffee break before commencing the second part in which the content of the presentations is reflected on. This format is typical of authors like Roxana Kreimer in Argentina. On a more modest level, there are Francisco Barrera's philosophical wine sessions in which yours truly participates as an assistant. Lasting less than Kreimer's sessions (90 minutes), between 10 and 15 minutes are given over to posing the main questions of the topic, followed by an hour-long discussion and a wine tasting during which the closing topic is chosen. This format is akin to that of the philo-cafés which Esther Charabati[139] has been organizing in Mexico City for over two decades now.

In both formats, the subjects to be broached during the session are decided on beforehand, which gives the philosopher several days to prepare them and to send those people interested in participating material and recommended reading.

Other cafés have a more open organization, since, bearing in mind that those participating in them can vary from session to session, the topics for discussion are chosen consensually at the beginning of each one. This format was employed by Arnáiz when, nearly 15 years ago, he started to organize sessions at La Casa del Libro in Seville.

Unlike workshops, the intention of philosophy cafés is to foster community and democracy, for which reason training in thinking skills takes second place, albeit without disappearing altogether, to dialogue. Phillips also advocates for recuperating those meeting places in any society with democratic aspirations. As if they were agorae, the intention of philosophical cafés is not to encounter an ultimate point on which all concur, but a diversity of answers and

---

[139] Esther Charabati, "La filosofía de café: el primer café filosófico en México," *Revista Internacional de Filosofía Aplicada HASER* 11 (2020): 63–91.

even self-criticism of one's own positions.[140] Considering the tendency towards fragmentation, individualism and the emergence of different worldviews in our open and globalized society, philosophy cafés facilitate the understanding and critical analysis of the discourses that raise a rainbow over our cities.

With a format akin to that of philosophy cafés, philosophy walks have begun to appear in recent years. Using the dynamicity of the Peripatetics, a topic is proposed in a specific location, where it is briefly reflected on by the group, before proposing another one and setting off for another place to discuss it.[141]

A word of warning: not everything that is called a philosophy café in its different formats (philosophical tea, wine, beer, chocolate or *atole*) has a philosophical nature. The most modest versions are those organized by people with a basic knowledge of the discipline, either because they have only taken a course on this methodology, lasting a few days or weeks, without holding a philosophy degree, or because they have not read the works of the major authors or have not trained in their reflective practice methodologies for years. There are also those with a philosophy degree who organize cafés because it is a socially or professionally appealing option, but lack the necessary practical training to bring them to fruition. Sessions become formal classes in which the diversity of thought inherent to meetings of this sought is prevented. Ideological or pseudo-religious[142] groups, which start sessions freely, but end up converting them into a platform for ideologically seducing adepts, also pose a danger. In all cases, we would encourage those attending such sessions to check the credentials of their organizers. They often do not hold a philosophy degree or, conversely, do

---

[140] Christopher Philips, *Socrates Cafe: A Fresh Taste of Philosophy* (New York/London: W.W, Norton and Co., 2002).

[141] Zoran Kojcic, "Socratic walk," *Revista Internacional de Filosofía Aplicada HASER* 8 (2017): 67–90.

[142] In the United States, Lydia Amir has warned about this danger in relation to the New Age movement: Lydia Amir, *Rethinking Philosophers' Responsibility* (Cambridge: Cambridge Scholar Publishing, 2017), 5–13.

indeed but are unfamiliar with the drift of the dynamics of philosophical practice and its most outstanding proponents, and lack training in this field.

6. Philosophy Workshops

Philosophy workshops focus on training those participating in them in specific currents or theories and, therefore, are not as entertaining as their café counterparts. If the latter are substitutes for cinema tickets, workshops are more like an alternative to educational classes, as is the case with the aforementioned prison workshops.

Together with the workshop format which revolves around a philosophical author, current or theory, there are established structures like Socratic dialogue, which can be summarized as follows:

(1) A question is chosen, usually with the structure, "What is X?" in which X has to do with concepts such as happiness, freedom, love, technology, deceit, friendship and theft, among others.

(2) The participants are asked to think about a simple example in their lives representing the concept in question.

(3) Each member tells his or her story.

(4) The participants choose one by *consensus* before performing an in-depth analysis on it. It is crucial that they all identify with it in some way or another.

(5) Then, the example is described in much greater detail by the person who has experienced it and who is also expected to answer any query that the others may have.

(6) All the participants help to divide the story into stages and to look for the specific place in which this concept is expressed.

(7) A definition of the concept is constructed.

(8) The validity of the definition for the stories of the rest of the members is verified. If this is not the case, the definition is modified until finding one that adapts to each specific case.

(9) The definition is refuted (and improved) with examples that are not represented in those of the group, but, nonetheless, are added to it.

As can be deduced, although philosophy workshops involve analytical thinking tools, they are also open to others like working with judicative and non-perceptive objectivities, to wit, the eidetic intuition practices inherent to the Husserlian approach.[143]

These and other philosophy workshops, which will not be described here because they have already been covered in previous sections, have been held in public and private institutions, including hospitals and health services in general. The "nursing care process" is a tool whose aim is to assess and address those aspects with which patients are unsatisfied, from the biological to the social sort, through the psychological, spiritual and philosophical kind (decision-making and value decisions). Hospitals offer an ideal setting for questioning that requires a philosophical approach: the empty feeling following the death of a loved one, the dilemma of confronting an operation with scant possibilities of success or accepting the certainty of a closer death, the hospitalization of family members with degenerative or chronic diseases or iatrogenesis in the face of death, questions about the epistemological certainty of certain treatments, recuperating existential meanings and reconstructing a life course after having been at death's door are just a few examples. Specifically, as to nursing diagnoses the tenth domain refers to life principles and is defined by the attainment of "principles underlying conduct, thoughts and behavior in relation to acts, customs or institutions regarded as true or possessing an intrinsic value". The first class refers to values and *as yet* there is no diagnosis. That "as yet" has

---

[143] Edmund Husserl, *Experience and Judgment*, 322ff.

been the case for over two decades now, evincing not only the discipline's lack of knowledge of philosophical aspects, but also the urgent need to remedy this state of affairs. In contrast, there are other known diagnoses in which philosophical practice plays a central role: the willingness to improve decision-making and to enhance knowledge, the risk of a decline in religiosity, spiritual and moral suffering, personal identity disorders and conflictive decisions, among others. Workshops have also been held in the corporate sector: at Norwegian companies, engaging philosophers for generating Socratic dialogues is a very widespread practice. Notwithstanding the activity's controversial nature, when compared with a Marxian approach, it would be reductionist and short-sighted to equate all institutions with those imbued with capitalist ideals. Honneth has recalled the existence of a social economy, together with the market economy.[144] Although the latter focuses on capital gains and measures any interest in employees on a profit basis, it should be recalled that, together with banks driven by those interests, there are also ethical banks and savings banks, whose profits are supposed to be invested in social projects, such as aid programs for the underprivileged. On the other hand, the term "company" does not only refer to major multinationals, but also to small enterprises that do not always link earnings to an increase in profits. These small enterprises can decide to employ profit surpluses for the benefit of their clients or different cultural interests. In Spain, for example, regional centers[145] tend to have restaurants open to the general public, but their profits are invested in broadening the citizenry's knowledge of them through activities funded in this way. Lastly, mention should go to institutions, like non-governmental organizations (NGOs), which, although they employ staff whose wages have to be paid by different means,

---

[144] Axel Honneth, *Freedom's Right: The Social Foundations of Democratic Life* (New York: Polity Press, 2014), 176–252.

[145] The country's 17 autonomous communities have centres or delegations in other regions which serve to promote them.

pursue diverse social objectives. In sum, it is important to be critical not only with those vested interests that convert employees into human *resources*, but also with that stance which, in an indiscriminate manner and without nuances, lumps together all institutions in the same category.

7. Annex. The Dissemination and Didactics of Philosophy

Two fields deriving from theoretical-practical philosophy and related to philosophical practice are the dissemination and didactics of philosophy.

Dissemination should not be understood as being tantamount to trivializing philosophy, but as a way of creating conscious mechanisms for the varied audiences at which sessions are aimed. In other words, the intention is to take philosophy to the people, while avoiding its generalization or, better said, its conversion into a discourse that consolidates the masses. Similarly, the intention of didactics of philosophy is to educate students in order that they should become critical and well-informed citizens and to provide them with an education that prevents their ideological, biased, polarized manipulation in which it is admitted, in a black and white fashion, that there is always a side that is blessed with all the bonanzas and another damned by its decisions.

Both disciplines are summarized by Adorno in the following terms: "However, whether someone is an intellectual or not is manifested above all in his relationship to his own work and to the societal totality of which it is a part. This relationship, not the work in specialized domains like epistemology, ethics, or even the history of philosophy, is what constitutes the essence of philosophy in the first place."[146]

There are certainly dissemination mechanisms closer to theoretical-practical philosophy, since the model involves the theoretical presentations of specialists in a language accessible to the public at large. However, this attempt to engage the largest number of people

---

[146] Theodor Adorno, *Critical Models*, 21–2.

evinces a commitment to abandoning the classical discourse pronounced *by* and *for* theoretical-practical philosophers.

II. Experiential Dimensions of Philosophical Practice

> A doctor per se, in contrast to whoever is well-versed in medicine, is characterized by having an experience that cannot now be rigorously formulated from a methodical point of view. Since in the diagnosis the subject who judges plays an important role. But therapy is more than 'applied science' [...]. This explains why the finest points of the art of medicine are so difficult to convey[147]

---

[147] Eduard Spranger, *La experiencia de la vida* (Buenos Aires: Realidad, 1949), 23.

CHAPTER 1
CONSTRAINTS OF LOGICAL-ARGUMENTATIVE PHILOSOPHICAL PRACTICE

1. Logical-argumentative Framework

A considerable number of authors writing about philosophical practice address it from a logical-argumentative perspective: they understand their work as if it were a way of honing analytical-conceptual skills or, in other words, of broadening skills in argument and concept analysis on a (formal or informal) logical basis. To illustrate this, two explanations, separated by almost 20 years, are cited below. On the one hand, in the proceedings of the 5th International Congress on Philosophical Practice Warren Shibles stated,

> Philosophical practitioners [...] facilitate activities as: (1) to examine arguments and justifications of their counselees; (2) to clarify, to analyze and to define important terms and concepts; (3) to expose and to assess underlying assumptions and logical implications; (4) to show conflicts and inconsistency; (5) to explore traditional theories of philosophy and its meanings related to counselees' issues; and (6) all activities that has [sic] been identified as philosophical.[148]

On the other, Lydia Amir identified the following function of philosophy in a work by Falzon:

> Any introductory book explains that philosophy teach us: "... to weigh up positions, beliefs and arguments, to ask whether there are good reasons for holding a belief or position, whether reasons that are put forward in support of them are adequate or relevant, and whether the arguments being presented conform to principles of sound reasoning. To question beliefs and positions that have become closed and

---

[148] Warren Shibles, "The philosophical practitioner and emotion," in *Thinking through Dialogue*, ed. Trevor Curnow (Oxted: Practical Philosophy Press, 2001), 51.

dogmatic, to show up the limits of such thinking, its failure or inability to deal with certain facts, considerations or arguments, and to open the way to thinking differently" (Falzon, 2007: 204–41).[149]

In a recent paper,[150] I have described how the vast majority of authors writing about philosophy for/with children focus on fostering skills pertaining to this frame: "improvement of reasoning ability",[151] "development of creativity",[152] "personal and interpersonal growth",[153] "development of ethical understanding",[154] "discovering alternatives,[155] impartiality[156] and consistency",[157] "discovering the feasibility of giving reasons for beliefs",[158] "discovering comprehensiveness",[159] "discovering situations",[160] "discovering part-whole relationships",[161] "eliciting views or opinions",[162] "clarification and restatement",[163] "explicating students' views",[164] "inferring logical implications[165] and what is suggested",[166] "seeking consistency",[167] "requesting

---

[149] Lydia Amir, *Rethinking Philosophers' Responsibility*, 239.

[150] José Barrientos Rastrojo, "La Filosofía con Niños como experiencia transformadora. Una propuesta en organizaciones sin ánimo de lucro," *Childhood & Philosophy* 15, no. 32 (2019): 1–28.

[151] Matthew Lipman, Ann M. Sharp, and Fredrick S. Oscayan, *Philosophy in the Classroom* (Upper Montclair, N.J.: Institute for the Advancement of Philosophy for Children, Montclair State College, 1977), 31–41.

[152] Ibid., 41–2.

[153] Ibid., 42–3.

[154] Ibid., 43–4.

[155] Ibid., 44–6.

[156] Ibid., 46–8.

[157] Ibid., 48–50.

[158] Ibid., 50–1.

[159] Ibid., 51–3.

[160] Ibid., 53–5.

[161] Ibid., 55–8.

[162] Ibid., 94.

[163] Ibid., 94–5.

[164] Ibid., 95–6.

[165] Ibid., 96–7.

[166] Ibid., 97–8.

definitions",[168] "searching for assumptions",[169] "indicating fallacies",[170] "requesting reasons",[171] "asking students to say how they know",[172] "eliciting and examining alternatives",[173] "grouping ideas",[174] "suggesting possible lines of confluence of divergence"[175] and "moving discussions to higher levels of generality".[176] In his philosophy sessions, the Frenchman Oscar Brenifier attempts to foster skills like "proposing concepts and hypotheses", "articulating, expressing and clarifying ideas", "understanding one's own ideas and those of others", "analyzing", "reformulating or modifying ideas", "working on the relationship between examples and ideas", "arguing", "practicing inquiry and objection", developing the "relationship between concepts, coherence and the legitimacy of ideas" and judgment, "creating and using conceptual tools: error, falsehood, truth, absurdity, identity, oppositions, categories", "singularizing and universalizing thought", "questioning oneself, discovering and recognizing one's own errors and incoherencies" and "understanding, accepting and applying working rules".[177] In this discursive training, the Mexican Eugenio Echeverría has stressed the need to acquire the following skills: "offering reasons", "distinguishing good reasons from bad ones", "constructing inferences and evaluating arguments", "generalizing and employing analogies", "identifying, questioning and justifying assumptions", "recognizing contradictions",

---

[167] Ibid., 98.

[168] Ibid., 98–9.

[169] Ibid., 99–100.

[170] Ibid., 100–1.

[171] Ibid., 101–3.

[172] Ibid., 103–4.

[173] Ibid., 104–5.

[174] Ibid., 105.

[175] Ibid., 105–6.

[176] Ibid., 106–7.

[177] Óscar Brenifier, *Filosofar como Sócrates* (Valencia: Diálogo, 2011), 132–3; Óscar Brenifier, *La práctica de la filosofía en la escuela primaria* (Valencia: Diálogo, 2012), 12–3.

"detecting fallacies", "attempting to be consistent", "making distinctions and connections (part/whole, means/ends, cause/effect)", "posing questions and finding problems", "making predictions and formulating and testing hypotheses", "proposing examples and counter-examples" and "detecting vagueness and ambiguity".[178] Similarly, the Portuguese Dina Mendonça notes that *filosofía para crianças* (philosophy for children) serves to "clarify questions", "to review beliefs" and "to formulate new hypotheses", among others.[179] Furthermore, the questions posed in workshops for children pursue three objectives: to ask for reasons, explanations and clarifications, to develop other points of view and to explore issues.[180] Lastly, it essential not to forget Carla Carreras' thinking skills table in the previous section, which clearly puts the accent on logical-argumentative rationality.[181]

This type of reason is not incorrect. On the contrary, it enhances skills that are necessary in a world whose inhabitants have difficulties in analyzing discourses and, as a result, are easily manipulated; a society in which the meta-narrative has exploded and in which the demands of decisions have become an existential analysis, without which the individual would be converted into a

---

[178] Eugenio Echeverría, *Filosofía para niños* (México DF: SM, 2006), 155.

[179] Dina Mendoça, *Brincar a pensar. Manual de filosofía para crianças* (Lisboa: Plátano, 2011), 21.

[180] Ibid., 26–27.

[181] Obviously, there are exceptions to this tendency in Lipman himself, such as the defense and explanation of careful thinking, with its emphasis on affective, empathetic or other types of thinking (Lipman, *Thinking in Education*, 265ff). However, most of his oeuvre focuses on the deployment of the thought cited here. Authors such as Angélica Sátiro, *Jugar a pensar. Recursos para aprender a pensar en educación infantil (4-5 años)* (Puebla: SEP, 2008) and Jordi Nomen, *El niño filósofo y el arte, Cómo favorecer que los niños desarrollen el pensamiento creativo* (Barcelona: Arpa y Alfil Editores, 2019) have substantivised creativity, leading to a greater deployment of this mode of reasoning. This does detract from the general hypothesis that the original, and still valid, sense of philosophy for/with children employs a logical-argumentative reasoning.

pawn of the masses. Having said that, restricting the application of philosophy to that rationality raises two problems: (1) the possibilities of philosophy are limited to the analytical avenue and (2) there is a risk of falling into a disagreement between what one thinks and what one desires.

Reductionism is not inherent to philosophical practice or philosophy for/with children, but, as a convenient derivation of general philosophy, results from the continental or analytical ways of doing philosophy which appear in the rest of the discipline's sub-areas. Namely, these tendencies surface in epistemology, ethics, aesthetics and the history of philosophy and political philosophy, among others.

The fact that thinkers understand that their task in workshops or counseling sessions is restricted to paying attention to arguments is owing to the fact that the education that they received at university prescribed that doing philosophy was inherent to the Oxonian school and other similar ones, that it did not include a "Contemporary Philosophy" module that integrated the thought of the principal contemporary authors, that the "Hermeneutics" module was taught at the faculties of literature or theology at their universities and that, by and large, the analytical tendency has not only consolidated its dominant position at education centers, but has also displaced other ways of doing philosophy.

This disregard, when it occurs in this way, not only implies the exclusion of continental philosophy from faculties of philosophy, but also that of others (which may also be derided by continental philosophy), such as the philosophy of indigenous peoples. However, that subject will be broached elsewhere.

2. Ontological Dissonances

The first logical-argumentative constraint occurs in the midst of ontological dissonances consisting in a lack of coherence between the different dimensions of the subject.

The first evidence of this reality appeared in several philosophical counseling sessions: the participants managed to guess the decision that they should make after an analysis of its appropriateness and the inappropriateness of its alternatives, but showed an *essential* inability to express this in their personal lives.

Those readers with an interest should consider the story about the quest of a patient with terminal cancer for the meaning of life, which occurred 15 years ago.[182] The basis of the distance between thought and volition or affections is illustrated in Yalom's novel *Quando Nietzsche chorou*. In the book, Breuer, Freud's mentor and, in the story, Nietzsche's philosophical counselor, complains about the philosophy of the hammer in the following terms, after logically understanding what was the best alternative for his existence: "Here is a truth with a supreme and irrefutable rationality. However, whenever I am really frightened, it does not calm my fears. This is the problem with philosophy: to teach it and apply it in real life are two very different endeavors."[183]

The rational conclusions of the main character and the grounds of his decision follow opposing and unfathomable paths. In point of fact, many people do not attend sessions to find answers or a solution to their personal problems, since they are already acquainted with it, but to provide their ideas and the rest of their essential dimensions with a sort of unique certainty. In other words, those who consider what is the best begin to prosper in their lives, without they themselves being the first to boycott it.

This intention is analogous to that of Paul the Apostle, who was troubled in the following terms: "For the good which I will, I do not; but the evil which I will not, that I do" (Rom. 7:19).[184] The saint knew the precepts that he should follow, but his perverse will

---

[182] José Barrientos Rastrojo, "Del pensar zambranista," 207–21.

[183] Irvin Yalom, *Quando Nietzsche chorou*, 220.

[184] All the biblical quotes appearing in this book are taken from John Reynolds et al., *The Holy Bible, translated from the Latin Vulgate* (Douay: English College, 1609).

did not adapt to them: he did not seek to resolve a dilemma, but a conversion that included an identity transformation. It was not a question of the need for new truths, but truths that substantiated his existence; truths that led to the transformation not only of his ideas, but that also sprung from the root, from the core of his realities, and pollinated the branches emerging from the depths of his being. On the basis of the Zambranian categories, it could be claimed that the objective would not be an analytical truth, but a piece of evidence (or a revelation, in the words of Ortega y Gasset). According to philosophy, evidence lays the foundations of the subject's identity, for which reason its change implies the whole or integral transformation of a person: "The evidence tends to be wanting, terribly wanting in intellectual content. But, however, in life it brings about a unique transformation that other richer and more complex thoughts were incapable of achieving."[185]

3. Logical-argumentative Handicaps for Understanding Existence

Dilthey cautioned that modern rationalism might be putting up walls against the subject's latent internal experience: "In the veins of the knowing subject, as it was conceived by Locke, Hume, and Kant flows no real blood [...]."[186] Life, the real blood, escaped from the major modern philosophical systems, whereby the sciences of the spirit cannot attempt to understand the human being exclusively through scientific analysis, but should access cultural expressions, namely, art and history, created in the heat of existence. The experience of freedom does not appear in the sterilized discussions of the bourgeois enclosed in the faculty, but on the sweaty bodies of those who have fought on the battleground; envy is understood in the cold, hostile gesture made to congratulate

---

[185] María Zambrano, *La confesión: género literario* (Madrid: Siruela, 1995), 69.
[186] Wilhelm Dilthey, *Gesammelte Schriften I* (Göttingen: Vandenhoeck & Ruprecht, 1973), xviii; Hans Peter Rickman, *Wilhelm Dilthey: Pioneer of the Human Studies* (London: Paul Elek, 1979).

an adversary; happiness is only perceptible in the outbreak of laughter or in the jocular smile of a young man who is happy to see his pet again, after having lost it for a few days.

The dissonance between modern reason and life is illustrated and explained in different areas of knowledge. Religion has expounded on the shortcomings of human reason when trying to attain divine truths, for how can a temporally and spatially limited entity understand what is beyond time and space, exclusively through its own efforts? In the words of Radhakishnan, an Indian philosopher and politician influenced by the Advaita, "Life cannot be comprehended in its fullness by logical reason. Self-consciousness is not the ultimate category of the universe. There is something transcending the consciousness of self."[187]

Ficinus answered the question on the basis of the incorporation of man into God and, consequently, contingent on an education that could become the subjective genitive, which will be examined further on. He compared God with sunlight; without Him, the eyes cannot see or contemplate truth.[188] Therefore, possessing eyes for seeing is not enough, for an adequate medium also has to exist. This idea is in line with what is being explained here, inasmuch as the logical-argumentative tool is, to our mind, insufficient for understanding some dimensions of reality.

Based on logical-argumentative rationality, it is unnecessary to reach out to the divine to come up against hermeneutic difficulties. Aesthetic experience leads us to the same impasse: when the subtle rays of the sun in the late afternoon caress us, informing us of its zenith, and consequently lead us to an understanding of the mortality of everything that exists, is it possible to say that an analytical intellection of the situation has taken place? Would it not be more correct to point out that the afternoon, playing the role of

---

[187] Radhakishnan cited in Trevor Curnow, *Wisdom in the Ancient World* (London: Duckworth, 2010), 206.

[188] Eugene F. Rice, *The Renaissance Idea of Wisdom* (Boston: Harvard University Press, 1958), 66–7.

the subject and, as a result, transforming us into the object, has understood itself, our understanding being a passive end user of the former? This example is akin to the case of a symphony, poem or novel: are we the subjects who interpret them or do they convert us into objects through which the act of understanding occurs and, by extension, we attain that discernment?

John Dewey reinforced these doubts about logical-scientific reason in *Art as Experience* by shifting towards aesthetic experience, in whose deployment the intellection that we are seeking here is revealed.

> Where should we look for an account of such an [aesthetic] experience? Not to ledger-entries nor yet to a treatise on economics or sociology or personnel-psychology, but to drama or fiction. Its nature and import can be expressed only by art, because there is a unity of experience that can be expressed only as an experience. The *experience* is of material fraught with suspense and moving toward its own consummation through a connected series of varied incidents.[189]

These frontiers of logical-argumentative rationality are revealed in counseling sessions: their intention is modify the subject by stressing a change in his or her ideas (see Figure 2.1). The problem is that ideas do not provoke a principal change in all the subject's dimensions, to wit, ideas do not directly act on the being of a person.

---

[189] John Dewey, *Art as Experience* (New York: Capricorn Books, 1958), 43, original emphasis.

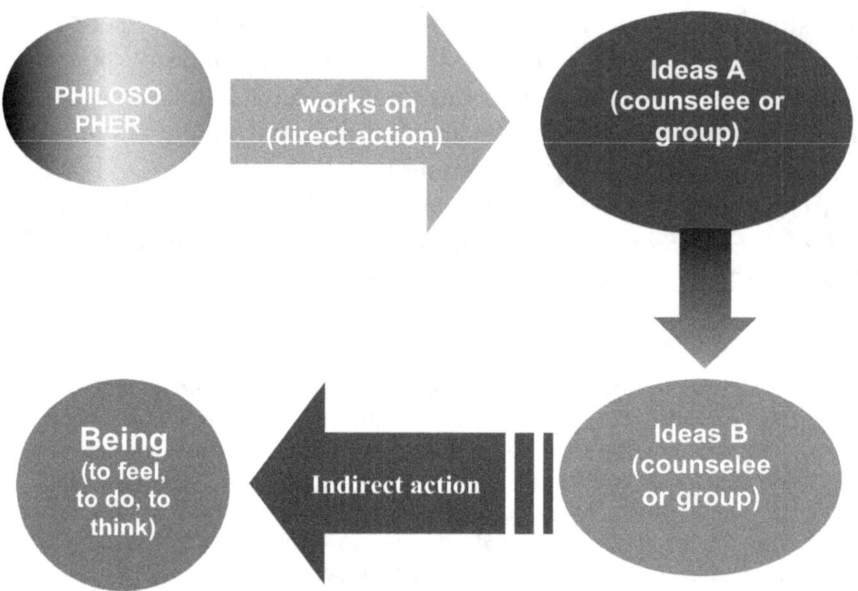

Source: own elaboration.

FIGURE 2.1 **Changing ideas in Philosophical Counseling**

The counselor hopes that if the subject's ideas are changed, his or her integrity will also be modified, assuming that the being springs from thought. Nevertheless, thought is only one of the dimensions deriving from the being, from the identity of the counselee. As a result, what is illustrated in the following graph, anticipated in a logical-argumentative session, cannot be achieved (see Figure 2.2):

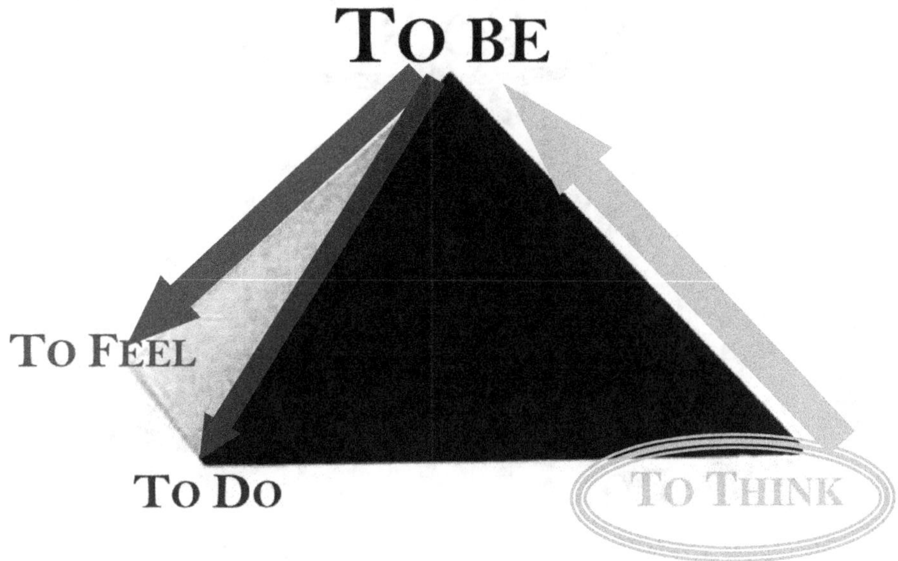

Source: own elaboration.
FIGURE 2.2. **First pyramid.**

As the being or identity of the subject is the starting point, it would be necessary to change this in order that the rest of his or her dimensions should accompany it (see Figure 2.3).
The problem involves encountering the mechanism modifying the being, and establishing that the transformation is brought about by a change in ideas is to be unaware of other rationalities with which the twentieth century has accessed entities concealed from logical-argumentative reasoning.

Source: own elaboration.
FIGURE 2.3. **Second pyramid.**

Ernst Cassirer,[190] Cirlot[191] and Mauricio Beuchot[192] have pointed to symbolic reasoning, María Zambrano[193] and Antonio Machado[194] to poetic reasoning, Miguel de Unamuno and Ortega y

---

[190] Ernst Cassirer, *An Essay on Man: An Introduction to a Philosophy of Human Culture* (New Haven and London: Yale University Press, 1977); Ernst Cassirer, *The Philosophy of Symbolic Forms, Volume 1: Language* (New Haven and London: Yale University Press, 1955).

[191] Juan Eduardo Cirlot, *Diccionario de símbolos* (Madrid: Siruela, 2018).

[192] Mauricio Beuchot, *Las dos caras del símbolo: el ícono y el ídolo* (Puebla: BUAP, 2013).

[193] María Zambrano, *Filosofía y poesía* (Mexico DF: Fondo de cultura económica, 2001).

[194] Tomaso Bugossi, "La poética de la luz y de la razón creadora: Antonio Machado y María Zambrano," in *Actas III Congreso Internacional sobre la vida*

Gasset[195] put narrative reasoning into practice, Sartre did so with a dramatic-existentialist-dialectic reasoning,[196] Kandinsky, with an aesthetic reasoning mediated by abstract art,[197] Marx, with an economic reasoning,[198] Mannheim, with a social reasoning,[199] Merleau, with a corporal reasoning,[200] Scheler, with a reasoning of metaphysical attraction through the *ordo amoris*,[201] Foucault, with an archaeological and biopolitical reasoning[202] and so on and so forth. Certainly, most explanations have been arrived at by means of logical-argumentative mechanisms, that is, by writing an essay or treatise on them, but their articulation does not correspond to that model.

The challenge would be to find a reasoning that encompassed all of them or, at least, one that provoked adequate changes in the being so as to break not only the ideological, but also the ontological and identity-related, system of the subject, a rationality that even

---

y obra de María Zambrano: María Zambrano y la "edad de Plata" de la cultura española (Vélez-Málaga: Fundación María Zambrano, 2004), 46–55; Martín Ruiz Calvente, "Antonio Machado en María Zambrano," *El búho* (2007), 23–50; Antonio Machado, *Juan de Mairena* (Madrid: Cátedra, 2006).

[195] "So, we should not say that man is, but that he lives ... reason consists of a narrative. Versus pure physical-mathematical reasoning, there is a narrative reasoning. To understand something human, personal or collective, it is necessary to tell a story. This man, this nation does such and such a thing and it is so because, beforehand, he or it did another thing in another such way. Life only becomes slightly transparent in the face of historical reasoning," Juan Ortega y Gasset, *Historia como Sistema* (Madrid: Alianza, 1999), 47).

[196] Jean-Paul Sartre, *Being and Nothingness: An Essay on Phenomenological Ontology* (New York: Philosophical Library, 1956).

[197] Wassily Kandinsky, *Concerning the Spiritual in Art* (New York: Dover Publications Inc., 1977).

[198] Karl Marx, *Capital: A Critical Analysis of Capitalist Production* (London: Swan Sonnenschein, Lowrey, & Co., 1887).

[199] Karl Mannheim, *Ideology and Utopia*.

[200] Merleau-Ponty, *Phenomenology of Perception*.

[201] Max Scheler, *Ordo amoris* (Madrid: Caparrós, 1996).

[202] Michel Foucault, *Discipline and Punish: The Birth of the Prison* (New York: Vintage Books, 1979).

aspires to make the subject something more, or something less, than he or she is.

Our proposal is experiential reasoning.

4. From Ideas to Beliefs

Moving on to another debate on logical-argumentative handicaps, there is Ortega y Gasset's theory that separates ideas from beliefs. The Spanish philosopher differentiated between the two, contending that ideas are things that we are, while beliefs are things that we inhabit.[203] Ideas, such as possession or predication subject to the substratum "I", can change. However, as beliefs are things that we are, "they do not have the nature of particular content",[204] that is, beliefs are the condition of possibility and constitution of that substratum "I". The character that we live, who we are, is based on our beliefs. Therefore, we cling to them like drowning cats.

The loss of our belief frame gives rise not only to "a sea of doubts", but also to an identity crisis or, what is the same, the loss of who we are, of confidence in who we believe we are or in the beliefs that underpin that edifice. Indeed, crises are always crises of beliefs: yesterday, I thought that I was a good student, but the exam failures of the past few months have ended up dissipating that confidence, making way for the possibility that, perhaps, I am not such a good student after all or even that this was a mere illusion in the past and that the authentic reality is that I am a "bad student". Each belief frame ("good student" and "bad student") gives all my ideas a musical tonality or a specific color. When "good student" was the frame that worked, the musical key imposed itself on all my confrontations with reality and I sensed that an exam was "something easy to pass", I was not afraid to present my work in class, because "it was always valued by my teachers", I dared to meet new challenges for I assumed that "I had the ability to

---

[203] José Ortega y Gasset, *Obras completas 8* (Madrid: Alianza, 1994), 383.
[204] Ibid., 384.

continue to make progress if I made an effort". When "bad student" becomes the belief frame, this gives rise to ideas like "I am incapable of passing the exam, even if I try", "I am a failure", "I will not pass the exam, however much I try", feelings of incompetence when faced with the difficulties that arise and an inaction motivated by my fears about how trivial I see myself. As in the case of a picture, what is important is not the object which is being painted, but the artistic approach from which it is executed: a flower can express the most somber abyss or the elevation of the human spirit above any setback. Many centuries ago, Epictetus explained this by distinguishing between reality and phantasy: controlling representations is the first step towards leading a happy life.[205] We wonder whether or not it would not be wiser to *introduce* the subject into happiness frames (the term being understood according to Stoic categories), before allowing him or her to control representations and phantasies.

Many people attend psychology or philosophy sessions with the aim of recuperating their previous belief frame (for instance, so as to become a good student again). It is also possible that they have noticed that the previous frame has deteriorated because of the new circumstances and are therefore seeking a new certainty.[206] For example, counselees may be confused because they have been abandoned by their partners who, after 30 years of marriage, have decided to live with someone of the same sex. The solution is not to design a set of thoroughly explained logical-argumentative reasons, but to achieve a consistent belief system into which it is possible to introduce new phenomena that were unacceptable before (e.g., homosexuality in the family), from which it is possible to accept a new reality (e.g., living alone) or to assume losses without having

---

[205] Epictetus, *Enchiridion* (Mineola, NY: Dover Publications, Inc., 2004), 1–2.

[206] It was precisely María Zambrano who cautioned that what was sought in crises were new pieces of evidence and certainties that kept the edifice of life functioning: María Zambrano, *Hacia un saber sobre el alma* (Madrid: Alianza, 2004), 99–121.

to accept meaninglessness (e.g., recognizing the temporality of love).

In conclusion, acquiring beliefs is not a question of organizing ideas or constructing an edifice whose frame is of the logical-argumentative kind.

5. From Intra-mundane Facts to Events

Claude Romano, a contemporary phenomenologist, has proposed a dichotomy that recuperates the Ortegian schema, albeit with a Heideggerian inspiration. According to the Frenchman, it is essential to distinguish between intra-mundane facts and factual events.

As with ideas, intra-mundane facts are realities that occur within the frame prescribed by a reality that happens to a specific person: "They happen to me, but they do not bring *me* into play"[207] or, in other words, they do not bring into play the self that identifies us during that period of our lives.

Experiences (or events) trigger an *"impersonal reshaping of my possibilities and of the world that occurs in an event and because of which my own adventure is flawed"*.[208] The appearance of new possibilities, or the "phenomenological transition",[209] is due to the fact that a reconfiguration of myself, of who I am, has occurred. For this reason, new possibilities appear in the world which were previously invisible. Similarly, others that were guessable disappear from my field of vision. The break produced by the event is clear when the text emphasizes the appearance of a flaw, without a solution of continuity. Not only myself has been radically modified, but also the future.

A few months ago, I made the acquaintance of an inmate who was serving a prison sentence for having murdered her husband, who

---

[207] Claude Romano, *El acontecimiento y el mundo* (Salamanca: Sígueme, 2012), 54, original emphasis.

[208] Ibid., 51, original emphasis.

[209] Ibid., 102, original emphasis.

owing to his alcoholism used to beat her under the cover of darkness and with malice aforethought. The reason behind her actions was the fact that he had attempted to stab their child when, one night, he would not stop crying. The tragedy was not the injustice of the sentence or the fact that she missed her child, but her yearning for the person who she had killed. Thus, her sorrow was threefold: her imprisonment, the feeling of guilt for what she had done and the incarceration to which her own passions subjected her. The widow was aware of how violent he had used to be towards her, but the character and ontological situation prevented her from forgetting her passionate feelings for her husband. A logical-argumentative approach (analyzing her arguments, justifications, the concepts involved, etc.) is rather inefficient in a counseling session: she knew that what she had done was not wrong and that her dependency was not "healthy". Nevertheless, the bedrock of her emotional dependency, which served as a belief frame, condemned her to live the facts in a previous world. Change requires an event or experience that "gives birth to a new world",[210] an experience that affects her in a particular way.[211]

In this case, there is a greater need to inquire into the category of birth[212] and into the mechanisms of its production[213] than into epistemological criteria of validity or into the coherence and gestation of the predication of judgments.

Versus all these constraints of logical-argumentative reasoning, we propose *experience* as a model. This overcomes ontological dissonance more efficiently, acts on beliefs rather than on ideas and links to the event.[214]

---

[210] Ibid., 50.

[211] Ibid., 51.

[212] Ibid., 108ff.; Claude Romano, *Lo posible y el acontecimiento* (Santiago de Chile: Ediciones Universidad Alberto Hurtado, 2008), 123–39.

[213] María Zambrano, *El sueño creador* (Madrid: Turner, 1986), 82; José Barrientos Rastrojo, *Vectores* zambranianos, 1074ff.

[214] Experience should not lead to experiential reductionism, opposing the former. In fact, there are experiential *conversations*. For philosophical work, moreover,

there is a need to resort to logical-argumentative dimensions, as I have explained in José Barrientos Rastrojo, *Resolución de* conflictos, 175–211.

CHAPTER 2
EXERCISES AND EXPERIENTIAL DISPOSITIONS

1. The experiential frame to Philosophical Practice

Experiential philosophical practice revolves around four aspects:
- (1) Exercises
- (2) Dispositions
- (3) Scenarios
- (4) Metaphors

The exercises are tasks that train subjects in philosophical skills and which serve as triggers for attaining evidential truths.

The dispositions allow the exercises to increase their transformative capabilities.

The scenarios are frames of the philosophical areas that change when making the transition from a logical-argumentative approach to an experiential one. For instance, in logical-argumentative epistemology truth coincides with the conclusion of the reasons of an argument, while in the experiential approach truth is identified with evidence, namely, it changes the frame in which it is incardinated, thus creating different types of truths.

The metaphors comprise the translational system in which the experiential process is integrated. Following this theory, there is the metaphor of pilgrimage that transforms subjects into pilgrims, the exercises into stages or days of the way, the goal into the place of pilgrimage, an existential transformation, and the fellow participants into travelling companions.

2. Experience. A Description

We will start by explaining "experience" employing two exercises proposed by two different authors: the German Walter Benjamin at the beginning of the twentieth century and the twenty-first-century Buddhist philosopher Daisaku Ikeda.

In *Experience and Poverty*, Benjamin explained how an elderly man, on death's door, manages to make his sons understand *experientially* the most important aspect of life.

> Our childhood anthologies used to contain the fable of the old man who on his deathbed, fooled his sons into believing that there was treasure buried in the vineyard. They would only have to dig. They dug, but found no treasure. When autumn came, however, the vineyard bore fruit like no other in the whole land. They then perceived that their father had passed on valuable piece of experience: the blessing lies in hard work and not in gold.[215]

The example has several interesting points: learning emerges from the sons, for their father merely creates the right conditions for this to happen; it is essential to perform an activity or exercise; the path is not predetermined but should be chosen by the apprentice; and the model of knowledge corresponds to a metaphorical or symbolic schema (it includes a material point of departure and a transcendental point of arrival).

Daisaku Ikeda, a Buddhist master who dialogues with Lou Marinoff in *The Inner Philosopher*, allows a mother whose son has died to change perspectives by proposing to her an exercise with a structure identical to Benjamin's.

> During Buddha's time, there lived a woman named Kisa Gotami. She married young and gave birth to a son. One day, the baby fell sick and died soon after. Kisa Gotami loved her son greatly and refused to believe that her son was dead. She carried the body of her son around her village, asking if there was anyone who can bring her son back to life. [...] She immediately went to the Buddha's residence and pleaded for him to bring her son back to life. "Kisa Gotami, I have a way to bring your son back to life." "My Lord, I will do anything to bring my son back." "If that is the case, then I need you to find me something. Bring me a mustard seed but it must be taken from a house where no one residing in the house has ever lost a family member." [...] Kisa

---

[215] Walter Benjamin, *Selected Writings/Walter Benjamin, Vol. 2, Part 2, 1927-1930* (Harvard: Harvard University Press, 2005), 731.

> Gotami went from house to house, trying to find the mustard seed. [...] Kisa Gotami finally came to realise that there is no one in the world who had never lost a family member to death. She now understood that death is inevitable and a natural part of life.[216]

Lastly, there is the case of a Mexican counselee with whom I worked some years ago. One of his problems was that, after going to bed, he would be overcome by an unbearable anxiety. I soon realized that his agitation increased whenever he attempted to control it, denying that it was getting worse for fear of its consequences. My proposal was acceptance, but I could not address the issue directly, as that would have been like asking someone in the midst of an anxiety attack to calm down. On the contrary, it was necessary to convert his suffering into a resource. Accordingly, I asked him to write a detailed account of the different phases through which he passed in a notebook. This exercise led him to accept the situation, inasmuch as he needed it to complete the task. It was the first time that he had accepted the situation as a reality on the basis of which he should develop his life. In the words of Ortega, life is a problem.

Experience or knowledge of experience is "knowledge acquired living [...]. Neither is it studied or learnt knowledge, nor the devised or constructed kind. It is not an intellectual knowledge, but the vital sort. And, on the other hand, it is personal, untraditional knowledge, inherited or sapiential".[217] Critical thought often helps to acquire it: a conservation can be experiential, that is, transforming; when that occurs, efficiency is not measured in the quality of the arguments deployed, but in their potential to reshape and metamorphose.

---

[216] Lou Marinoff and Daisaku Ikeda, *The Inner Philosopher: Conversations on Philosophy's Transformative Power* (Cambridge, MA: Ikeda Center for Peace, Learning, and Dialogue, 2012), 64.

[217] José Luis Aranguren, "La experiencia de la vida," in *Experiencia de la vida*, VV. AA. (Madrid: Alianza, 1969), 36.

Spranger explains the transformation that experience brings about in a physician by underscoring a type of knowledge that is not acquired through the theoretical memorization of the "well-versed in medicine": "A doctor per se, in contrast to whoever is well-versed in medicine, is characterized by having an experience that cannot now be rigorously formulated from a methodical point of view. Since in the diagnosis the subject who judges plays an important role. But therapy is more than 'applied science' [...]. This explains why the finest points of the art of medicine are so difficult to convey."[218]

Experiential training would not focus on understanding the structures that correctly link conclusions, reasons or assumptions, or on improving concepts or definitions, but would seek to access how experiential discourses or activities provoke an identity-related or ontological change. In the following sections, these avenues will be described in further detail, but it is first necessary to distinguish between experience and other phenomena like insight.

Not all the actions that we perform bring about an essential change in our being. Perhaps the conversation held with a specialist in the thought of Nezahualcoyotl convinces us of the need to shift our lives towards an Nahual ethic; despite the fact that a previous conversation with a specialist in Kant did not led us, months before, to embrace an ethics. The validity of the arguments deployed by the Mesoamerican and German specialists may have been analogous, but that of the expert in Nahual thought turned on a light (a piece of evidence) that substantially transformed us. Insight corresponds to the situation of the Kantian, while experience is present in the Mexican case.

The dichotomy between insight and experience is repeated when considering two youngsters who, before going up to university, attend an informative talk in which the value of nursing is explained. One leaves enthused, for he has discovered and recognized his calling in the words of the speaker and wishes to

---

[218] Eduard Spranger, *La experiencia de la vida*, 23.

relive the narrated experiences in his existence. In sum, he leaves the talk transformed. His perplexed companion stares at him: he was bored by the talk, the explanations seemed a chimera far removed from his interests and he even browsed social media because he could not stomach the talk's humanitarian message. The departure point (i.e., the talk) was identical, but this led to a dual reality: the former attended an experience, while the latter only gained a few insights into the situation which, as Romano would say, did not bring into play his self or reshape his possibilities.

Beyond the distance between insight and experience and the challenge of expressing an experiential philosophical practice, it is useful to understand the mechanisms and conditions that would help the former to become the latter. The *dispositions* of the subject and the *scenarios* of the action underpin this path.

3. Experiential Dispositions
3.1. Description

All farmers know that growing tomatoes depends on factors that they can control in order to obtain a good harvest, without that meaning that they are able to control all the growth factors: "You cannot pull on a seed to make it emerge from the earth. The only thing that you can do is to provide it with warmth, humidity and light; then it will have to grow."[219]

Experiential truth – proof – requires a similar amount of care as does a plant or the education of a child. It is impossible to program experiential conclusions. As occurs with logic, the result is inferred and prescribes on the basis of reasons. However, it is possible to create dispositions and scenarios that facilitate that emergence, situations that increase the possibility that the discourse heard by the young may set into motion a metamorphosis.

The role of the experiential guru can be explained as follows. In the middle of a forest, the neophyte wants to see the sunlight (i.e.,

---

[219] Ludwig Wittgenstein cited in François Julien, *Un sabio no tiene ideas o el otro de la filosofía* (Madrid: Siruela, 2001), 78.

experience), but the leafy branches of the trees prevent him from doing so. The guru would increase the possibility that the sun may illuminate his face if he took him to a clearing, that is, a glade without any trees nearby, a place where the shadows cannot exercise their power. Nevertheless, this action does not immediately guarantee that he will see the sun (just as the guru's action creates the right conditions for experiential maturation but does not guarantee it). Factors that we do not control may hinder our intentions, for example, a cloudy day, the inadvertent blindness of our initiate or the simple fact that he closes his eyes because he does not want to see. This might have happened to the sons of Benjamin's elderly father, to Kisa Gotami or to the Mexican counselee with his nocturnal anxiety.

There are 11 dispositions the we have detected to date which prompt experiential evidence to emerge:

    (1) Age replete with lived and vivid experiences.
    (2) Bravery in the face of dangerous events.
    (3) Courage to cross thresholds that do not allow a step back.
    (4) Patience, delay and deployment of experience.
    (5) Opening. Play and fascination in the face of problems: "surprise is welcome".
    (6) Commitment to authenticity and self-criticism.
    (7) Preparing oneself for subtlety.
    (8) Humility until the subjective genitive.
    (9) Accepting the possibility of the dissolution of the self (subjective genitive) and the ontological act.
    (10)   Withdrawal.
    (11)   Balance.

Owing to the fact that the aim of this work is experiential philosophical practice and not experience, which we will cover in another book, we will not dwell on them here. However, we will describe them is sufficient detail in order to facilitate, on the basis of our description, the design of sessions to the rhythm of their music.

3.2. Age Fulled with Lived and Vivid Experiences

Before starting, rather than a disposition, a word of warning: age is not sufficient on its own for attaining knowledge deriving from experience. Experience is often equated with life and age. Even the book of Job defends the superior wisdom of the elderly: "What knowest thou that we are ignorant of? what dost thou understand that we know not? There are with us also aged and ancient men, much elder than thy fathers."[220]

This identification comes unstuck all too frequently. Robert Nozick eloquently observes, "Wisdom [the result of life experiences] need not be geriatric."[221]

This assertion is supported by the classics, such as Seneca's writings. The Cordovan philosopher noted that age and wisdom *should* concur, since it would be indicative of a life devoted to the philosophical work of prudence. Unfortunately, the parting of ways between the two tend to be very frequent, whereby the following complaint: "Often a man who is very old in years has nothing beyond his age by which he can prove that he has lived a long time."[222]

Julián Marías ventures to offer a reason for that experiential deficit: because of not having dared to take risks: "Peasants and women with a poor education occasionally display a surprising accumulation of life experiences, combined with a dearth of 'experiences': they are people who have always done the same, people to whom nothing has happened."[223]

---

[220] Job 15:9–10.

[221] Robert Nozick, *The Examined Life: Philosophical Meditations* (New York: Simon & Schuster, 1989), 278.

[222] Lucio Anneo Seneca, *Minor Dialogues*, 261.

[223] Julián Marías, "Un escorzo de la experiencia de la vida," in *La experiencia de la vida*, VV. AA. (Madrid, Alianza, 1969), 116.

Certainly, the passing of the years makes it possible to have a greater number of experiences: a 10-year-old usually has less experience than a 30-year-old. Nevertheless, age does not guarantee the accumulation of experiences: it is not uncommon to observe how a child from a poor neighborhood has had more experiences than a young, middle-class philosophy degree holder. The philosopher's arrogance will prevent him from understanding the child's stifled laughter when he begins to talk to him about the meaning of existence or the value of good and evil in life.

In short, it is life experiences and not age that allow us and make us willing to acquire experiential knowledge.

3.3. Bravery in the Face of Dangerous Events

Ortega y Gasset linked *per*, the root of experience, to *peligro* (danger), *"perigro"*.[224] Decades later, Claude Romano would establish the same link through the German root: experience is the translation of *Erfahrung*, deriving from *Gefahr*, which means danger.[225]

The main danger of experience emerges from the end that assails whoever suffers from it: the death of the self, of the pervious person so as to allow for the emergence of the other. It should be recalled that this is tantamount to saying that the previous belief system perishes in order to establish a new existential legality. In her *Notas de un método*, María Zambrano observes that "a certain amount of adventure, and even a certain amount of perdition in experience, a certain amount of lost wandering have been essential for the subject that is gradually formed".[226] Without that losing herself, the subject would still cling to her beliefs, the crisis would not have been triggered and, borrowing an example from Panikkar, the young woman would never change her status of daughter for that of mother: "Mothers learn to be mothers not in hygiene and

---

[224] José Ortega y Gasset, *Obras completas 8*, 175.

[225] Claude Romano, *El acontecimiento y el mundo*, 213.

[226] María Zambrano, *Notas de un método*, 18.

child psychology classes (useful, on the other hand), but by giving birth to children, breast-feeding them and living with them."[227] This begs the question of how to confront the abyss without obliterating it. Indeed, this incapacity encourages the most reiterated attitude: flight.

Experience places people in the dilemma of having to decide on whether or not to take the plunge into the abyss without a safety net, where death is not only foreseeable but also expected: just as the silkworm has to relinquish its life as a cocoon to become a butterfly, so too does the individual have to plunge off the cliff as a neophyte in order to return to the summit as a hero. Wounds and scars not only bear witness to his struggle, but are also the constituent elements of his new identity, those that give him character and personality.

Two Stoic texts narrate the frame of mind of the sage when faced with this harsh molding: to accept pain with courage in light of the heroism that our makeup and strength of spirit request of us. To this should be added an epithet: trust in that freedom is obtained if it is fought for and provided that it is maintained by oneself.

> "I must die: must I, then, die groaning too? I must de fettered: and wailing too? I must go into exile: does anyone, then, keep me from going with a smile and cheerful and serene?" [...] "But I will fetter you." What is that you say, man? fetter *me*? My leg you will fetter, but my moral purpose not even Zeus himself has power to overcome. "I will throw you into prison." My paltry body, rather! "I will behead you." Well, when did I ever tell you that mine was the only neck that could not be severed? These are the lessons that philosophers ought to rehearse, these they ought to write down daily, in these they ought to exercise themselves.[228]
>
> "What aid, then, must we have ready at hand in such circumstances?" Why, what else than the knowledge of what is mine, and what is not mine, and what is permitted to me, and is not permitted to me? I must

---

[227] Raimon Panikkar, *Iconos del misterio. La experiencia de Dios* (Barcelona: Península, 1999), 76.

[228] Epictetus, *The Discourses*, 13.

die: must I, then, die groaning too? I must de fettered: and wailing too? I must go into exile: does anyone, then, keep me from going with a smile and cheerful and serene? "Tell your secrets." I say not a word; for this is under my control. "But I will fetter you." What is that you say, man? fetter *me*? My leg you will fetter, but my moral purpose not even Zeus himself has power to overcome. "I will throw you into prison." My paltry body, rather! "I will behead you." Well, when did I ever tell you that mine was the only neck that could not be severed? These are the lessons that philosophers ought to rehearse, these they ought to write down daily, in these they ought to exercise themselves.[229]

This spirit depends on a gymnastic conception of one's own strength and a gladiatorial one when confronted with the task of plotting one's own personal path: the attainment of experiential truths comes at a price, "from which none can be exempt. Experience here is something that is part of the historical nature of man".[230] Scars are an element of regard and prestige for warriors and plastic surgery is shameful and ignominious for this conception, for it erases the external signs of the struggle. Little wonder that an excess of facial plastic surgery ends up eliminating all traces of expression, condemning people undergoing it to become slaves to smooth skin that does not reflect any heroic story of the past. Scars amaze those displaying them because they are marks of a struggle of cosmic dimensions from which those emerging victorious now exhibit them as if they were medals: "Just as you too do not say that the cock which has one a victory, even though he be severely cut up, has fared badly, but rather the one who has been beaten without suffering a blow. Nor do you call a dog happy when he is neither in pursuit or toiling hard, but when you see him sweating, suffering, bursting from the chase."[231]
It should be noted that a badly healed scar can be synonymous of hideousness, as occurs in a mental illness in which that mark can be signified by a denial of reality. Thus, rather than idealizing its

---

[229] Idem.

[230] Hans Georg Gadamer, *Truth and Method*, 319.

[231] Epictetus, *The Discourses*, 287.

possession, the accent should be placed on its proper healing: "'Even in the mind of the wise man, a scar remains after the wound is quite healed.'"[232] This adequate management has given rise to philosophical exercises that, over the centuries, the Stoics, among others, have bequeathed us.[233]

3.4. Courage to Cross Thresholds that Do Not Allow a Step Back

Deriving from the foregoing is courage. According to the *Merriam-Webster Dictionary*, it is the "mental or moral strength to venture, persevere, and withstand danger, fear, or difficulty".[234] That action implies crossing thresholds that do not allow a step back or reaching a mountain pass or a seaport offering a new anchorage, that is, new belief system coordinates with which to scan the horizon. Continuing with the etymology of "experience", according to Ortega y Gasset the root *per* is connected with *"peiro"*: *"Peîro* [...] appears yet again when Ernout-Meillet deals with the word *portus*, door. *Portus* and *póros* mean a 'way out' which, when walking in the mountains, we encounter," and also signifies "the *channel* in a reef and the *entrance* to a cove, for which reason it is called a *port*".[235]

Romano links *per* to the Greek *peiro* (to cross), *perao* (to pass through) and *peraino* (to pass through to the edge).[236] He thus underscores the tension inherent to a person who seeks knowledge from experience, someone who places himself between two incompatible extremes or two universes with possibilities and rules that cannot be reconciled. This tension can only be resolved with death. Thus, Spranger contends that "life experience reaches its

---

[232] Lucio Anneo Seneca, *Minor Dialogues*, 68.

[233] A book on philosophical practice in prisons, which I am in the process of finishing, describes the performance of these activities in over 100 pages.

[234] *Merriam-Webster Dictionary*, *s.v.* "Courage," accessed December 23, 2020, https://www.merriam-webster.com/dictionary/courage.

[235] Ortega y Gasset, *Obras completas 8*, 175.

[236] Claude Romano, *El acontecimiento y el mundo*, 213.

peak is this secret of 'perishing and becoming', in an always new becoming oneself, disintegration and rebirth",[237] a passage that recalls Dante's *íncipit vita nuova*.

Furthermore, the impossibility of returning also appears, according to Romano, in *perás*, the Greek for "limit", a "beyond". So, it makes sense that *peratés* should be a traveler or, better said, a *per-egrino* (Spanish for pilgrim) or he who walks "through" (*per*) a field or fields (*argos*). The two mortal sins of whoever commences his experiential life are *flight* and *apathy*. One reason for flight derives from vulgar entertainment or the yearning for pleasure that disregards personal development through the often painful discovery of evidential truth. This is the case of the *tourist*, who embarks on his experiential journey not as a means of gaining experience, but as an excuse for taking selfies of himself in front of the most highly recommended monuments on the most popular travel websites. In contrast to the *pilgrim*, the tourist is protected by insurance policies that prevent him from being sufficiently adventurous in the full existential evolution that death requires. That sense of security hinders the challenging contemplation of the abyss. Tourists cannot even put their hands out of the windows of the coaches taking them to the Iguaçu Falls so as to prevent them from being scratched by an inopportune branch. All other possible risks, like feeding the coatis – since they might bite – are prohibited. Accordingly, this eradicates the adventurous nature of the experience, which is the basis of the creation of one's own identity. However, tourists amuse themselves on their trips as if they were living in an ersatz theme park, going around and around on the same attraction like sleepwalkers trapped in their self-imposed security or in their flight from risk, thus activating a false courage.

Tourists go on their trips to flee from monotony. Their alleged salvation is to satisfy their *curiosity* for adventures: "There are different forms of flight, one of which is curiosity, consisting in

---

[237] Eduard Spranger, *La experiencia de la vida*, 56.

wanting to see, but not wanting to do so in order to gain a greater and better understanding, but wanting to see something in order to lose sight of it immediately and to continue searching for novelties."[238]

Although he lives so securely, so placidly, so far removed from danger, to the point that his body ends up yearning for anxiety and uncertainty, paradoxically the subject, in his ambivalence, expects an anxiety without anguish. Leaving aside the needs of those suffering from chronic illnesses, it is akin to when we purchase milk without lactose, coffee without caffeine, sweetener without sugar, juice without pulp and bread without gluten.

> "There is nothing so unbearable for man as living in complete tranquility, without passions, without chores, without amusements, without anything with which to occupy himself. Then, he feels his nothingness, his abandon, his dependency, his impotence, his emptiness." Here, nothingness and emptiness are apparently related to what Pascal called "tedium" and what we would nowadays call anguish or distress. Man realizes that in his solitude he comes face to face with his own nothingness and, in order to set aside that mirror, continuously seeks to enjoy himself and to keep himself occupied. [...] Entertainment is characterized by a sort of flight that ultimately consists in losing oneself.[239]
>
> Ordinary experience is often infected with apathy, lassitude and stereotype. We get neither the impact of quality through sense nor the meaning of things through thought. The "world" is too much with us as burden or distraction.[240]

The *promise* of these experiences tends to be unsatisfactory, thus increasing the burden, for the "welcome change" intended with a life change occurs infrequently, for it would seem that the purpose of travel insurance is that tourists should return home without any physical or, or course, existential damage. This unsated thirst

---

[238] Josep Maria Esquirol, *La resistencia íntima. Ensayo para una filosofía de la proximidad* (Barcelona: Acantilado, 2015), 61.

[239] Ibid., 30.

[240] John Dewey, *Art as Experience*, 260.

encourages constant travel consumption with the hope that the destination will bring about the long-desired metamorphosis. The final product is the same sensation of emptiness and with the sole satisfaction of posting travel photos on Instagram or having a new banality about which to talk in the next get-together with one's friends. At best, tourism has become a social status symbol.

John Dewey has put forward aesthetic experience as a mechanism for shaking off that *apathy* or "complete tranquility". It is the first step in performing exercises for encouraging us to muster up enough courage to live experiences.

> Yet apathy and torpor conceal this expressiveness by building a shell about objects. Familiarity induces indifference, prejudice blinds us; conceit looks through the wrong end of the telescope and minimizes the significance possessed by objects in favor of the alleged importance of the self. Art throws off the covers that hide the expressiveness of experienced things; it quickens us from the slackness of routine and enables us to forget ourselves by finding ourselves in the delight of experiencing the world about us in its varied qualities and forms. It intercepts every shade of expressiveness found in objects and orders them in a new experience of life.[241]

Aesthetic experience involves understanding the artist's experience, immersing oneself in it[242] and, as at a concert, ending up feeling the same passion as the first violin when the last note sounds or as the members of an audience or readers who hold their breath when the main character of a film or book takes the plunge. It is precisely the distance between the first violin and the spectator that mediates between direct and indirect experiences or narratives, but that will be covered in another book.

Aesthetic experience possesses the same traits as a pilgrimage: one can live as a tourist who sees the *Mona Lisa* with the urgency of having to comply with a predetermined itinerary or as a person who, once he has arrived at the altar of his inner quest, becomes

---

[241] Ibid., 104.
[242] Friedrich Scheleiermacher, *Los discursos*, 67.

rapt and is only interrupted by the guard telling him that it is closing time.

3.5. Patience, Delay and Deployment of Experience

Aesthetics encourages contemplation, respect for the more leisurely paces of the other in order to allow the truth of a work of art to open up from itself. Haste and the irruption of options have provided opportunities for choice, but have degraded decision-making by impoverishing experience: the availability of experiences has trivialized them all by preventing us from dwelling on them, respecting their sacral status. When there is only one book, its repeated reading transforms it into a fetish; when it is multiplied by a million, the possibility of dwelling on each one of them is reduced because the rest demand urgent attention. Their sheer number calls for horizontal and sequential dynamics, like, for example, watching a large number of films and series on cable television platforms. Exiguity favors the enjoyment of details and depth. In relation to a dichotomy explained above, insights are synonymous of point sequences, but experience is developed from within, to the point that, owing to its depth and density, it becomes eternal.

In his *Art as Experience*, Dewey explains how speed is inversely proportional to the cultivation of experience: "Zeal for doing, lust for action, leaves many a person, especially in this hurried and impatient human environment in which we live, with experience of an almost incredible paucity, all on the surface. No one experience has a chance to complete itself because something else is entered upon so speedily."[243]

It is important to note that this trait formed part of the last phase of the workshops envisaged in the hermeneutic practice project. The participants lost themselves in a sole phrase, allowing the words to take shape, without seeking an objective alien to this. Indeed, "To look at a work of art in order to see how well certain rules are

---

[243] John Dewey, *Art as Experience*, 44–5.

observed and canons conformed to impoverishes perception."[244] This way of acting implies the imposition of the legitimacy of the subject (the objective of seeing if the rules are complied with) on the work of art and, therefore, silencing its own way of occurring. A correct approach has been covered above using the Heideggerian example of the peasant's shoes or ore.

Aranguren concurred with this point when remarking, "Life experience requires abiding and having patience, giving time to time; life experience has to ensue, it cannot be provoked or anticipated."[245] His contemporary Julián Marías started by recommending that "haste" be eschewed and concluded by assuming the unfruitfulness of achieving one's own ends, for perhaps it is better to abandon them so as to attain other unimagined superior ones: "The man with life experience is never 'hurried' – in contrast, he requires a certain amount of calmness and tranquility, but has the haste of he who does not need to reach the end of each thing."[246]

This protraction should also be applied to the tempos of the realities with which we relate. It is a beginner's error to program the reading of the pages of a book in a homogeneous fashion, namely, to expect to take the same amount of time to read 20 pages of Descartes' *The Discourse on the Method* as 20 pages of Heidegger's *Vorträge und Aufsätze*[247] or Husserl's *Experience and Judgment*. Each book possesses its own tempo that must be respected, as if it were a living being, so as to avoid not understanding its content. Gadamer recalled this in his *The Relevance of the Beautiful*: "Every work of art imposes its own temporality upon us [...]."[248] For this reason, one of the first

---

[244] Ibid., 205.

[245] Jose Luís López Aranguren, "La experiencia de la vida," 34.

[246] Julián Marías, "Un escorzo," 118.

[247] Martin Heidegger, *Vorträge und Aufsätze* (Stuttgart: Klett-Cotta Verlag, 2003).

[248] Hans-Georg Gadamer, *The Relevance of the Beautiful and Other Essays* (Cambridge: Cambridge University Press, 1986), 45.

hermeneutic steps consists in discovering the rhythm of reading or of contemplation of a painting, monument or stranger. As with any authentic experience, this is learnt by traveling down a path that does not exist, for, as Machado declared in his *Proverbs and Songs*, "Wayfarer, the only way is your footsteps, there is no other."[249] Gadamer and Dewey have explained the articulation of this existential placement. On the one hand, it is a question of letting oneself be penetrated by the work of art per se, circling and entering into it. Meanwhile, without being aware of it the work penetrates us:

> To do that, we have to go up to the building and wander round it, both inside and out. Only in this way can we acquire a sense of what the work holds in store for us and allow it to enhance our feeling for life. […] we must learn how to dwell upon the work in a specific way. When we dwell upon the work, there is no tedium involved, for the longer we allow ourselves, the more it displays its manifold riches to us.[250]

And, according to Dewey, "One must move about, within and without, and through repeated visits let the structure gradually yield to him in various lights and in connection with changing moods".[251]
This path is akin to the reality of a person deaf from birth who recuperates his hearing when an adult. The acquisition of hearing would initially enable him to hear articulated sounds; however, he will not understand them. Deep contemplation of each sound will allow him to distinguish nuances that will progressively become phonemes and all the lengthy grammatical syntax and semantics. Experiences, and in particular aesthetic experience, continue that path that opens up a world with an inclination to infinitude, which will remain a mystery for those who do not learn to tarry. Jauss explains this in the following terms: "Whoever aesthetically

---

[249] Antonio Machado, *Proverbios y cantares* (Madrid: Ediciones El País, 2003).
[250] Hans Georg Gadamer, *The Relevance of the Beautiful*, 45.
[251] John Dewey, *Art as Experience*, 220.

perceives a painting, namely, whoever acquires new knowledge through sight, must cope with the inclination to identify or recognize with haste and, instead of this, to be aware of how, for the beholder, significance – the object of imagined reality – is gradually constituted from some colored blotches that are strange at first sight."[252]

The procedure happens in two enabling spheres: (1) *to let experience unwind* and (2) to learn to tarry. These actions can yield therapeutic results, since, as has been seen with the Mexican counselee and his nocturnal anxiety, painful coloration stems all too frequently from denying and obstructing the deployment of experience.

Accordingly, María Zambrano proposed descending into the abyss as a way of emerging from a crisis. Going over and over a problem removes the problematic interpretation of the situation. In other words, dwelling at length on an issue without denying it ends up breaking the curse on the individual. On the contrary, flight or entertainment (turning in the opposite direction so to avoid looking the monster in the eyes) are partial solutions that, unlike descending into the abyss, do not abrade the conflict. It is important to remember that an oasis can only be found by wandering through the desert. This, however, does not detract from the fact that many painful circumstances do not need to be lived to be resolved and that it is not a good idea to go wandering through some deserts because of the strong likelihood of dying from thirst. Nonetheless, flight not only avoids confronting a problem or obtaining the answer to a question, but also prevents us from attaining the identity constituting us. Dewey explains the deployment of experience as follows:

> In contrast with such experience, we have *an* experience when the material experienced runs its course to fulfilment. Then and then only is

---

[252] Hans-Robert Jauss, *Pequeña apología de la experiencia estética* (Barcelona: Paidós, 2002), 69.

> it integrated within and demarcated in the general stream of experience from other experiences. A piece of work is finished in a way that is satisfactory; a problem receives its solution; a game is played through; a situation, whether that of eating a meal, playing a game of chess, carrying on a conversation, writing a book, or taking part in a political campaign, is so rounded out that its close is a consummation and not a cessation. Such an experience is a whole and carries with it its own individualizing quality and self-sufficiency. It is *an* experience.[253]

Although explaining the task is a simple matter, the preparation for undertaking it calls for high standards. The first step involves practicing the habit of tarrying: "If certain meanings are combined, *to tarry* is both to defer and to remain in some place during a certain time: to remain in some place deferring the end. The term comes from the Latin *demorari,* which means 'to wait' or 'to be late'."[254]

Zambrano distinguished two methods for accessing the truth: the architectonic and that of the serpent. The former was more direct and was represented by an arrow heading towards its target, which, during its trajectory, avoided looking the realities appearing to its left and to its right in the eyes. The latter was slower, trod unexpected paths, moved three step forward and two back, established objectives that it did not meet, slithered like a snake avoiding the straight path and creating bends when leaving the pre-established route.[255] The path of life is that of the serpent: our being is determined by a set of unpredictable experiences pregnant with truths, which are the crucial milestones of our biography. Experiential philosophical practice helps to discover that evidence which signals the path towards the constitution of the subject, assists him when he loses his frame of certainties (beliefs) and when it urges him to build another identity underpinned by a new evidential pillar.

---

[253] John Dewey, *Art as Experience,* 35, original emphasis.

[254] Josep M. Esquirol, *La resistencia íntima,* 49.

[255] María Zambrano, *El pensamiento vivo de Séneca* (Madrid: Cátedra, 1992), 48.

3.6. Opening. Play and Fascination in the Face of Problems: "Surprise Is Welcome"

An aforementioned text compared two situations: tedious familiarity with the given versus the activating dimensions of art: "Familiarity induces indifference, prejudice blinds us […]. Art […] quickens us from the slackness of routine and enables us to forget ourselves by finding ourselves in the delight of experiencing the world about us in its varied qualities and forms."[256] Certainly, routine protects us from injury, although it also prevents us from learning the different and the appearance of evidence.

Imagine three young men at the entrance of the Faculty of Medicine of the National Autonomous University of Mexico (hereinafter UNAM). Over the past years, they have been studying day and night, but, after having sat their exams, none of them have reached their long-awaited objective: one studies for another year to prepare his exams and to make another attempt, while the other two decide to start studying nursing at the UNAM. Of these last two, one sees the situation as a way of being better prepared to make a further attempt at studying medicine (like his companion), while the other lets himself be seduced by nursing, because of the possibility of acquiring knowledge that he did not expect. Indeed, he is fascinated by nursing, discovers that the way in which this profession relates to patients was what he was seeking and what, he claims, he cannot find in medicine (more closely associated with the biomedical model than with its humanistic counterpart). A year later, the horizons of the three young men can be clearly distinguished. The first continues to be engrossed in his studies, for which reason he has not broadened his horizons. The second has had the opportunity to abandon the initial context, but his tenacity to take a degree in medicine has prevented him from enjoying the advantages of nursing, which he continues to view from the perspective of what it may contribute to prepare him for medicine. Only the third has broadened his horizons.

---

[256] John Dewey, *Art as Experience*, 104.

According to Martín Velasco, experience is only acquired if "the eyes allow themselves to be filled with the contemplated, without having any other activity to perform than opening themselves to it, eliminating the obstacles in the way, paying attention to it".[257] The last student has given himself the chance to integrate other worldviews. This does not mean to say that he has abandoned his desire to study medicine, which he could do the following year like his companions, but that he now has a disposition to open up to whatever happens. Even though the three manage to study medicine, the experiential learning of the third has been possible thanks to his disposition. In the words of Gadamer, the last student was willing to "accept some things that are against myself, even though there is no one else who asks this of me".[258] This is where the essence of experience lies:

> The truth of experience always contains an orientation towards new experience. That is why a person who is called "experienced" has become such not only through experiences, but *is also open to new experiences*. The perfection of his experience, the perfect form of what we call "experienced", does not consist in the fact that someone already knows everything and knows better than anyone else. Rather, the experienced person proves to be, on the contrary, someone who is *radically undogmatic; who, because of the many experiences that he has had and the knowledge he has drawn from them is particularly well equipped to have new experiences and to learn from them*. The dialectic of experience has its own fulfilment *not in definitive knowledge, but in that openness to experience* that is encouraged by experience itself.[259]

When Mª Carmen Paredes analyses *erudite ignorance* in Nicolás de Cusa, she understands that the wisdom attained through experience involves a path which calls for maintaining the candle of knowledge alight, to wit, the possibility of always being open to

---

[257] Juan Martín Velasco, *El fenómeno místico. Estudio comparado* (Madrid: Trotta, 2003), 325.

[258] Hans Georg Gadamer, *Truth and Method*, 319.

[259] Ibid., 223, emphasis added.

knowing more: "More than a possession, ignorance is a disposition of the spirit towards knowledge and is equivalent, since Socrates, to a state of opening."[260]

Even when there is nothing for it but to accept the circumstances because it is impossible to change them, as Epictetus noted,[261] we are not proposing pure resignation in the face of life's painful vicissitudes, for that may lead to bitterness. On the contrary, this opening involves converting suffering and pain into a resource, for discovering the crisis, as with any loss, is a chance to become strong. Moreover, it is a question of climbing another step and enjoying the aesthetic condition of the tragedy, laughing at one's own fall and, although pained, enjoying oneself. In point of fact, in his *Of Anger* Seneca taught that a mechanism for overcoming anger was to laugh at oneself or at the situation: if someone tries to box our ears, to reply with a "it was a pity a man could not tell when he ought to wear his helmet out walking".[262]

This fascinated and ludic disposition in the face of difficulties helps to attain experiential knowledge because it fosters another, which will be examined further on: balance. Our passions convert us, as the term itself indicates, into passive beings and, consequently, it is impossible for us to act for ourselves. But if we deactivate that possibility through fascination in the face of pain and suffering, we will remain sufficiently judicious in order that we should be able to discover the secret that experience wishes to reveal to us.

This theory calls for philosophical exercise and training to obtain results, but it is not impossible to achieve this. The first step, when faced with difficulties or the unexpected, would be to utter in a sharp, subtle and ironic voice, "Surprise is welcome. I am here to enjoy it."

---

[260] María del Carmen Paredes, "El concepto de 'sabiduría' en *Idiota* de sapientia," *Anuario filosófico* 28 (1995): 675.
[261] Epictetus, *The Discourses*, 175.
[262] Lucio Anneo Seneca, *Minor Dialogues*, 128.

3.7. Commitment to Authenticity and Self-criticism

One of the paradoxical phenomena that can be detected in many faculties of philosophy is the high level of dogmatism of the students or their inability to think for themselves. Unlike students taking other degree courses, like teacher training or information science, future philosophers cling to their ideas and beliefs, employing a series of argumentative tools learnt in the lecture hall and, similarly, have great difficulty in questioning them or in detecting the traces of truth embedded in the different. This reality is not only evinced in Spain, but I have also witnessed it the lecture halls and passages of the aforementioned faculties on several continents.

This is well illustrated by one of the philosophy workshops that I have organized from Tokyo to São Paulo, through Mexico City, Rome, Evora and Madrid. Called "What is a good question", the participants should pose three questions with a growing level of excellence. Afterwards, they should contend why each one of them is better than the rest that they have noted down themselves. At a certain moment, the philosopher asks some of the participants to think against the reasoning that they have prepared; in other words, they should argue that their worst question is the best and vice versa. To date, *all* those participants in my sessions who have found it hard to turn their train of thought upside down have been philosophy degree holders or students. There have been some exceptions of people holding or studying other degrees, but even in those cases some have found it harder than others. What is even worse is that those students closer to doctoral research have come up against greater difficulties, whereas those who completed their studies some years ago and have devoted their time to teaching middle or high school students have not found this such a challenge. Lastly, the students in these faculties are accustomed to attempting to impose their ideas on the group and when failing to achieve this, remain silent until the end of the session, showing indifference to the incapacity of the rest. After the session, they criticize the rest of the participants for their lack of argumentative thinking or the workshop itself for not having assimilated the truth of their assertions or for having permitted arguments that, from their perspective, are erroneous. It should be noted that, here, the philosopher does not feel angry, but despairs over the line taken with our students (and with ourselves), feeling anxious about the drift of the system's "good students" and the "chosen" in their quest to reach the pinnacle of academic philosophy.

The problem of dogmatism, especially when it is mediated by arrogance, is the inability to continue learning from difference. This does not mean to say that the aforementioned students or professors should not continue to delve deeper into their lines of thought. However, the decline in their mental flexibility and, as a result, their capacity for listening to the other are both matters of concern. This is troubling because it paves the way for disrespect (in the words of Honneth)[263] for whatever does not conform to their philosophical ideology and prevents them from creating plural communities or from taking philosophy beyond the limits established by constituent and constituted power.

Experienciality and knowledge of experience can only be forged if, in addition to opening up to the other, as has been seen with Gadamer, they facilitate two elements: (1) commitment to authenticity and (2) self-criticism. Some contend that both are antagonistic: commitment to authenticity would make us close ranks around ourselves and would hinder self-criticism. Having said that, that commitment is not to a monadic myself (to the authentic *me*) that alienates the rest, but to *the* authenticity. Commitment does not occur in relation to the *myself*, but to *the itself* in which we all participate, for which reason it has to be done despite the fact that it does not correspond to one's caprices. This is the difference between doing *what I feel like* and doing what is suitable and timely.

---

[263] Axel Honneth, *Disrespect*, 101–24.

When a person does *what he feels like*, his decision is mediated by passions that make him impassive to the desires that control him. In opposition to this attitude, the Stoic world proposed doing whatever best suited the rational principle.[264] Faced with a dilemma, one should not wonder, "What do *I* feel like doing?", but "What is the most just and suitable *thing* that should be done?" The answer is obtained by reflecting on the just actions of our venerated masters or what a person, who for us is a model of wisdom, would have advised us to do (this connects with experienciality, since it constructs wise human beings). In sum, timely decisions stem from commitment to what we should authentically be, notwithstanding out passions.

A good way of gauging the level of progression with respect to the assumption of the authentic path is to be found in our determinations in the face of external criticism. When rebuked for an action, the most habitual solutions for the neophyte are denial and excuses. In contrast, mature individuals treading the path to wisdom use it as a basis for reflection and change. After rebuking them, parents or professors tend to encourage young people to ponder on the issue in order to change. If the quarrel is taken seriously, namely, if it is considered as valid for reflection, this can lead to metamorphic ascension. In order to produce that metamorphosis, moreover, that reflection has to emerge as an experience. As we progress up the experiential and sapiential scale, it will be unnecessary for an external agent to admonish us: this depends on daily reflection on the improvement of actions (without this leading to a demoralizing or perfectionist obsession). As already noted, Seneca proposed the following analytical exercise at the end of the day:

> It was the custom of Sextius when the day was over, and had betaken himself to rest, to inquire of his spirit: "What bad habit of yours have

---

[264] Marcus Aurelius, *Complete Works of Marcus Aurelius* (Hastings: Delphi Classics, 2015).

you cured to-day? what vice have you checked? in what respect are you better?" Anger will cease, and become more gentle, if it knows that every day it will have to appear before the judgment seat. What can be more admirable than this fashion of discussing the whole of the day's events? How sweet is the sleep that follows this self-examination? how calm, how sound, and careless is it when out spirit has either received praise or reprimand, and when our secret inquisitor and censor has made his report about our morals? I make use of this privilege, and daily plead my case before myself: when the lamp is taken out of my sight, and my wife, who knows my habit, has ceased to talk, I pass the whole day in review before myself, and repeat all that I have said and done: I conceal nothing from myself, and omit nothing: for why should I be afraid of any of my shortcomings, when it is in my power to say, "I pardon you this time: see that you never do that any more?" [...] A good man delights in receiving advise: all the worst men are the most impatient of guidance.[265]

Philosophy for/with children, one of the most advanced philosophical practices, establishes self-correction as a principal characteristic of critical thinking.[266] Lipman relies on Peirce when stressing that this is a crucial element so that reason should discover its basic weaknesses and for improving.[267] The members of the community of inquiry are an essential resource for progressing; although it is first necessary to *dispose them*, to encourage that disposition in each one of them.

3.8. Subtlety

The *distracted tourist syndrome*, if we may say, has been encouraged by the abuse of social networking sites and their instantaneous availability via mobile devices that take photos and post them immediately. This state of affairs means that the time devoted to dwelling on nuances has been substituted by the activity of selecting Instagram filters or messages to send via WhatsApp.

---

[265] Lucio Anneo Seneca, *Minor Dialogues*, 154–5.
[266] Matthew Lipman, *Thinking in Education*, 212.
[267] Ibid., 218.

A century ago, John Dewey noted the incapacity of sightseers at the time: "The hasty sightseer no more has an esthetic vision of Saint Sophia or the Cathedral of Rouen than the motorist traveling at sixty miles an hour *sees* the flitting landscape."[268] At that moment, fugacity was already an ontological determination of travelers, but they still had time. The current problem is that entertainment robs the subject of the chance to be bored and the tourist that of tarrying. The most serious consequence is that we miss nuances of reality and the capacity to penetrate them:

> A crowd of visitors steered through a picture-gallery by a guide, with attention called here and there to some high point, does not perceive; only by accident is there even interest in seeing a picture for the sake of subject matter vividly realized. For to perceive, a beholder must *create* his own experience. And his creation must include relations comparable to those which the original producer underwent.[269]

Versus this lost perspective, "Therefore the sages got their knowledge without travelling; gave their (right) names to things without seeing them; and accomplished their ends without any purpose of doing so."[270]

The relevance of this loss of subtlety is owing to the fact that the depth of experiential truths requires intuiting that which surrounds us with finesse. The young man who was transformed in the talk described above maintained a level of attention that his colleague, amusing himself on social media, was incapable of maintaining. The latter not only lost information, but also disqualified himself from enjoying the nuances of the message and its presentation.

Without a shadow of doubt, new ways of learning have been opened thanks to social media, but, nonetheless, it should be recalled that it is complicated to access a teaching in which full

---

[268] John Dewey, *Art as Experience*, 220.

[269] Ibid., 54.

[270] Lao-Tse, *The Tao Teh King, or the Tao and Its Characteristics* (New York: The Project Gutenberg EBook, 2008).

attention, the Stoic *prosoche*, has not been expunged for many people.

Understanding derives from perception; if this is restricted, the reasons for attaining the former cannot yield fruit and, consequently, the path to experience is blocked.

Art, philosophy and mysticism are conducive to experience, for which reason they have inquired into the development of contemplation and meditation (the Stoic *meletai*). Each one will now be exemplified in order to discover the alignment between their visions of this resource: "An artist, in comparison with his fellows, is one who is not only especially gifted in powers of execution but in unusual sensitivity to the qualities of things. This sensitivity also directs his doings and makings."[271] "And this means learning how to listen to what art has to say. We shall have to acknowledge that learning to listen means rising above the universal levelling process in which we cease to notice anything – a process encouraged by a civilization that dispenses increasingly powerful stimuli."[272] "The perception of what is small is (the secret of) clear-sightedness; the guarding of what is soft and tender is (the secret of) strength. Who uses well his light,/Reverting to its (source so) bright,/Will from his body ward all blight,/And hides the unchanging from men's sight."[273]

The loss of subtlety is synonymous of the abandonment of the world and reality: "The flavours five deprive the mouth of taste."[274] Hume distinguished between two categories of subtlety: the delicacy of passion and that of taste. Maturation implies moving from the first to the second; in other words, from a coarse sensitivity, without specifications or autarchy, to a sharp, subtle one, with the philosophical fortitude that allows us to know how to discern and act in light of the correct and incorrect.

---

[271] John Dewey, *Art as Experience*, 49.

[272] Hans Georg Gadamer, *The Relevance of the Beautiful and Other Essays*, 36.

[273] Lao-Tse, *The Tao Teh King*.

[274] Idem.

> Some people are subject to a certain *delicacy* of *passion*, which makes them extremely sensible to all the accidents of life, and gives them a lively joy upon every prosperous event, as well as a piercing grief, when they meet with misfortunes and adversity. [...] There is a *delicacy* of *taste* observable in some men, which very much resembles this *delicacy* of *passion*, and produces the same sensibility to beauty and deformity of every kind, as that does to prosperity and adversity, obligations and injuries.[275]

The English thinker's definition of delicacy of taste coincides with subtlety: "Where the organs are so fine as to allow nothing to escape them, and at the same time so exact as to perceive every ingredient in the composition: this we call delicacy of taste, whether we employ these terms in the literal or metaphorical sense."[276] The work in which he develops this concept puts forward suggestions for organizing a gastro-sophical workshop that serves to foster subtlety through gastronomy. "A good palate us not tried by strong flavours, but by a mixture of small ingredients, where we are still sensible of each part, notwithstanding its minuteness and its confusion with the rest."[277]

James observes that subtlety is not only the readiness to attain experiential knowledge, but also its consequences. After having certain experiences, the capacity to penetrate reality in a previously unknown way is intensified. "One must have musical ears to know the value of a symphony; *one must have been in love one's self to understand a lover's state of mind*. Lacking the heart or ear, we cannot interpret the musician or the lover justly, and are even likely to consider him weak-minded or absurd. *The mystic finds that most of us accord to his experiences an equally incompetent treatment*."[278]

---

[275] David Hume, *Essays Moral, Political and Literary* (London, Edinburgh, Glasgow, New York and Toronto: Henry Frowde, 1904), 3, original emphasis.

[276] Ibid., 240.

[277] Ibid., 241.

[278] William James, *The Varieties of Religious Experience: A Study in Human*

3.9. Humility until the Subjective Genitive

In the Bible, Proverbs directly establishes a relationship between wisdom and humility: "where humility is, there also *is* wisdom".[279] There are several reasons behind this link.

Firstly, arrogance serves to block the truths presented by people, situations and discourses. In their absolutist belief, they hold that they possess all knowledge and close their senses to the other. At the other extreme, the humble open themselves and accept the unexpected as a mechanism for learning about the unknown by becoming receptacles that adapt to any type of truth that may occur. All in all, it makes sense that the first step for experiential learning should be to assume one's own limitations and the awareness of the need for what one does not possess: "experience is experience of human finitude".[280]

Humility consists in a Socratic type of ignorance. Plato uttered his famous statement, "I know that I know nothing", in an attempt to render evident something differing from mere stupidity; it is about abandoning the throne of truth. Thus, through maieutics, questions – the authentic opening of the ignorant – are chosen instead of answers, the reserve of those who believe that they know. The Greek philosopher placed himself on the same level as he who seeks it so as to elevate it, from below, in order that he should find his own solutions.

This dynamic occurs in philosophical counseling sessions and philosophy workshops. When a counselee arrives at a session with his questions and ends up demanding a line of action, the philosopher returns the questions to him in order that it should be he who plots his own path with his own answers. This does not mean to say that the role of the philosopher should be passive: he

---

Nature (New York, London, Bombay, Calcutta and Madras: Longmans, Green & Co., 1917), 380, emphasis added.

[279] Prov. 11:2, original emphasis.

[280] Hans Georg Gadamer, *Truth and Method*, 320.

should pay due attention to the rational and experiential processes through which the person moves. Philosophy for/with children works in a similar way: it helps pupils not only to find their own answers, at a higher level, but also their own questions.

All considered, philosophical practice involves a paradigm shift with respect to other ways of doing philosophy. The first obligation of transformation is to separate the specialist from his staff of command and to provide him with a humble seat next to those who he has always disrespected. Thus, in addition to changing expository forms, which often disregard the discourse of the inferior, an attempt should be made to approach distained universes, such as prisons, or interlocutors who inhabit the most conflictive neighborhoods in society. It is not a simple task, but, two millennia ago, Seneca observed that whoever claimed that philosophy was an "effeminate and easy kind of soldiering"[281] would be deceiving us.

By opening up to these plundered and scorned discourses, humility has pollinated philosophy in recent years. The approach to philosophy taken by women and indigenous peoples' proximity to the discipline have brought us close to metaphysical salvation by means of an aesthetics included in nature as the Nahault "flower and song" or the understanding of the *xapiris* in the world of the Yanomami. Nonetheless, there are still fields to be ploughed which require this humble and attentive attitude. So, it makes no sense that philosophy should construct a reflection on women's thought to create a feminine philosophy, because it is necessary that these philosophies be formulated by their own agents, that they be allowed to have their say. This task is complicated for those who have been trained in a philosophy of elevated daises, academic feudalisms and accommodated youth. But as this topic goes beyond the scope of the section, it is now time to move on.

---

[281] Lucio Anneo Seneca, *The Complete Moral Letters*, 100.

3.10. Accepting the Possibility of the Dissolution of the Self (Subjective Genitive) and the Ontological Act

One of the pinnacles of humility is accepting the possibility of the dissolution of the self. This disposition does not pursue the annulment of the self so as to let the other impose itself, but seeks to impose on individuals an experience surpassing all subjects. It is not a question of reducing *my* notion of "friendship" to accept *yours*, but using that of both to attain *the* "friendship" in transcendental terms. That experience is not legitimized on the basis of me or the other, but implies accepting one's own reality. To this end, all that remains is to reduce myself to myself.

The dissolution of the self has been conceptualized by Panikkar as the "subjective genitive". In the subjective genitive, the subject abandons his status as substratum, of the center of adjective reality, to become a predicate or predication or, better said, genitive: he becomes transformed into a reality that lives *off* and *from* (the genitive) another reality that surpasses him:

> Another way of saying the same thing is to interpret the expression "experience of God" as the subjective genitive and not as the objective genitive. Namely, it is not *my* experience *on* God, but the experience of God – in me and through me – and of which I am aware [...]. Experience understood as the subjective genitive would be my participation in the experience *of* God. It is my conscious answer and my participation in that experience whose ultimate subject is precisely God. I understand my participation in this experience as a communion, a communion between God, who is the subject, and this experience *of* God which is *mine* insofar as I am aware of it.[282]

This adjusts to the mystical experience in which one does not live for oneself, but through God: only he provides certainty and the necessary breath to continue living. This idea appears in The Epistle of St Paul to the Galatians: "With Christ I am nailed to the cross. And I live, now not I; but Christ liveth in me. And that I live

---

[282] Raimon Panikkar, *Iconos del misterio*, 78, original emphasis.

now in the flesh: I live in the faith of the Son of God, who loved me, and delivered himself for me."[283]

The dissolution of the self requires disarming oneself and not even setting out on the quest, plus, as with courage, creating the conditions so that experience may hurl its darts at us until converting us into a bloody target: "To do experience with something [...] means: to let it approach us [...], reach us, pounce on us, turn us upside down and transform us."[284]

This is a mode of experience: mystics. Others may have art or certain emotions as their subject. Thus, experientially understanding love implies letting oneself be swept away by it, to be trapped by falling in love and, *from there*, to comprehend the world, discovering previously concealed nuances in the couple, in oneself and in reality. The experience of art would be analogous: to comprehend the sensitive qualities, letting them envelop and subsume us like a mother with her fetus: "Sense qualities are the carriers of meanings, not as vehicles carry goods but as a mother carries a baby when the baby is part of her own organism. Works of art, like words, are literally pregnant with meaning."[285]

As Dewey noted, works of art are literally *pregnant* with meaning: when the subject is subsumed in its scope of action, he abandons his limited spatiotemporal perception and acquires aesthetic vision, freed from these constraints. Far from destroying human beings, this immersion in aesthetics, broadens them, opens their eyes or gives them ones capable of comprehending new realities, just like the lover registers realities in the beloved, inaccessible to those who do not love her.

In fact, experience does not only not destroy the subject, but is the basis on which he is constructed: Nishida and Romano concur on the same point: "It is not that there is experience because there is an

---

[283] Gal. 2:19–20.

[284] Martin Heidegger cited in Claude Romano, *El acontecimiento y el mundo*, 212.

[285] John Dewey, *Art as Experience*, 118.

individual, but that there is an individual because there is experience."[286] "It is not man who has an experience, but ex-per-ience that makes man."[287] The face of the individual is mortgaged by the experience lived: his biography is not forged by the days (or experiences) that pass by, but by the experiential milestones determining his biography. "Nothing happens to me but to the extent that I make myself […]. 'I' am my history understood in a factual way on the basis of the events that *make history* for me, namely, that open a history for me and the dimension of *its meaning*."[288]

Similarly, Julián Marías recalled this with peasants: a human being without experiences lacks his own face. He will possess what he has inherited from his forefathers, his family or the ideology of the system. This implies that neither is he distinguishable nor does he have his own features, but possesses those received from a vicarious mold. He has not generated his self, but has remained a shapeless being.

The difference between children and adults is precisely the detachment of latter from the image of their parents. The answers of preschool children reproduce the worldview of their parents because they have yet to formulate their own arguments, whereas teenagers and adults forge their own destinies. Firstly, there is a stage of rebelliousness against what they receive and, subsequently, they become integrated into their own paths.

Romano is more caustic when claiming, "Only in it [experience] and owing to it does man access his humanity."[289] This humanity, which is understood here as that which provides an identity, is not accessible to animals because they are incapable of recuperating their self and, therefore, of forging their identity on the basis of

---

[286] Kitaro Nishida, *An Inquiry into the Good* (New Haven and London: Yale University Press, 1990), 19.

[287] Claude Romano, *El acontecimiento y el mundo*, 230.

[288] Ibid, 138, original emphasis.

[289] Ibid., 230.

their experiences. Experience becomes a condition of existential creation inherent to man; thanks to it, a person acquires a being that distinguishes him from the rest.

Returning to the subjective genitive, it is possible to see the profound coherence that is achieved from among these philosophical and mystical dictates with the mystics of Antón Pacheco. For this professor of the University of Seville, "It is not man who makes art, but rather art that presents itself to man. Art precedes man."[290] Panikkar explains this in a hermeneutic sense: each and every one of us are a way of making God exist inasmuch as we accept that he should care for us. "The experience of God is so personal because each one of us is no more than that same experience *of* God in me, in which I discover myself precisely as the "you" of that "I" which calls me and, calling me, made me be."[291]

The same happens in experiential workshops: people end up becoming a version of the philosophical experience, as occurred in the last stage of the hermeneutic practice workshops.

This state of affairs brings us to a crucial point for understanding experiential philosophical practice: its action is not anthropological, personal or ideational, but ontological. Despite the fact that counseling sessions or workshops start with the questions, problems or ideas of counselees or participants, their objective and end result transcend them since they do not cling to people but aspire to their dissolution in experience. Sessions revolve around experiential comprehension and not their particular and subjectivist problems. Experiential philosophical practice requires that they surrender to or ex-pose themselves to experiences. As a hermeneutic act, it is not a question of gaining a subjective understanding of reality, but of relinquishing the self to the powers of experience. If our intention is to understand the meaning of life

---

[290] José Antonio Antón Pacheco, *El ser y los símbolos* (Madrid: Mandala, 2010), 355.

[291] Raimon Panikkar, *Iconos del misterio*, 125, original emphasis.

of another person, we must submit our own capacity for understanding to the world of that person and, from there, scan the horizon from where he understands the world. Furthermore, if we want to understand the meaning of freedom, it is not enough to design different approaches to this concept, for it is also necessary to transfer ourselves to its *eidos* in order that our actions, affections and, therefore, ideas and evidence should be constructed from there.

Whether that determination is subsequently therapeutic or damnatory is something that escapes the purposes of the discipline. Notwithstanding this, repeating what has been noted above, the manifestation of experience and its truth does not depend exclusively on the subject (he may prepare himself so as to increase the possibilities of its emergence). "The (experiential event) occurs without an agent: it occurs if the agent, 'Is the "taking place" of the event, which leads to the "thing", and not vice versa; it is the verbality of the verb from which the subject derives.'"[292]

3.11. Withdrawal and retreat.

Withdrawal is the capacity to avoid the din of the multitude, the uproar in dispute with the necessary balance to attain knowledge of experience. This should not be understood as isolation, for neither is it possible to learn anything, nor to confront anything, in a vacuum.

Festugiere has explained how contemplation was a suspicious element in Classical Antiquity because it involved antisocial practices.[293] Petrarch justified that position on the basis of the maxim of Genesis: "It is not good for the man to be alone."[294] Lastly, Bruni proposes that the philosopher should lead an active life: he will be perfected by his family, political and economic

---

[292] Caude Romano, *El acontecimiento y el mundo*, 17.

[293] Trevor Curnow, *Wisdom, Intuition and Ethics* (Hants: Ashgate, 1999), 45.

[294] Rice, *The Renaissance Idea of Wisdom*, 37–8.

activity,[295] consuming the Renaissance idea of *"nunquam privatum ese sapientem"*.[296]

Esquirol renounces a withdrawn life when it becomes "a totally sterile reclusion and isolation".[297] Accordingly, he distinguishes between "isolation" and "solitude".[298]

This should not encourage us to throw the baby out with the bathwater, since a taxonomy of withdrawal that encompasses both of the extremes cited by Esquirol often occurs. Even though one of them should be avoided, the other forms the basis for acquiring experiential knowledge.

Comte-Sponville lists the different forms of withdrawal: from that of the hermit to that which is produced within society:

> As to solitude [...], the sage is closer to his own as he comes closer to truth. But solitude is not isolation: it is true that some live it like hermits, in a cave or in a desert, but others live it in a monastery, and even others – the majority – among their families or collectively .... To be isolated is to be without contacts, without relationships, without friends, without love, and that, of course, is a misfortune.[299]

The silence of withdrawal is productive, focusing and not conducive to boredom or to enjoying activities that end up breaking self-absorption. In pathological cases, silence creates a noise that alters, namely, that place in an alter (or other), as Ortega y Gasset observed, but neither does it return to the self, nor allows experience to impose itself on us. On the contrary, timely withdrawal expunges passions and reorders: this is how Zoran Kojcic explains it in his PhD thesis, following Marcus Aurelius: "If we have ordered souls this place will be fine for us, we should take care of that inner place, keep it tidy (Aurelius 1996, 39–40). This also follows some Socratic principles of taking care of the Self.

---

[295] Ibid., 46.

[296] Ibid., 47.

[297] Josep María Esquirol, *La resistencia íntima*, 12.

[298] Ibid., 8.

[299] André Comte-Sponville, *El amor. La soledad* (Barcelona: Paidós, 2000), 29.

What they both suggest is that running away from the Self in solitude or remote places does not truly help, not unless we already could deal with the issues on our own."[300]

For his part, Trevor Curnow turns the classical idea upside down: it is not a question of taking life to withdrawal, "the aim of meditation was not to facilitate withdrawal from the world, but to spiritualise the individual life."[301]

In short, Panikkar cautions that solitude has nothing to do with escaping from the world; on the contrary, it is to return to the cited self, albeit relatively speaking: "To enter silence is not a flight from the world, a dichotomy between the essential and the relative. It is to discover that the essential is only so because I am speaking from the relative; and the relative is only so because I discover that there is a relationship that enables me to remain in silence from an essential point of view."[302]

Withdrawal makes us return to the source, to focus on experience, and thus allows its deployment owing to the fact that attention explores it in its stages of development. Furthermore, "Only he who is capable of solitude can truly be with the rest."[303]

Meditation (or the Stoic *meletai*), attention to detail (the Stoic *prosoche* and *akroasis*), those moments of isolation from professional or personal obligations, writing confessional diaries and putting aside a daily moment for performing these activities give rise to the conditions that allow withdrawal to take shape and make our days existentially relevant. Esquirol has explained withdrawal as a mechanism of struggle against that which is established by the powers that be: "Whoever goes to the desert is not a deserter [...]. Whoever goes to the desert is above all *resistant*. He does not need courage for expanding, but for

---

[300] Zoran Kojcic, "Performance oriented method in philosophical counseling" (PhD diss., University of Sofía, 2019), 80.

[301] Curnow, *Wisdom, Intuition and Ethics*, 135.

[302] Raimon Panikkar, *Iconos del misterio*, 44.

[303] Jose María Esquirol, *La resistencia íntima*, 9.

withdrawing, thus resisting the harshness of the exterior conditions. A resistant person does not yearn for domination, colonization or power. More than anything else, he does not want to lose himself, but to serve the rest in a very special way."[304]

Pierre Hadot has urged us to recuperate the practice of philosophy retreats, insofar as they were created by the Hellenistic schools before their appropriation by religion.[305] In the field of experiential philosophical practice, we organized one with Ran Lahav in 2005. Subsequently, both he and Francisco Barrera have continued to do so sporadically in Spain and abroad, alike.

3.12. Balance

Imagine a lover who has a date with her beloved at 6 pm. The bus taking her there is delayed because of a protest march along its route. The young woman loses her temper and is gradually overcome by anger. The time passes by with insufferable slowness while she mentally curses the driver, the bus company, all living beings who have had the unfortunate idea of creating such companies and, of course, the unknown inventor of the wheel. Obviously, the young woman is in a lather, it being the other in which the feeling of impotence linked to the misfortune that she is suffering is installed.

At that moment, if we asked the afflicted lass what she is learning from the experience, her murderous look would be sufficient to understand that experiential learning is the last thing occurring within her. What is regrettable about this situation is not that she has lost her temper, that she has become angry or that this has contributed to reduce her life expectancy and that of her relationship, but that she has wasted the opportunity of learning from a painful experience owing to the fact that her balance has vanished and that she has done nothing to avoid it.

---

[304] Idem.

[305] Pierre Hadot, *Philosophy as a Way of Life* (New Jersey: Blackwell, 1995).

If we videoed the situation and if in a subsequent encounter in which she were calmer we viewed the video, she would probably be able to learn lessons for the future. What is the difference that makes learning possible in the second case? Her balanced disposition. Anger and passions have plunged her into such a passive state by completely catching her attention, thus clouding her judgment and vision and preventing the experiential evidence from emerging.

We are not of course saying that emotional outbursts[306] should be avoided at all times, since they can be useful for accessing the direct understanding of some circumstances and people. We only affirm that they often hinder the vision necessary for experiential learning.

In view of the foregoing, small wonder that Seneca dedicated a full chapter to *Of Peace of Mind*.[307] In this regard, according to the Tao, "In the opening and shutting of his gates of heaven, cannot he do so as a female bird?"[308] or that the encounter with beauty calls for "serenity of mind": "A perfect serenity of mind, a recollection of thought, a due attention to the object; if any of these circumstance be wanting, our experiment will be fallacious, and we shall be unable to judge of the catholic and universal beauty."[309]

In the mystical dimension, the same recommendation is repeated: "The attainment [...] of mental tranquility. Freedom from care, freedom from nagging conscience, freedom from the effects of the passions, all make it possible for the mind to be at rest and keep its attention in the heart. The implication is that only when attention is kept there can anything significantly mystical begin to happen."[310]

---

[306] It is necessary to distinguish between the passion that leads to passivity and the emotion that the movement of a person provokes.

[307] Lucio Anneo Seneca, *Minor Dialogues*, 250–87.

[308] Lao-Tse, *The Tao Teh King*.

[309] David Hume, *Essays Moral, Political and Literary*, 237.

[310] Trevor Curnow, *Wisdom, Intuition and Ethics*, 96.

Summing up, the acquisition of experiential knowledge implies mastering ones passions to a minimum degree, at least at the moment when the deployment of its truth is expected. If the situation were not propitious, it would be preferable to leave the task for another more favorable moment. As noted in Ecclesiastes, "The words of the wise are heard in silence, more than the cry of a prince among fools."[311]

---

[311] Eccles. 9:17.

CHAPTER 3
EXPERIENTIAL SCENARIOS AND METAPHORS

1. Experiential Scenarios
1.1. Description
Dispositions are linked to the *subject*; scenarios comprise the *frames* in which the philosophical action of workshops and counseling sessions takes place. Its purpose is akin to that of dispositions: to increase the proclivity of insights to become experiences. In the main, this implies that logical-argumentative epistemology becomes experiential, the dynamics of the sessions shift from the rationalist play performed in a laboratory or classroom to become a pilgrimage, journey or entertainment, ontology is not affected by argumentation but is factual, hermeneutics is anagogic and action is ontological and not psychological or anthropological. In sum, the following scenarios will be examined:

    (1) Migratory or wandering processuality.
    (2) Anagogic hermeneutics.
    (3) Evidential epistemology.
    (4) Ontological and factual world.

1.2. Migratory or Wandering Processuality
We have already referred to some of the etymological links of the word "experience". We connected the root *per* to danger and divined its association with pilgrimage, understood here as a journey through (*per*) the fields (*agros*).

The connection with the journey was to be found, moreover, in the German term *Erfahrung* (experience): its root verb, *fahren*, signifies to travel or, as Ortega y Gasset added, to navigate. That journey is not interesting for its destination, as with current travel, but because of what happens (to us) during it, because that is where the face of the hero is forged. "The phoneme *per* implies ¡to travel¡, insofar as it is abstracted from its eventual purpose [...], the journey is taken inasmuch as *to be travelling* [...]. So, the content of ¡to travel¡ is what happens to us during it; and that is, principally, to encounter curiosities and to face dangers."[312] Following the Machadian maxim, these journeys manage to create a path that did not exist before: "In *per* what was *originally* involved was a journey, to wander over the world when paths did not exist, but all journeys were more or less unknown and dangerous. It was to travel through unknown lands without a previous guide."[313]

Secondly, the journey obliges the hero to pass through trials (*peîra*), for *per* is also linked to this term. If he is successful, they will leave marks on him which will provide him with a face. Its mechanism coincides with the right of passage in which young men acquired the status of adults, after defeating a monster, which was usually themselves.

Likewise, the hero has to return home and, to that end, has to have acquired a series of tools and a profile differing from that with which he embarked on his journey. According to Foucault,

> Finally, from this idea of navigation I think we should keep hold of the idea that this dangerous journey to the port, the port of safety, implies a knowledge (*savoir*), a technique, an art, in order to be undertaken well and to arrive at its objective. It is a complex, both theoretical and practical knowledge, as well as being a conjectural knowledge, which is very close, of course, to the knowledge of piloting.[314]

From its own context, art explains this adventure that bears fruit with the acquisition of knowledge of experience:

> The artist is compelled to be an experimenter because he has to express an intensely individualized experience through means and materials that belong to the common and public world. [...] If, instead of saying

---

[312] José Ortega y Gasset, *Obras completas 8*, 175.
[313] Ibid., 176.
[314] Michel Foucault, *The Hermeneutics of the Subject: Lectures at the Collège de France 1982-82* (New York: Palgrave MacMillan, 1994), 249.

> "experimental" one were to say "adventurous," one would probably win the general assent—so great is the power of words. Because the artist is a lover of unalloyed experience, he shuns objects that are already saturated, and his therefore always on the growing edge of things. By the nature of the case, he is as unsatisfied with what is established as is a geographic explorer or a scientific inquirer.[315]

The expedition is driven by a double convergent displacement: "displacement of the subject towards himself and his return to himself".[316] It is a self-absorption in which the subject encounters a face which he extracts from his interior.

All these statements explain why it is more convenient to talk about *pilgrimage* than about travel in relation to experience. Pilgrimage consists in a deepening transition in which external confrontation nests in and shifts towards the interior. Walking feet become a metaphor of the very path towards the innermost abyss. Each stage increases the density. The face which is sought is that which was already possessed, although comprehended with an intensity never envisaged before. Lastly, the destination is an amplified self that resists egocentricity, due to the wandering departure from the absolute self to find oneself again in the other.

The pilgrim's journey possesses an aspect that should not be overlooked: suicide. Experience calls for renouncing the previous belief system and that signifies the death of the previous character so as to acquire another. All crises hang over this death of the previous identity or over the impossibility of being able to continue living with it in a new context that has just commenced.

Suicide cannot be imposed on anyone, whereby it is important that, throughout the whole process, the person is reminded of his commitment to the direction that he has taken. It is essential to be "open to the event".[317] Beliefs or fear of taking the plunge without

---

[315] John Dewey, *Art as Experience*, 144.

[316] Adriana Atencio Antoranz, "El cuidado de sí desde la ética del psicoanálisis" (PhD diss., Universidad Complutense, 2018), 249.

[317] Claude Romano, *El acontecimiento y el mundo*, 42.

a safety net can drive him to, or make him doubt about, doing so. If the plunge is not taken, the metamorphosis will fail, as in the example of someone who takes a parachute jump. There cannot be any birth if before there has not been a real death.

To the journey and the pilgrimage should be added the metaphor of entertainment as a frame of experiential philosophical practice. The idea derives from the Stoics who understood the philosophical path as an entertainment for learning to live and not to succumb to the blows of life. This world would be generated according to metaphors of the activity and development of whoever joins a gym. Both philosophical activity and physical training bring to the surface initial weaknesses (the first criticisms of the rest or muscle cramp), involve lessons (existential or physical due to the desire to reach goals for which one is not yet prepared or to overtraining), provide moments of enjoyment that highlight progress or periods of stagnation in which one cannot find reasons to continue (degree programs anticipated as impossible to finish or philosophy exercises whose complexity leads to discouragement), require a trainer who indicates how exercises should be done and moments of solitude in which they are performed autonomously and involve the appearance of external obstacles that make it difficult to do so (the winter cold, the struggle against the system, apathy per se, the craving for subjecting the body/existence to an exertion for which it is not prepared). Two types of preparation (physical and philosophical) fuel each other: philosophical ascesis (for example, the Stoic kind) helps to obtain the existential fortitude necessary to complete a physical test, while training the body stimulates that of philosophical resistance.

The workshops of BOECIO, the philosophical practice project in prisons, rely heavily on this metaphor down to its tiniest details: the philosopher does not ask whether or not the tasks have been undertaken, but how the training of strength is progressing; when laziness raises its head, the philosopher assimilates it to that which appears three months after having joined a gym; he talks of overtraining if a person wishes to reach excessively high goals and injuries when the performance of a philosophy exercise has had a strong impact on a participant.

1.3. Anagogic Hermeneutics

Experiential anagogics explains the meaning of the following sentence: "Philosophy 'conceives', wisdom *traverses*."[318] Understanding transcendental realities such as God, the truth of art or experience exceeds the spatiotemporal limits of the cognizant subject, for which reason there is the need for an interpretive mode that comprehends entities beyond time and space. But how can logical-argumentative intellectual forces understand infinite entities? The answer has already been insinuated above: it is not the subject who understands, but the entity that understands itself *through* the subject. In effect, this brings us to the subjective genitive.

In this anagogic movement, the person comes into contact with a knowledge that facilitates, but never creates or possesses. The epistemic journey is an ascent with a point at which the self is left behind so as to reveal the transcendent. This play is the pivotal point of anagogics. According to Antón Pacheco, "The word anagogics comes from the Greek *anagoge*, which signifies the action of leading upwards [...]. So, anagogics would be that factor which, inscribed in things, is capable of referring us, by rising, to the ontological determination of the thing itself."[319]

Anagogics assimilates the subject to the cognizant entity through a series of sentences: "Each revealed meaning will be tantamount to ascending a level, an assimilated ontological state. So, hermeneutics is both a knowledge and spiritual process."[320] In mysticism, closeness to God is directly proportional to the

---

[318] François Julien, *Un sabio no tiene ideas*, 57.
[319] José Antonio Antón Pacheco, *El ser y los símbolos*, 168.
[320] Ibid., 152.

knowledge of him, up until the point of vanishing and comparing oneself with him during the mystic union.

There are several metaphors for understanding anagogic union. Antón Pacheco highlights the aforementioned assimilation: "to know is to assimilate oneself" in medieval thought.[321] Bovelles prefers the term "absorption": "For Bovelles, the acquisition of knowledge is a process of absorption, and absorption is itself a process of transformation of the individual. According to him, by swallowing and consuming whatever is in the nature of things, he becomes all those things."[322]

For his part, Julien describes it as a "bath" and pollution, "like an oil stain" insofar as this liquid infiltrates into porous fabric: "Instead of forcing thought, they infiltrate into it and, dissolving, "bathe" and pollute it. And, then, a sense (taste) spreads in a continuous, imperceptible and progressive way. What is said extends *like an oil stain*."[323]

Lastly, Bernard of Clairvaux resorts to participation, a Platonic term: "For Bernard knowledge is participation. Participation involves a community or communion with nature. The great principle now appears, which will smooth out all differences in level: 'the similar seeks the similar'."[324] As Panikkar remarks, "When I experience, to wit, when I touch the totality of the Being with my being, I am enjoying the experience of God."[325]

Assimilation, bathing, pollution and participation (to which should be added osmosis) describe the entry into experience (or into God) slowly but surely, until the last fiber of the element. Just as it is difficult to remove an oil stain from fabric, so too will it be difficult

---

[321] Idem.

[322] Trevor Curnow, *Wisdom, Intuition and Ethics*, 123.

[323] François Julien, *Un sabio no tiene ideas*, 49, original emphasis.

[324] Bernard of Clairvaux, *Obras completas de San Bernardo V. Sermones sobre el Cantar de los cantares* (Madrid: BAC, 1983), 18.

[325] Raimon Panikkar, *Iconos del misterio. La experiencia de Dios*, 19.

for anagogic-experiential learning to be separated from whoever has acquired it.

Antón Pacheco's spiritual hermeneutics, which is equal to anagogics, is that which produces a "normalization between degrees and levels of reading and the degrees of the Being; and, in turn, the degrees of the Being coincide with those of knowledge [...]. In the spiritual hermeneutics of the Book, the *modi essendi*, the *modi cognoscendi* and the *modi interpretandi* coincide".[326] When this is produced in the subject, the schema is reiterated, namely, its ontological or identity-related, epistemic and hermeneutic spheres move at the same rhythm. Thus, the lack of harmony of the logical-argumentative approach is not produced here.

Assimilation is concomitant to a progression or ascension in the degrees of the being. It gradually enables us to see with greater subtlety, distinguishing hitherto invisible nuances.

> So, in all religious traditions, the mystic is he who, at a specific moment in his life, confesses, "With hearing of the ear I have heard thee, but now my eye seeth thee" (Job 42:5) [...]; "As we have heard, so we have seen" (Ps. 47:9). This is what the mystics are referring to when, attempting to communicate what they have lived, they appeal to the experience of their recipient as an indispensable condition for them to understand: "If anyone has seen it, he knows what I say," Plotinus said. "Whoever has not experienced this will not understand it well."[327]

Antón Pacheco underscores the singular character of this anagogic experientiality, already seen above: "Hermeneutics is more than an interpretative technique: hermeneutics is a spiritual journey. The Transfigured World is the full insertion of the sensitive world into the intelligible world through the symbolic world. This insertion [...] brings about a radical transformation in the sensitive world,

---

[326] José Antonio Antón Pacheco, *El ser y los símbolos*, 151.
[327] Juan Martín Velasco, *El fenómeno místico*, 290.

which is converted into an environment of light and transparency, into a Transfigured World."[328]

This journey highlights the *spiral* deployment of experiential philosophical practice sessions. Different sessions repeatedly address common topics, although each new approach offers a deeper perception. In other words, the counselor formulates the same question in successive sessions, while the counselee receives a different reply to his question each time he poses it anew. As to groups, the sessions are intertwined, it being possible to repeat the same exercise in greater depth in several of them. The activity of echoes and the repeated reading of the same phrase in hermeneutic practice workshops expedites this intention: the participants always listen to the same text and, at the same time, deeper sounds that are closer to them, or to which they are closer, appear, until they cease to utter it so that it can read them.

In brief, this scenario distances itself from understanding that seeks conclusions on the basis of reasons by employing mechanisms of induction, deduction or abduction. On the contrary, it inquires into and makes hearing conscious of the truths inserted in any text, in people or in reality. In this way, it is possible to see more clearly the real with the objective, it is given more weight and its truth is accumulated. Thus, the importance of the conclusion leads to evidence.

1.4. Evidential Epistemology

If anagogics provides the keys to experiential understanding, evidence is its type of truth.

As has already been seen, evidence is not the result of a line of argument that links reasons to conclusions, but of an occasional or protracted event that is produced in conversation. According to Zambrano, "the evidence tends to be wanting, terribly wanting in intellectual content. But, however, in life it brings about a unique

---

[328] José Antonio Antón Pacheco, *El ser y los símbolos*, 94.

transformation that other richer and more complex thoughts were incapable of achieving."[329]
Those who criticize it from the standpoint of intellectuality or laugh at it because it lacks a complex and sufficiently erudite analytical structure, are mistaken. Their error is grounded in the fact that they attempt to impose a criterion of validity that is inadequate for the evidence: "For that reason, proverbs of wisdom are so wanting in their formulation and appear to be disappointing, but they offer food for thought, because in their simple banality they come close to the fundamental (same) level that makes everything communicate."[330] Theoretical content can repeat what is already known, but progress is not made in the horizontality of increased knowledge, but in the verticality of increased depth and transformation. "It is rediscovery. It is not a new truth, but a form that takes something that is already known and which now penetrates life, shaping it; it is something that did not operate before, but has now become operative."[331]
Progress in verticality can be made by means of variation: "Wisdom gives rise not to progression but to variation [...]. Wisdom is not explained (there is not much to understand in it)."[332]
In fact, Husserl's mechanism of eidetic variation is a resource that should be included in phenomenological practice workshops. This variation was analogous to Dewey's aesthetic action that explores experience (aesthetics) repeatedly in order to allow oneself to be impregnated with its truth in successive explorations; although an imaginative dimension was added by means of phantasy so as to jump from the empirical to the transcendental.
A criterion for verifying the validity of the evidence obtained is the *coherence between its content and life*. Theoretical learning is verified in written exams in which students demonstrate their

---

[329] María Zambrano, *La confesión: género literario*, 69.
[330] François Julien, *Un sabio no tiene ideas*, 212.
[331] María Zambrano, *La confesión: género literario*, 69.
[332] François Julien, *Un sabio no tiene ideas*, 24.

ability to memorize content; experiential learning should be perceived in a nodal change in the individual. This is due to the fact that truth, existence, life and the cognitive knowledge of the mind coincide in evidence. "Evidence is the point at which truth, a truth of the mind and of life, come into contact. The truth of evidence is imposed and, on doing so, produces security, certainty. It is firm and transparent at the same time."[333]

Owing to this connection, Aranguren is fully aware that the ways of acquiring it cannot be theoretical, as has been observed above: "Therefore, life experience is the knowledge acquired living […]. Neither is it studied or learnt knowledge, nor the devised or constructed kind. It is not an intellectual knowledge, but the vital sort. And, on the other hand, it is personal, untraditional knowledge, inherited or sapiential."[334]

Zubiri is more specific: acquisition takes place "in the *real* and *effective* course of a lifetime" and the subject of such acquisition is not the mind but the spirit, for it consists in "the credit that the *spirit* collects in its *effective trade* with things".[335] He even goes so far as to claim, "Experience signifies something that has been acquired in the real and effective course of a lifetime. It is not a set of thoughts that the intellect forges with or without truth, but the credit that the spirit collects in its effective trade with things."[336]

The evidential frame explains why understanding does not depend on an intellective act, but on an ontological one, that is, to become that which one is attempting to understand. When a student complains to a professor that he knows the text that is being read in class, the latter could reply that the idea is not know it, but to understand it:

---

[333] María Zambrano, *La confesión: género literario*, 69.

[334] José Luís López Aranguren, "La experiencia de la vida," 36.

[335] José Luis López Aranguren citing Xavier Zubiri in José Luis López Aranguren, "La experiencia de la vida," 30, emphasis added.

[336] Xabier Zubiri, "Sócrates y la sabiduría griega," *Escorial* 2 (1940): 189.

> The simplest rudiment of mystical experience would seem to be that deepened sense of the significance of a maxim or formula which occasionally sweeps over one. "I've heard that said all my life," we exclaim, "but I never realized its full meaning until now." "When a fellow-monk," said Luther, "one day repeated the words of the Creed: 'I believe in the forgiveness of sins,' I saw the Scripture in an entirely new light; and straightway I felt as if I were born anew. It was as if I had found the door of paradise thrown wide open." This sense of deeper significance is not confined to rational propositions. Single words, and conjunctions of words, effects of light on land and sea, odors and musical sounds, all bring it when the mind is tuned aright.[337]

The pinnacle of the experiential-evidential process is the recognition of the authority of the rest. A person's words will not be gauged by the validity of his arguments, but by a profoundness that deserves to be heard: "It [mystic experience] would provide the believer with a criterion of the truth of his life as such, which would extract him from the authority of texts, tradition and teachers and would lead him to underestimate all historical and ecclesiastic mediations and not to believe anyone but the God spawned immediately in the inner experience of the subject."[338]

This is no trivial matter, since evidence offers (humble) freedom from any imposed ideology. Having experienced a situation gives one the authority to question whoever acts within it and is still a neophyte on that painful path. It is the authority of a father who advises his son to avoid certain paths owing to the hardships that he will suffer, without this implying any prohibition. Thus, experiential evidence, despite its authority, does not entail dogmatism or absolutist tyranny, for authority is not imposed but received;[339] moreover, it should be recalled that experience is the awareness of one's own limitations. This awareness not only derives from prudence that averts all absolutism, but also knows that truth does not *emanate* from oneself, but is *received* from a

---

[337] William James, *The Varieties of Religious Experience*, 372.

[338] Juan Martín Velasco, *El fenómeno místico*, 285.

[339] Hans Georg Gadamer, *Truth and Method*, 294ff.

superior entity. As a matter of fact, that entity could reveal new truths to us in the future or perhaps there are still truths hidden from and invisible to our eyes at our present level of development. Furthermore, listening to the other and otherness can facilitate intellective training that allows for accessing those truths that we do not possess. Consequently, it would be anti-experiential to believe obstinately to be in egocentric possession of the supreme truth.

Ending with Julien: "On being hollow, *it allows things to pass*: it does not lead to the coagulation of meaning",[340] "It is the word that is always available and is limited to *beginning* to say."[341]

1.5. Ontological and Factual World

Anagogic hermeneutics and evidential epistemology are consumed in a factual ontology.

Claude Romano has distinguished between intra-mundane facts and inherently factual events. As to the former: "They happen to *me*, but they do not bring *me* into play."[342] Intra-mundane facts act as insights, for which reason they are not decisive in the positioning of reality. On the other hand, events give rise to an *"impersonal reshaping of my possibilities and of the world that occurs in an event and because of which my own adventure is flawed"*.[343] The event "has already given birth to a world",[344] a new world that "concerns me in particular".[345] As this has already been discussed, let us continue with what has not yet been addressed.

Sessions are initially based on the subjectivity of the group or counselee: their questions, their problems or determining issues contextualized in their lives. However, the philosophical ambition

---

[340] François Julien, *Un sabio no tiene ideas*, 214, original emphasis.

[341] Ibid., p. 219, emphasis added.

[342] Claude Romano, *El acontecimiento y el mundo*, 54, original emphasis.

[343] Ibid., 51, original emphasis.

[344] Ibid., 50.

[345] Ibid., 51.

of the workshops is to move on, first of all beyond particular aspects and then towards the transcendental and metaphysical realms. Specifically, the particular conflict arising from an emotional breakdown is addressed conceptually and analytically before carrying out exercises that phenomenologically open the *eidos* of "love" or on the basis of analyzing the maxim, "Killing is reprehensible", after a murder in the neighborhood, until transporting the group or counselee to the experience in order that they should attain an anagogic understanding.

This step does not disconnect a person from the particular owing to the fact that it is impossible for him to withdraw from his spatiotemporal circumstances. However, instatement is not synonymous of dependency, for which reason a person can break free from it without abandoning it. This can be explained with the following example. When a person falls in love with someone else, he embarks on his path with an important subjectivist impression: he focuses *his* gaze on his beloved without this leading him to abandon himself, since he can end up falling in love with the image that he projects on her and not with her. The first quarrels occur precisely because of that imposition of himself on his partner, of his model of reality which clashes with his ideal. If this happens in both directions, the relationship will be condemned to failure. Nonetheless, if the growth of the relationship implies their progressive distancing from themselves in order that, helping each other mutually, they are driven towards a love that surpasses the individuality of both, the subject will break loose from his blinding ego, without abandoning his spatiotemporal circumstances. This ascent, which starts with a dance between the two lovers, attains the experience of love, which ends up becoming the conductor. The moment when they notice this, they will know that neither was the performance in one of them (first phase), nor in the dance between them both (second phase), but in the symphony of the orchestra that makes them dance on the center stage (third phase).

A second example: when an author considers the possibility of writing a novel, he has a general idea of the plot and the main characters and even a specific denouement. The approach is deeply influenced by the writer. However, as the text develops, the narrator feels that the characters require unplanned scenarios, that the planned actions do not chime with the psychology that the characters have acquired and that the imagined denouement is the stuff of which dreams are made and totally inadequate for the novel. Indeed, if the author stubbornly stuck to his guns, readers would soon realize that the novel does not flow, for the demands of the text itself have not been respected by him. Here it can be observed that the initially powerful author has become a transcriber or copyist of the dictates of his creations. If his editor asked him for a happy ending, the author would not be able to humor him unless the main characters gave their consent. The dynamics of experience are similar: an individual can activate it, but there comes a time when it takes control and pronounces, "If you want to continue to delve deeper into me, you should follow the path that I set out." In short, the subject loses the potency that the experience acquires. To assume an experience involves humility and the acceptance of this potency that the experience has over the subject.

This loss of potency does not imply the subject's denial, but, paradoxically, his expansion: as seen above, he will be consumed by the experience and, as a result, will form part of an entity that sees more deeply and which surpasses him in all of its dimensions. Thus, the lover acquires a vision of the experience of love that enables him, for instance, to sense the suffering of that which was previously hidden from him. The novelist achieves the perspective of his own characters by broadening his own: in his approach to life, to his role as a novelist should be added that of a plumber, that of a doctor or that of any other of his creations.

In workshops, this can be implemented by means of simple techniques such as the game of transferring realities. For example, when it is necessary to answer a question and a participant suffers a mental block, he is asked to reply from the perspective of his mother, from that of a sage, from that of a stone or a trampled flower in a field, from that of the voice of a text or from that of freedom (all this in a progression moving from the particular to the most generic).

All this explains why experiential philosophical practice does not focus on particular psychological explanations, but intends to transport the subject to external experiences and entities from which to understand reality and himself.

2. Metaphors
2.1. Description

All metaphors possess a material and transcendental profile. The former, which is the most clearly visible, consists of the alliance, understood as a metal ring, the cross understood as a piece of wood or the physical sensation of a caress. The transcendental plexus is flight that gives a new meaning to that materiality. Thus, the alliance is transformed into a commitment, the cross into the synthesis of a faithful life and the caress into a promise of affection or love between couples.

The metaphor shapes a web of meanings that allow for redefining the material elements. For example, a math course can be experienced as a metaphor, understanding it as a way of planting the seed of knowledge of calculation in students. This new semic network will then give shape to a new renovated global meaning and, moreover, will give each element of the situation a new coloring. These four elements possess specific meanings in relation to the materiality of mathematical knowledge. The sun implies providing knowledge at a timely moment and in an appropriate medium in order that it should *flourish*; the fertilizer can be compared to the incentives that will have to be offered at moments of greatest difficulty for growth; and the water is tantamount to knowing how to teach in such a way as to prevent the death of the plant, whether this be due to overwatering or to a lack of that vital liquid. The role of the teacher is analogous to that of a gardener and that of the student to that of the plant's pot.

The implementation of the metaphorical frame requires a deep understanding of metaphor and each one of its elements and, subsequently, the connection of each element with another of material reality. It is also necessary to be able to go down the opposite path, namely, to ask which transcendental element corresponds to the materiality of a class, for example. Both paths transport the material and the transcendental and allow for encountering solutions to problems or to fly beyond the tedious plain of what is given at first sight.

2.2. Voyage and pilgrimage

The first two metaphors have been glossed as scenarios, although they can be studied as metaphors.

Within this analogical figure, philosophical practice does not only involve undertaking occasional rhetorical or dialectic tasks, as occurs in the logical-argumentative approach. Rather, experiential workshops require that subjects be traversed by the experience of the voyage or pilgrimage.

The pilgrimage reveals its truths progressively. Progress is made insofar as subjects are gradually possessed by each stage, as the group or individuals are enveloped by the experience that they are living. The experience's domination over subjects enables them to see it more profoundly through its own eyes, as with the lover who begins to see reality in a different way when he contemplates it through the eyes of the experience of love.

Due to the foregoing, the experiential path is not trodden with physical feet, but with inner activation. Although the lower limbs move, there is no progress if the act of going beyond boundaries is detained and if the inner self of a person is not given deeper paths. In this vein, it is discovered that the hermitage or cathedral of pilgrimage in the experiential approach is equated with this personal construction. Experiential pilgrims do not only travel down existing paths, but also create new ones and, consequently, new personal horizons.

Pilgrimage involves different images. The first and most obvious are based on the fact that the subject mutates into the pilgrim, the teacher into the path and the manuals into instructions (whether they be human, textual or situational). In addition, other images appear which encounter their analogues in counseling sessions and workshops: the sandals, the backpack, the deserts crossed, the miles covered, the inns at which accommodation is sought, the travelling companions, the sun that beats down, the rain that constrains, the loneliness, the blistered feet, the color that the skin can turn, the sunburns, the risk of straying from the path, the robbers along the way, the blows received from the aggressors, the shadows of the path, the bruises, the food eaten, the strategies for coping with the way, the discouragement and the fatigue, among others. All have a specific deployment in an experiential project.

2.3. Training

Training has been the metaphorical inspiration of the BOECIO project, as will be explained in further detail below.

When resorting to training, each element is reinterpreted using the gym metaphor. The philosophical act is converted into an exercise and the teacher into a training companion, the weights are diaries in which the participants reflect, progress is measured by the ability to cope with misfortune with greater fortitude and, as in any gym, care is taken not to under- or overtrain. The participants wear sports clothes to the sessions, they are asked what they have strengthened each week, mechanisms are employed so as to allow them to analyze moments of reluctance, the possibility of injuries are evaluated and the training is not based on the teachings of the trainer accompanying the process, but on philosophy whose teachings serve to improve their breathing capacity when some or other difficulty robs them of oxygen.

2.4. Cultivation

The last metaphor described here has to do with cultivation, which should be understood in terms of both gardening and agriculture or rearing.

This metaphor can be expressed by giving the participants in sessions a plant that they must nurture throughout the process. In this way, the metaphorical transitions performed by the trainer are added to those perceived by the students when looking after their plants.

In this connection, to the previous metaphors are added images like pests, death by overwatering, the symptoms with which plants express suffering (which are then contrasted with the mechanisms employed by the human body to reflect illnesses and their causes), understanding the specific needs of each plant and even knowledge of when they should be transplanted or that each one has its own needs that should be learnt and to which it is necessary to conform.

If the metaphor of the voyage gives strength to confront dangers, training increases stamina in the face of difficulties and cultivation enhances sensitivity and acuity to understand silences or that which habitually remains concealed. Each one of these capabilities appears in all the metaphors; however, each metaphor is more susceptible to some than to others. For this reason, the selection of metaphors in experiential work is no trivial issue, but should be consistent with two elements:

(1) The target audience of the sessions.
(2) The objectives pursued.

CHAPTER 4

EXPERIENTIAL PHILOSOPHICAL PRACTICE IN THE BOECIO PROJECT

1. Description

Experientiality can materialize in both counseling sessions and group workshops.

In counseling sessions, exercises are proposed, the participants are encouraged to develop the indicated dispositions and the scenarios shape the type of truths pursued. Since we have offered a detailed description of this elsewhere (Barrientos, 2009), we will focus on how to supplement the model in philosophy workshops. Specifically, we will make the most of the explanation to broaden the experiential aspects of the BOECIO project.

2. Exercises

BOECIO is based on training in Stoic exercises and critical thinking. This requires a brief theoretical training session in each encounter, which only takes up a fifth or a sixth of the time. The rest is akin to a physical gym exercise, including explanatory sessions in which communal, reflective, critical and synthesis capabilities are honed. Furthermore, the accent is placed on two exercises in each encounter: an initial one and another based on weekly training.

For example, the initial exercise in the BOECIO session focusing on *enkrateia*, or governing one's own passions, consists in picking up a heavy object and holding it aloft. With time, the participants start to feel how their fatigue, pain and suffering increase. Meanwhile, the trainer divides the blackboard into three or four blocks representing the stages which they go through. The participants are first requested to focus on their ideas and sensations, which should then be listed below each stage, thus reflecting the emotions, passions and expressions to which the process has given rise. A real session resulted in the following table:

FIRST STAGE (INITIAL)	SECOND STAGE (DEVELOPMENT)	THIRD STAGE (INTENSIFICATION)	POST-EXERCISE
Tension	Heavy	Struggling with fury	Relief
No	Readjust	Struggling on the	Tiredness
problems	Struggle	basis of reason	Liberation
Not heavy	Numbness	Aggressiveness	Agreeable
Light	Discomfort	Trying to lift the	Nice
Trusting	Effort	object higher to	Persisting
Fun	Pain in shoulders,	prevent it from	pain
Enjoyment	arms and wrists	falling	Pleasant
	Bracing your elbows	Encouraging oneself	pins and
	for greater comfort	Breathing with the	needles
	Tiredness	whole body	Need to
	Pain	Exercises of control	recover
	"The exercise should	Despair	Returning
	be made less	Wanting to carry on	at last to
	demanding"	Searching for peace	the
	"I didn't imagine it	of mind	previous
	would last so long"	"Goddamn it!"	reality
	Divert the focus of	The pain spreads to	Hands
	attention	another part of the	recuperate
	Unnatural posture	body	their
	"I think my arm will		normal
	hurt in an hour"		color
	Rigid position		
	Learning to sustain it		
	better		

This activity allows for becoming aware of the difficulty in coping with efforts and the weakness of those who do not control their emotions or possess *enkrateia*.

The initial exercise in the session addressing *prosoché* and acceptance, whose intention is to improve the capacity to perceive and accept the unbearable and immutable, involves looking at a painting or listening to disagreeable music in order to explore it. As the works of art are traversed, the supportable feelings and, subsequently, the necessary and desirable ones are gradually identified. This enables people to reach the objectives that they have established.

The advantage of the weekly exercises is that those deprived of their freedom have more time to perform them. In the BOECIO project, the main exercise consists in keeping a personal diary to which 20 minutes should be dedicated each day. Resembling Marcus Aurelius' *Meditations*, the participants first recover the ability to write manually. Secondly, it helps them disconnect from virtuality and the daily hustle and bustle for a time each day. And, thirdly, it prompts them to embark on their own path of profoundness and attention. In sum, as María Zambrano (2004: 35) observed, it serves to defend the personal solitude in which we encounter ourselves.

Another exercise involves analyzing a problem by contemplating it from an increasingly greater distance. Henceforth, the capacity to distance oneself and, by extension, to deactivate the potential of passions, is trained.

Lastly, critical thinking exercises involve analyzing written and visual arguments, so as to become accustomed to dealing critically with the opinions of others.

3. Dispositions

Disposition are addressed transversally throughout BOECIO.

The program does not oblige anyone to become involved in training. Its organizers are aware that prisoners are often obliged to attend or to appear at the sessions to obtain prison privileges. The trainers know that there will always be participants who do what they are told, but without showing any real commitment.

Notwithstanding this, no one is expelled from, or invited to leave, the sessions, for BOECIO is aware of the consequences that this may have in a prison. They are merely asked to listen in silence from the back of room. If at any moment they want to participate, they are quite welcome to do so.

Despite the foregoing, BOECIO proposes a leap of faith that requires courage and daring. The trainers determine the participants' level of commitment and the moment when they should advance through the different stages. Indeed, the content of the different sessions indicates that individuals have their own rhythm and that being too hasty will lead to overtraining as prejudicial as apathy or like training with exercises that do not create any tension. For which reason, those participants who get involved should learn to wait patiently for truths or evidence, to be willing to delay matters. The aim is not to reach the goal before the rest, but to make progress in one's own critical competencies and in governing one's own passions. As in the poem by Kavafis, which has been employed in some of the program's different editions, it is not important to reach a free port, but to learn not to be shipwrecked along the way and to enjoy the passage despite the difficulties.

In this sense, the formal proposals of the workshops facilitate the occurrence of events that are just as unexpected for the prisoners as they are for the trainers. Each new edition of the program includes unprecedented discoveries. Thus, the trainers or philosophers never repeat the same experiences with each group, but are open to new ones with their own nuances deriving from the events experienced by each individual.

Certain exercises, such as *prosoché*, are conducive to subtlety. Additionally, they foster acuity for contemplating reality in depth so as to understand on the basis of the body or critically on that of critical thinking.

Some exercises serve to hone discursive capabilities, others leverage images or music, while all of them facilitate some type of understanding that polishes the hermeneutic, gnoseological and, in general, comprehensive simplicity of the prisoners.

Governing one's passions avoids personal excesses like arrogance. By exercising the *physis*, Stoics understood that the human being was an entity that mediated between gods and animals. In this way, humility presides the meetings. On the other hand, that the trainers vacate the throne of truth and look to the teachings of sages (whether they be philosophers or participants who have progressed or have discovered evidence worthy of praise) gives rise to truths that constrain the vanity and self-conceit of whoever believes that they are in possession of all truth.

Lastly, when they grasp the temporal limitations of the human being through texts like Marcus Aurelius' *Meditations* and Seneca's *The Complete Moral Letters to Lucilius*, the participants will learn to place themselves in that temporal levity and humility.

Withdrawal finds its best expression in diaries. Writing becomes that place where the recovery of oneself is defended, where one finds one's balance amidst the daily hustle and bustle and where one prepares oneself for the blows of daily life.

In this brief summary, readers will find a description of the practical application of the dispositions dealt with in previous chapters or, alternatively, can recap them in order to recall each one of them and to contrast them with the foregoing.

4. Scenarios

Experiential scenarios are consistent with the results obtained in the BOECIO project.

In the first place, the workshops attempt to bring about a transformation in the participants in which (anagogic) understanding is only possible if they gradually change. Whoever does not follow the exercises will have difficulties in attaining the project's intimate truths. They will manage to understand the texts discursively, but, as BOECIO is not a program of theoretical classes, they will not have obtained the proposed training: like athletes who claim to have prepared themselves to run a marathon by exclusively reading a dozen manuals.

The insufficiency of theory is evident from the word go and in the continuous evaluation of the encounters: if the participants do not train, that is, if they do not perform the exercises or keep a diary, they will not acquire the knowledge or transformation expected. On the contrary, if they do train, they will be surprised by the acquisition of not only new theoretical knowledge, but also new ways of thinking, of initiating relationships with people who were previously invisible and, through these actions, of encountering a renovated way of connecting with reality.

Discoveries highlight anagogic epistemology and hermeneutics. Some prisoners have discovered a new existential meaning, others have understood the constraints imposed on them by their dogmatism and still others have managed to re-establish relationships by accessing communication capabilities which they are unaware that they possessed.

Attaining this evidence requires performing the exercises, which introduce themes differing from the discursive ones as types of truth, the way of relating with the world (people understand that they form part of reality and abandon their centrality) and the participants see themselves as travelers in an existence in which they can make progress.

These scenarios are fostered when the participants are encouraged to write their diaries from the heart and, even more so, when they perform exercises like generating their own maximum vitality on the basis of a leisurely analysis of their previous reflections. Likewise, this is achieved by employing the metaphor of the voyage, namely, encouraging the participants to see BOECIO as an inner voyage and by showing them that it serves to open unexplored paths and, by extension, to explore and construct blocked faces.

5. Metaphors

Although BOECIO alludes to the four aforementioned metaphors, it is especially geared to training. The first reason for this is that it coincides with the Stoic way of understanding philosophy. Seneca and Epictetus united philosophical action with gymnastics. For instance, Epictetus alluded to weights and athletes to explain the progress made in philosophy.

> Come now, show me what progress you're making in this regard. Suppose I were talking with an athlete and said, Show me your shoulders, and he were to reply, "Look at my jumping-weights." That's quite enough of you and your weights! What I want to see is what you've achieved by use of those jumping-weights. "Take the treatise On Motivation and see how thoroughly I've read it." That's not what I'm seeking to know, slave, but how you're exercising your motives to act or not to act, and how you're managing your desires and aversions, and how you're approaching all of this, and how you're applying yourself to it, and preparing for it, and whether in harmony with nature or out of harmony with it. If in harmony, give me evidence of that, and I'll tell you whether you're making progress; but if out of harmony, go away, and don't be satisfied merely to interpret those books, but also write some books of that kind yourself (Epictetus, 2014: 11).

Prisoners are familiar with the gym metaphor as it is one of the common activities in many male prisons and modules, while not being unknown in those of women.[346]
The metaphor of training is stimulating and makes the program easier to understand. The participants thus see the sessions as an existential preparation and establish relationships between training

---

[346] In recent years, we have thought that it would be appropriate to introduce the dance metaphor in women's prisons, given its greater acceptance. In this regard, philosophical practice would become a dancing art and the BOECIO project, a program for learning to dance and to make life a model and an artistic modelling. This proposal has been put forward in sessions in which the participants have perceived that the training serves to shape not only their bodies, but also their souls and even their movements. This is tantamount to understanding philosophy as a purification of bodily movements facilitated by dance.

muscles to make them stronger and training life in order to be better prepared for the blows that they receive on a daily basis. They perceive that, if they do not train for a week, part of the work that they have performed will be lost or, at best, they will have ceased to make progress. They connect overweight with that configuration of spirits without form, of individuals who cannot control their desires. As a matter of fact, one of the exercises of the first sessions involves holding an object aloft (as has been seen), running or doing press-ups or abdominal exercises, before analyzing the stages through which the participants pass until the exercise becomes intolerable.

Meticulous attention is paid to the training metaphor. Firstly, the participants are encouraged to bring – within the possibilities offered by a prison – some or other sports symbol, like, for example, a pair of trainers, a T-shirt or, simply, a pair of laces. Secondly, the monitor's language is replete with sports-related references. His words of welcome usually include questions like the following: "How has training gone this week? Has anyone injured themselves? Has anyone over-trained? What weights have you used? Have you received any blows? Which muscles have you trained? Seneca employs similar gymnastic terminology in his writings, for instance, to underscore the need to receive blows to win:

> […] no prizefighter can go with high spirits into the strife if he has never been beaten black and blue; the only contestant who can confidently enter the lists is the man who has seen his own blood, who has felt his teeth rattle beneath his opponent's fist, who has been tripped and felt the full force of his adversary's charge, who has been downed in body but not in spirit, one who, as often as he falls, rises again with greater defiance than ever. For manliness gains much strength by being challenged […] (Seneca, 2013: 31).

In the BOECIO project, the trainers are equated with sports instructors: their purpose is not to offer themselves as models of knowledge, but as training companions who, obviously, are in better physical shape at the beginning, but who can lose it to the point of being surpassed by the rest. The instructors are aware that each new edition of the program offers them the chance to train with new participants. This is an opportunity to learn from them and to be open to new proposals for meeting the objectives of the exercises. They will establish a specific way in which the exercises should be performed, but will be open to any modifications that are suggested, provided that they respect the spirit and objectives of the activity. In this sense, BOECIO has evolved thanks to the recommendations of those who have shown a commitment to the program.

The participants perceive the injuries, overtraining and fatigue after months of work, as well as the existence of weeks during which they have not performed the tasks that they should have undertaken owing to excess work (as in a real gym). Similarly, there is the possibility of training in pairs (that is, supporting each other in the performance of the exercises). Their muscles increase in size and shed the "fat" that only serves to cause pathologies.

The classroom is also transformed, abandoning its nature as a place for rote learning content and breaking with its bidirectional structure to assume that of a gym. The participants perform exercises as if they were in a spinning or Zumba class and, bit by bit, learn to use the different machines (or philosophical devices). This helps them to integrate the competencies acquired into their lives, according to the needs of each moment. In fact, by the time that the program has ended, they will have acquired competencies for a second level at which they analyze which exercise is the most adequate for what they have experienced each week.

The metaphor is closed with the results. As with athletes who seek to prepare their muscles for the effort required in competition and for making their movements graceful, the participants in the BOECIO project learn how to govern their passions and, by extension, not to lose their peace of mind despite the challenges of life. In addition, they learn to cope with their surroundings in a more critical and profound way. This leads them to the third objective: to prevent their actions from being limited to their personal interests, in order that they should become authentic communicative actions, in line with Habermas' theory and the "we-ness" community of Tojolabal thought. *The Complete Moral Letters to Lucilius* summarizes other results:

> It is not pursued in order that the day may yield some amusement before it is spent, or that our leisure may be relieved of a tedium that irks us. It moulds and constructs the soul; it orders our life, guides our conduct, shows us what we should do and what we should leave undone; it sits at the helm and directs our course as we waver amid uncertainties. Without it [philosophy], no one can live fearlessly or in peace of mind (Seneca, 2013: 42).

As in a gym, BOECIO does not promise happiness or make it possible to perform its exercises in comfort. On the contrary, it makes it clear that its purpose is training for a life plagued with difficulties. Indeed, the most deft and artful is very close: one's own passions. For this reason, the participants are encouraged to control them through aversions finely trained with texts like Letter No. 37 of *The Complete Moral Letters to Lucilius*. This letter facilitates matching the oath of the philosopher with that taken by he who was prepared to die in the Roman circus, to wit, the philosophers and participants of the BOECIO program are likened to gladiators:

> You have promised to be a good man; you have enlisted under oath; that is the strongest chain which will hold you to a sound understanding. Any man will be but mocking you, if he declares that this is an effeminate and easy kind of soldiering. I will not have you deceived. The word of this most honourable compact are the same as the words of that most disgraceful one, to wit: a "Through burning, imprisonment, or death by the sword" (Seneca, 2013: 100).

III. EXCURSUS: ALLEGATIONS AGAINST PHILOSOPHICAL PRACTICE

> It might even transpire that by attempting to inject some health into a 'sick' society, philosophy itself would experience the beneficial effects of its own therapy[347]

---

[347] César Moreno Márquez, "De ida y por principio," 168.

CHAPTER 1
ANALYSIS, BLINDED POSITIONS AND ANSWERS

1. Philosophical Practice Normalizes and Does Not Promote Criticism of the System

The reproach that philosophical practice *normalizes* counselees within the system, instead of making them question it, is based on the over-generalization of some of the discipline's texts, on superficial and biased readings and, by and large, on a lack of knowledge of the discipline's tradition, its different orientations and its current practices. In posts financed by the very system that they are reproaching, their authors determine that the critical character of the system is an essential element of philosophy. Therefore, all philosophy that does not possess this characteristic violates the discipline's essence.

Even if philosophical practice were restricted to the development of an instrumental reason, the argument would be so inadequate as to reject philosophy in general. In this respect, Jesús Mosterín establishes an analytical mechanism for generating a rational life plan in his *Racionalidad y acción humana*,[348] a device that does not challenge the ideological presuppositions on which it is built. This is also the case with F. Schick in his *Making Choices* and Ramón Queraltó in his *La estrategia de Ulises*:[349] both recreate strategies for maximizing and minimizing solutions to problems, without critically analyzing the presuppositions.

On the other hand, it would be rather incoherent to claim that philosophical practice normalizes when the profession, whether it is pursued in middle or high schools or at universities, is funded by the state, and without assuming that the greatest criticism of the system would be to oppose it and, consequently, to reject being paid a salary. However that may be, if we continued along that

---

[348] Jesús Mosterín, *Racionalidad y acción humana*.

[349] Ramón Queraltó Moreno, *La estrategia de Ulises o ética para una sociedad tecnológica* (Sevilla, DOSS, 2008).

path, we would be indulging in the *tu quoque* fallacy. Therefore, before continuing, it is necessary to justify the impropriety of this accusation that has been levelled against our discipline.

After reading *Plato, Not Prozac!*[350] (or at least part of it or a summary of the book), some thinkers have given a pragmatic and instrumental character to all their oeuvre and, without any solution of continuity, to the discipline as a whole. However, Marinoff, the author of the aforementioned book and a professor at the largest university in New York (College University of New York), is plainly aware that the critical dimension of philosophical practice has to include the fundamentals in order to become not instrumental reason,[351] but an authentic struggle against the ideology of colonizing and dictatorial systems. Several passages in his most recent works point in this direction: "As expressed by Hugo Ball, the founder of the Cabaret Voltaire: 'For us, art is not an end in itself … but it is an opportunity for the true perception and criticism of the times we live in.'"[352]

The suggestion of combating ideology is not of the individualist kind, but a social one: in a Adornian[353] and Foucaultian[354] spirit, it advocates for deconstructing predatory and imperialist capitalism: "Simply stated, philosophical practitioners stand united in protest against the occupation and colonization of the human mind itself, by a congeries of forces including cultural imperialism, economic colonialism, and predatory capitalism."[355]

Ran Lahav, the founder and organizer of the 1st International Congress on Philosophical Practice, stresses the same line, albeit

---

[350] Lou Marinoff, *Plato, Not Prozac!: Applying Eternal Wisdom to Everyday Problems* (New York: HarperCollins Publishers, Inc., 2000).

[351] Max Horkheimer, *Eclipse of Reason*.

[352] Lou Marinoff, "Dada as Philosophical Practice, and Vice Versa: Reflections on the Centenary of the Cabaret Voltaire," in *New Frontiers in Philosophical Practice*, ed. Lydia Amir (Cambridge: Cambridge Scholar Press, 2017), 5.

[353] Theodor Adorno, *Minima Moralia*, Madrid, Akal, 2004.

[354] Michel Foucault, *Discipline and Punish*.

[355] Lou Marinoff, "Dada as Philosophical Practice," 10.

from a more intimist perspective: "The true philosopher is an agitator, a revolutionary, and for a very good reason: the search for wisdom requires questioning the obvious, forsaking our previous convictions, sacrificing our self-content and security, turning our back to perceived needs and values, and venturing into an uncharted terrain."[356]

Marinoff has been bold enough to confront one of the most powerful lobbies in the United States, that which pathologizes life. A proponent of anti-psychiatry, he rejects the reductionism that converts all behavior that does not comply with the normality established by constituent and constituted power into a mental illness.

> APPA [...] intended to utilize philosophy as a medium to elevate public consciousness. [...] APPA protests the economic and cultural imperialism that emanate from the pathologization of non-medical human problems by the psychiatric, psychological, and pharmaceutical industries, abetted and empowered by governments. These industries have exacerbated the spread of epidemics of culturally-induced illnesses – e.g. depressions, anxieties, attention deficits, among a host of other "disorders" afflicting affluent nations – to the extent that some of their proffered "cures" appear to be contributing causes.[357]

Although this does not lead to a denial of mental illness in all cases, as occurs with other philosophical counselors like Peter Raabe[358] and Shlomit Schuster,[359] who both note that, in a fully Foucaultian

---

[356] Ran Lahav, *Stepping out of Plato's Cave. Philosophical Counseling, Philosophical Practice and Self-transformation* (Vermont: Lovey books, 2016), 73.

[357] Lou Marinoff, "Dada as Philosophical Practice," 14. His posture in the interview that he gave in 2017 is very enlightening. The first part was entitled, "Political correctness is a Form of Insanity", which can be consulted at: https://www.youtube.com/watch?v=e4HjZ5weGwc (accessed December 29, 2019).

[358] Peter Raabe, *Philosophy's Role in Counseling and Psychotherapy* (Maryland: Rowan, 2014), 131–230.

[359] Shlomit Schuster, *Philosophy Practice: An Alternative to Counseling and*

spirit, mental illness is the result of biopolitical systems, it being possible to treat all problems from a philosophy-based approach.

This is not tantamount to saying that philosophical practitioners more attached to the system, like their academic counterparts, do not exist. As a matter of fact, within the movement they have been the target of criticism, it being claimed that they have not been engaged in authentic philosophical practice. This is the case with Ran Lahav for whom the profession is a medium for delving deeper into life, rather than for resolving problems. Notwithstanding the fact that he does not reject this other way of doing philosophy, he considers it to be at best second rate, since, as he himself notes, its potentialities are inferior to those of his deep philosophy,[360] previously understood as contemplative philosophy. The author himself explains this in the following terms:

> However, as time went by, most of us philosophical practitioners found ourselves doing philosophy on a much *smaller scale*. For the most part we found ourselves counseling counselees for very mundane problems: *how to deal with the boss, how to find a more satisfying job, what to do about one's lack of self-confidence, or about the fights with the husband or the wife*. This kind of philosophy no longer attempts to *elevate life*, *because it accepts life for what it is* and tries to deal with problems

---

Psychotherapy (Westport: Praeger, 1999).

[360] To assume that the only way of doing philosophy is one's own is a recurring problem for philosophers. Their Adamism, that is, their constant obsession with starting from scratch (i.e., Descartes and Heidegger) or with claiming that their own position is the only valid philosophy (which recalls the ideas of those philosophers who restrict the discipline to the Western current or to the aforementioned criticality) evinces their contempt for other ways of doing philosophy. The accusations among analytical and continental philosophers derive from this contempt for the opposite, as well as highlighting their inability to listen to the different and the absolutist obstinacy of the powerful. Obviously, not everything goes in philosophy or philosophical practice, for which reason their actions should be justified. These justifications stem from the tradition in which philosophers are trained. However, tradition should not become a cell that blinds, but wings that make it possible to fly according to justified philosophical models.

within life. It does not seek to transform the foundations of life, but to address specific needs or difficulties and to fix problems. Indeed, the philosophical counselor's aim is that at the end of the counseling, after two or five or twenty meetings, the counselee would deal more efficiently with her problem, and get back to everyday life with greater satisfaction.[361]

Initially, Lahav accepted this philosophy in the discipline, calling it "Small Philosophical Practice" (versus "Grand Philosophical Practice") or "philosophy-inspired counseling":[362] "This kind of philosophy is therefore basically a *normalizer, a problem-solver*, and a satisfaction-provider. I call it Small Philosophical Practice because it gives philosophy a limited task – to deal with specific elements within life, and also because its aspirations are small: it aims at little more than producing satisfaction."[363]

Lahav soon began to assert that philosophy should aspire to higher goals: wonder, criticism, opening the conscience. This is where his inflexibility leads him to exclude all philosophy that does not correspond to his own model:

> Of course, there is nothing wrong with wanting to make people feel better. *But this is no longer philosophy*, in the original sense of philo-sophia. Philo-sophia is a critic of people's perceived needs, not a satisfier of needs. Its aim is to arouse intellectual and existential discontent, not to offer satisfaction. It seeks to evoke perplexity and awe, not to produce solutions and complacency; to encourage appreciation of the infinite complexity and richness of life, not to simplify life into solutions and bottom lines. True philo-sophia seeks to

---

[361] Ran Lahav(2018): "Philo-sophia is a way of life (Reflection 11)", emphasis added, accessed November 15, 2019, http://www.trans-sophia.net/115845/Reflections.

[362] Ran Lahav, "Mexico ICPP 2018: The boundaries of philosophy," accessed November 15, 2019, https://philopractice.org/web/blog/mexico-iccp-2018-the-boundaries-of-philosophy.

[363] Ran Lahav, "Much More than Critical Thinking," accessed January, 15, 2006, http://www.geocities.com/ranlahav/Reflection_4.html.

question all that is "normal" not to lead people to (apparent) normality.[364]

This passage is sufficient to discredit academic criticism of philosophical practice as normalizing, above all because, as already noted, it does not hail from the periphery but from one of the most well-regarded authors of the movement: "The goal of philosophical practice as I see it is not to solve and satisfy, but rather to awaken forgotten dissatisfactions and yearnings, to transcend our everyday needs, arouse wonder, awe, even confusion, and in this way open for us new doors towards greater horizons of understanding and life."[365]

According to the myth, philosophers cannot work in a cave, but should help counselees or groups to see beyond its bounds: to assist them in abandoning the shadows of the real so as to approach authentic reality.[366]

The path is trod by inquiring deeper into the "transforming philosophers",[367] leaving the "perimeter" imprisoning and determining us[368] and the "models" themselves under which we apathetically construct our existence.[369] "To sum up, to philosophize is, as a first approximation, to investigate basic issues of existence by creating networks of ideas in a reasoned, creative, and dialogical way. Therefore, when we say that philosophizing can help us step out of the Platonic cave, we are in effect saying that reflecting philosophically on basic life-issues can be a way of personal growth and self-transformation."[370]

Leon de Hass, a Dutch philosophical practitioner who began his career more than 50 years ago and co-managed the 10th

---

[364] Idem.

[365] Ran Lahav, *Stepping out of Plato's Cave*, 18.

[366] Ibid., 6.

[367] Ibid., 8–9.

[368] Ibid., 26.

[369] Ibid., 34.

[370] Ibid., 15.

International Congress on Philosophical Practice, elaborates on its critical dimensions. Its origin connects with the May 1968 movements, when Marcuse would abandon theory for action in the Frankfurt School and when Habermas wrote his famous book in which he hoped that the young would hail in the beginning of the emancipation of society from its intellectual enslavement.[371] According to Haas, this initial impression never abandoned the profession, but has remained down to the present day.

> Philosophical practices are called "philosophical" not by chance. The international movement of philosophical practice came into being when academic philosophers made critical evaluations of the situation of philosophy in the 1960's, seventies and eighty's. The criticisms were about the loss of practical bonds with ordinary life and society. Simultaneously, these critics started experimenting forms of philosophical interventions in society, i.e., outside the walls of the academy. So, philosophical practice is philosophy, seeing itself as a (or even, the) contemporary way out the supposed dead ends of philosophy.[372]

Despite the fact that his counseling approach is phenomenological, the critical approach constantly resonates in his sessions and theories. For instance, in his *Skeptical Interventions*, he stresses, "The guest is challenged to distrust his or her familiar thoughts and thinking, and to keep searching for new possibilities and perspective."[373]

The same is repeated in the works of Elliot Cohen. Another classic author of the discipline and one of the founding fathers of philosophical practice in the United States, the director of the *International Journal of Applied Philosophy* and of the National Philosophical Counseling Association also in the United States, Cohen recalls that the intention of counseling is to enable

---

[371] Jürgen Habermas, *Toward a Rational Society*, 120–2.

[372] Leon de Haas, *Skeptical Interventions. A Critical View of Philosophical Practice* (Roermond: Platopraktijk, 2018), 14.

[373] Ibid., 106.

counselees to reply autonomously, without the mediation of ideas imposed from without, not even by experienced philosophers: "I did not enter into the counseling relationship with the idea that I was going to serve as an "expert" advice-giver who would lecture my clients on the principles of a good marriage. Rather, I saw my clients as *autonomous* beings who had some questions to answer for themselves."[374]

Lastly, citing the ETOR group, in which I embarked on my own path with the help of Professor José Ordóñez and Francisco Macera, for nigh on 20 years now the mission of the philosophical counselor has been "to work on opening possibilities": "It is important not to forget that the *counselor indicates, but never conducts*; the counselor *suggests, but never says*; he works on the opening of possibilities, but *never decides*. It should be taken very much into account that the *autonomy of the other* and, therefore, his *self-confidence* are thus cemented."[375]

All this does not make us blind to the existence of people who use the label of philosophical counselors/advisors and who are too close to a normalizing model. I believe that it would be opinionated to claim that they are not authentic philosophers or philosophical practitioners, since this would imply indulging in the aforementioned arrogance. Certainly, we do not feel comfortable with this position, but this does not discredit the profession as a whole. On the contrary, it undermines the credibility of those who employ this over-generalization in our discipline and not in philosophy in general, in spite of the fact that even philosophers of critical theory have proven themselves to be extremely incongruent, as will be seen below.

---

[374] Elliot D. Cohen, *Philosophers at work. An Introduction to Issues and Practical Uses of Philosophy* (New York: Sanders College Publishers, 1989), 345, original emphasis.

[375] VV.AA., *ETOR: Definición y metodología* (Sevilla: XXI, 2002), 3, original emphasis.

2. Normalizing and Acritical Dimensions of Some Academic Philosophies

After mounting the defense above, the time has come to analyze whether or not philosophers critical with philosophical practice, and more specifically those who have patented critical theory, were (and still are) coherent with their criticism.

The writings of Max Horkheimer put us on guard against an instrumental reason that annuls (critical) thinking. The reason for this is that many professions teach techniques, but do not challenge their assumptions. For instance, a lawyer who has been trained to defend any criminal or administrative case, but has not been provided with the tools for determining which cases he should ethically choose or for devising a fairer alternative system. Thus, the lawyer becomes another cog in the system, without challenging it. The system's functionalization, to wit, the instrumentalization of its agents without implementing strategies of criticality, led to the disaster of Auschwitz. The Nazi concentration camps have been heavily lambasted for the injustice in which those who suffered and perished in them were plunged. However, the vileness of the members of the SS who were not aware of their evil deeds has not been so extensively analyzed. This was the case with Eichmann,[376] a German-Austrian *SS-Obersturmbannführer* during the war who was tasked with managing the Final Solution to the Jewish Question and who, when questioned about the death of millions of people, considered that he was free of blame because he had only been following orders, for which reason he did not feel responsible whatsoever for any evil doings. That absence of critical thinking not only resulted in this "banality of evil" during the Second World War, but has been repeated in other contexts, such as the Milgram experiment(s) on obedience to authority in 1965 or refusing to rescue people who are drowning at sea because that is what the current legislation establishes. This is the essence of instrumental

---

[376] Hannah Arendt, *Eichmann in Jerusalem: A Report on the Banality of Evil* (London: Penguin Classics, 2006).

reason opening its wings: "[…] it is not only the business but the essential work of reason to find means for the goals one adopts at any given time".[377] Also according to Horkheimer, "Workers today […] do not question the rules in themselves. They have learned to take social injustice—even inequity within their own group—as a powerful fact, and to take powerful facts as the only things to be respected."[378]

Critical theory assumes that bowing to this reason has its advantages, since the system rewards whoever follows its guidelines and disfavors whoever opposes them: "Anyone who looks at the world soberly will see that the individual must adapt and subordinate himself. Such education to realism, too, the goal of every good pedagogy in the more developed phases of bourgeois society, was anticipated in the Protestant conception of the family."[379]

These dynamics have consequences for the constitution of subjects, namely, reification or commodification: reality (including the subjects) becomes a useful (human) resource for specific purposes. This is eloquently explained in Horkheimer's description of the commercial resignification of Christmas: "The child who knows Santa Claus as an employee of a department store and grasps the relation between sales figures and Christmas, may take it as a matter of course that there is an interaction between religion and business as a whole."[380] The resignification of nature is similar: "The story of the boy who looked up at the sky and asked, "Daddy, what is the moon supposed to advertise?" is an allegory of what has happened to the relation between man and nature in the era of formalized reason."[381]

---

[377] Max Horkheimer, *Critique of Instrumental Reason* (London & New York: Verso, 2012), Kindle, 5.

[378] Max Horkheimer, *Eclipse of Reason*, 107.

[379] Max Horkheimer, *Critical Theory: Selected Essays* (New York: Continuum, 2002), 100.

[380] Max Horkheimer, *Eclipse of Reason*, 30.

[381] Ibid., 74.

In the spirit of the first generation of the Frankfurt School, Horkheimer and Adorno concurred that there was the need for an emancipatory revolution, brought about by critical thinking for the former and by an aesthetic break that fragments unity for the latter. On this basis, Horkheimer established a role for philosophy that, in light of the foregoing, most philosophical practitioners would endorse:

> The real social function of philosophy lies in its criticism of what is prevalent. That does not mean superficial fault-finding with individual ideas or conditions, as though a philosopher were a crank. Nor does it mean that the philosopher complains about this or that isolated condition and suggests remedies. The chief aim of such criticism is to prevent mankind from losing itself in those ideas and activities which the existing organization of society instills into its members. Man must be made to see the relationship between his activities and what is achieved thereby, between his particular existence and the general life of society, between his everyday projects and the great ideas which he acknowledges. Philosophy exposes the contradiction in which man is entangled in so far as he must attach himself to isolated ideas and concepts in everyday life.[382]

Regrettably, Stuart Jeffries' novel *Grand Hotel Abyss*[383] about the Frankfurt School reveals how its members did not always practice what they preached and that some features of their discourse evince that theirs was an armchair philosophy, backing off when the time was ripe for revolution. Four situations described by Jeffries illustrate this well.

Firstly, the members of the first generation of the Frankfurt School belonged to wealthy families who had amassed their fortunes in the system that they criticized. Far from taking a stance akin to that of a twentieth-century Diogenes, their offspring decided to use capitalist profits to cover their basic needs. They left home late,

---

[382] Max Horkheimer, *Critical Theory*, 264–5.
[383] Stuart Jeffries, *Grand Hotel Abyss: The Lives of the Frankfurt School* (London and New York: Verso Books, 2016).

with Adorno, for example, asking his parents for money to pay for his flat when he was already over 30.

Secondly, when the members of the Institute for Social Research moved to the United States, fleeing from the National Socialist menace, they established themselves in the center of capitalism (New York), so maligned in their writings. Although they did not want to renounce their principles, most of the funding that the institute received came from foundations that fostered and respected the instrumental structures which they condemned. Continuing with their discourse in English seriously jeopardized the grants and subsidies that organizations of this type obtained. Horkheimer came up with a simple solution: to encourage his colleagues to write in German, a language very difficult to access for those who granted the subsidies, but also in order that the social critique should be effective.

Thirdly, to the risk of ending up penniless should be added the persecution of Marxism in the country of freedoms. Therefore, Horkheimer established another basic principle for the Frankfurt School: the prohibition of employing terms, such as Marxism and revolution, that might be associated with them.

The fourth and last deplorable situation came to pass years later after the end of the war. Just before May 1968, several currents of the Frankfurt School discovered in youth the revolutionary ambition that the institute had proclaimed. On the one hand, Habermas' (about whom Horkheimer would have his doubts because of his break with the indiscriminate criticism of the system) chapter *Technology and Science as "Ideology"*, in *Towards a Rational Society*, was an impassioned argument in favor of students as a means of achieving this: "Neither the old class antagonism nor the new type of underprivilege contains a protest potential whose origins make it tend toward the repoliticization of the desiccated public sphere. For the present, the only protest potential that gravitates toward the new conflict zone owing to identifiable interests is arising among certain groups of university, college, and high school students."[384]

Similarly, on the other side of the Atlantic, Marcuse sent letters to Adorno from the United States inviting him to join the revolutionary movement. Nonetheless, the latter not only voiced his opposition, claiming that it was a new form of authoritarianism akin to that which had led to the Second World War, but also decided to dispute its emancipatory doctrine as a whole. In 1968, a group of students occupied the Institute for Social Research. He had inherited its directorship and now found himself in the dilemma of having to make a difficult decision. Unfortunately, his resolution did not challenge the system, but was compatible with it: he rung the police (the symbol of constituent and constituted power) to get them to vacate the building.

These four examples are similar to the position of philosophers and, specifically, of quite a few university and academic ones.[385]

On the one hand, they devote their time to pronouncing grand discourses on the need for critical thinking and on the urgency of the untimely in our lives in order to avoid being manipulated and consumed by the system and, on the other, cling to their armchairs,

---

[384] Jürgen Habermas, *Toward a Rational Society*, 120.

[385] It is crucial to note that this characterization cannot be applied to all philosophy professors. There are clear examples of the selfless social commitment of many of them, whose philosophy admittedly is not a mere imposture within the system. In this regard, mention should go to Peter Singer and Bertrand Russell when they actively participated in protests or when they proposed clear political options. In Spain, there are also relevant cases, like that of Jorge Riechmann and his struggle for environmental ethics, plus thinkers of both sexes who understand the deliberate struggle for the rights of sectors scorned by society as a commitment surpassing their professional lives. This is taken to higher level by those who, in addition to devoting their time to philosophical practice, have decided to work (1) for free and (2) in sectors that society has decided to treat with disrespect not only to impose a discourse on them, but also to help them to make their discourse part of the constituent flow of society.

thus playing out a tragicomedy that transforms philosophy into cynical irony.

Moreover, even when they voice their criticism more than they should, many of these philosophers keep shtum when the constituted powers threaten their salaries and lives. In other words, they are Marxist while their regional, research and teaching allowances remain intact.

Similarly, they deliver conferences and courses only when they are remunerated (in cash or in conditions that favor their position of power), but offer excuses when there is no remuneration in the offing and let alone when they are expected to do so at their own expense.

On the other hand, their commitment to philosophy is only visible in spheres in which the normalizing security of the system provides them with sufficient immunity and protection. For those academic (or non-academic) philosophers who voluntarily decide to work in prisons, where their criticism of the criminal ideology puts their lives at risk, at schools where drugs (literally) fly over the walls or with the young homeless, are exceptions to the rule.

This abandonment or flight signifies that the disrespected are excluded from the benefits distributed by the emancipatory postulates of philosophy proclaimed from university pulpits, thus giving rise to a strange situation in which a criticism that does not bother anyone is produced. Those inflammatory discourses become a pantomime tolerated by the system and which, as a result, make us question their critical dimension.

After all, did not Socrates drink hemlock and Seneca slit his wrists due to the imperatives of constituted power?[386]

---

[386] I have developed this idea in an essay posted on the Spanish philosophy portal Filosofía & Co. in 2020.

3. Philosophical Practice for People at Risk of Social Exclusion in Response to a Normalized Philosophy

3.1. Background

Working with people at risk of social exclusion and the dangerous consequences for philosophers are indicative of the emancipatory potential of the activity described in these pages. Needless to say that these actions do not entail placing their lives in the hands of drug traffickers, due to the critical training of inmates in order that they should kick their drug habits: it is sufficient that they devote their time to freeing other sectors subjected by constituted power.

According to the line of the Frankfurt School, the power that should be defeated is capital or, better said, the reifying uses to which it is chiefly put. Habermas would call for the conversion of actions aimed at particular purposes or interests into other communicative ones that facilitate humanistic sociability. Honneth would stress the need for avoiding disrespect by recognizing the excluded. Thus, power is characterized as a force employed to foster that disrespect and non-recognition of the excluded. Versus this stance, we propose the following as a possible emancipatory solution, in opposition to the objectifying normalization of power and capital: (1) returning the discourse to the disrespected and (2) free and emancipatory philosophical action (or, at least, that action which, even though it is remunerated, turns against the payer and performs actions that are not based exclusively on a salary), thus annulling the dominance of the powerful. This would bring about a shift towards the importance of listening, humility and adjusting one's own rhythms to those of the other, all basic aspects of philosophical practice, as has been explained above.

The BOECIO philosophical practice project got underway with these prerogatives in mind, for solidary and free action were perquisites for joining the team. Even though we can profit from our work, this entry requirement means that technicians and researchers do not join the team exclusively for obtaining financial or professional rewards. In this way, we have converted the free-of-charge concept into a mechanism for critical and effective resistance against the reifying tendencies of the system. This criterion has highlighted the real intentions of many philosophers with profound discourses who understand philosophy as critical social action: most of these philosophy degree holders and professors have only accepted to join the project when they have received proof of some or other remuneration for their work.[387]

Together with this contempt for financial gain, effective interest (namely, applied and not merely practical) in the disrespected facilitates emancipation. Honneth has defined the processes of social exclusion and contempt in *The Struggle for Recognition and Disrespect: The Normative Foundations of Critical Theory*, two of his most important books. He defines them in the following terms:

> Processes of cultural exclusion consist of strategies that limit opportunities for articulating class-specific experiences of injustice by systematically withholding the appropriate linguistic and symbolic means for their expression. These strategies are applied through agencies of public education, the media of the culture industry, or forums of political publicity. They undermine the ability to articulate perceptions, which is a prerequisite for the successful thematization of the consciousness of social injustice.[388]
>
> Negative concepts of this kind are used to designate behaviour that represents an injustice not simply because it harms subjects or restricts their freedom to act, but because it injures them with regard to the

---

[387] It should be stressed that I consider that philosophical work should be remunerated and that the situation of many of its practitioners is so precarious that they cannot devote their time to philanthropic works until they have covered their own basic needs. However, it is striking that it is professional philosophers earning a monthly wage who have usually abandoned the project when discovering that no kind of gain was to be had, thinkers who maintain a theoretical position that encourages criticism of the system. At the other extreme, many people in a more precarious situation have accepted to join BOECIO, even defraying costs out of their own pockets. I would like to pay tribute here to the latter, for they have restored hope in the coherence of a sector of philosophy.

[388] Axel Honneth, *Disrespect*, 136.

positive understanding of themselves that they have acquired intersubjectively.[389]

The disrespected do not have the means to demand their own rights in the face of those powerful discourses that establish the canon of what is legitimate, valid and reasonable. The philosophical discourse that denies the legitimacy of Mesoamerican or Oriental philosophies, branding them as "mere" wisdom, those that undervalue the philosophy of women, indigenous communities, children or prisoners fall into this exclusive category. Philosophers of this kind often resort to persuasion, defending their conclusions on the basis of the authority that their knowledge and rhetorical skills give them (which is only another form of will-to-power), instead of being favorably disposed to re-establishing the voice of those who have been intellectually conquered. They generate an imperative in opposition to a subjective genitive or, as required, endorse the apparently compassionate maxim of enlightened absolutism, *"Tout pour le peuple, tien par le people"* ("Everything for the people, nothing by the people").

It is disturbing how the mechanisms of social exclusion have evidently colonized the philosophical discourse appearing in newspapers and pronounced in many lecture halls and conferences. Honneth identifies the following instruments:

    (1) Deverbalization.

    (2) Fostering individualism.

    (3) Fostering the ideology of performance.[390]

    (4) "The institutional repression of cultural traditions and processes of resistance".

    (5) "Atrophying the sociopolitical interests of wage earners by means of material compensations", namely,

---

[389] Axel Honneth, *The Struggle for Recognition*, 131.
[390] Axel Honneth, *Disrespect*, 137.

maintaining the welfare state ("income, free time") and making struggle a undesired malaise.[391]
(6) Adopting the stance of the selfless intellectual.[392]
All these aspects will now be briefly summarized below.

3.2. Deverbalization

Deverbalization occurs when people are not equipped with the educational tools for writing, expressing themselves or developing their own critical thinking. On the contrary, they are provided with models of truth, beauty, knowledge or philosophy that should be learnt by rote and described in exams. Even though some educational programs intend to be critical, it is the professors who have the last word and the ultimate authority to censor heterodoxies that do not coincide with their own thought. Occasionally, the censors do not have to be professors: in recent years, students themselves have censored each other, defending a philosophical ideology that remains unquestioned and unquestionable. In this sense, the difficulties that philosophy undergraduates and postgraduates have in engaging in self-criticism should be recalled. One of the problems of the historicist teaching of philosophy lies in the fact that, in the lecture hall, there is an obligation to study authors who do not connect with the students' own reality or that this connection is made by their professors. This has led some sectors of philosophical practice to criticize academia, contending that the history of philosophy, rather than philosophy per se, is taught in the lecture hall. This claim is excessive insofar as the analysis of the thought of authors who have studied an issue during decades offers food for thought that paves the way for the criticism of those who listen to them or read their works. Even when in philosophy cafés reference has been made to their theories, this has opened reflective channels that have broken with the monologic line of the group. Problems arise when those theories are not

---

[391] Ibid., 140.
[392] Ibid., 87.

connected with real practice and, above all, not converted into a philosophical practice, for, in such an event, philosophy can become a sort of archaeology that narrates a past disconnected from the subject and reality. In the preceding pages, philosophical practice workshops have been described as an experience in which participants are not only acquainted with the theory of an author, but are also taught to think through that author, with a view to opening up unimagined personal possibilities.

The difference between a banking and dialogic pedagogy provides keys for understanding the difference between these two ways of approaching philosophy. As Paulo Freire[393] noted, in banking education students blindly assume the dictates of their professors. The overcrowding of lecture halls and, basically, the need to address individually student realities that are increasingly more extreme, promotes exams based on theoretical-practical content for evaluation. Even when professors adopt critical and practical evaluation criteria, their ability to establish those that do not depend on their own whims is greatly hindered, for which reason students learn to reflect according to their dictates. The complaint is that students do not learn to make comments on philosophical texts in the lecture hall, but to comment on them according to the personal tastes of each professor.

The alternative is to be found in a dialogic education which, as its name suggests, implies promoting dialogic channels. The dialogue would be orchestrated following criteria of philosophical depth which, as in the case of Lipmanian philosophy for/with children workshops,[394] could be determined by the students themselves. Likewise, this kind of teaching is more likely to include philosophical practice sessions in class. It tends to be more commonplace in the high school stage in which, as could not be otherwise, there is also more openness to philosophical practice and philosophy for/with children.

---

[393] Paulo Freire, *Pedagogia do oprimido*.
[394] Matthew Lipman, *Thinking in Education*, 211ff.

These techniques not only facilitate the description of verbalizing (and critical thinking) processes, but also their implementation and, consequently, the emancipation of the individual.

3.3. Fostering Individualism and the Ideology of Performance

The one-way nature of master classes[395] and the tendency to reading without performing a contrast in the social medium give rise to socially withdrawn and individualistic students who have difficulties in orally presenting their thoughts.

When comparing a teacher training lecture with a philosophy lecture, notable differences can be observed.[396] First and foremost, philosophy students have greater difficulties in performing group or collaborative work. In point of fact, these proposals are treated with contempt, perhaps as a defense mechanism that shifts the responsibility on to someone else's shoulders. It could be claimed that this does not pose a problem, since the career opportunities of students taking these two degrees are dissimilar. This claim could not be further from the truth: the most typical career opportunity for philosophy postgraduates is teaching (as in the case of teaching training), while very few of them manage to pursue a career in research. Moreover, philosophy students regard teaching and working at schools as a lesser evil, perhaps weighing this up against the possibility of becoming a hermit in the Sahara or, more likely, because of their complete ignorance of the reality surrounding their future.

This individualism is also glimpsed at higher levels. For instance, most philosophy papers are written by a sole author, in contrast to those on pedagogy or psychology, which are usually co-authored

---

[395] It is not a question of rejecting the value of master classes: they have a series of educational advantages alien to other models, which cannot be covered here. As before, what is being criticized here is the reductionism or exclusivity revolving around an education grounded in them.

[396] This description does not imply that some have priority over others. Each degree program has its own shortcomings, although we are focusing now on the former due to the nature of this book.

by work groups. Similarly, philosophy research teams are usually formed by people specializing in the discipline, unlike their pedagogy or psychology counterparts. Lastly, the evaluation systems of university research penalize those papers written by two or more authors.[397]

Obviously, if philosophy degree programs are far removed from social reality, if workshop organization is not taught, if there are no internships or if these do not require previous training that facilitates the transition from a theoretical-practical philosophy to philosophical practice, students will have a hard time. It is important to stress that it is not fully the responsibility of the system, as courses and training sessions are organized outside the university system, but few students avail themselves of them while at university.

3.4. Abandoning Sociopolitical Interests and Adopting an External Vision

It is in those countries most influenced by capitalism where sociopolitical interests usually gain the upper hand. In Mesoamerican and South American countries there is a great interest in sociopolitical philosophy, but in Western societies metaphysical and epistemological works on the fundamentals of philosophy (whether they be continental or analytical) fill most of the shelf space in university libraries. This interest makes it more likely that philosophy will permeate spheres of social struggle. A

---

[397] See, for example, the evaluation criteria established by Spain's National Commission for the Evaluation of Research Activity (Comisión Nacional Evaluadora de la Actividad Investigadora, CNEAI) for the six-year research periods of university professors. The following is expressly indicated: "Unless fully justified by the complexity of the topic, methodological demands and the length of the work, *more than two authors may reduce the rating assigned to a contribution*" (BOE November 26, 2019. *Resolution of November 12, 2019, of the National Commission for the Evaluation of Research Activity, by virtue of which the specific criteria approved for each one of the fields of evaluation are published.* Emphasis added).

recent case has been the inclusion of philosophy as a human right in Article 3 of the Mexican Constitution, an unprecedented milestone in the history of humanity. Similarly, philosophical work with indigenous communities, homeless children or those belonging to the guerrilla or attending schools in poor neighborhoods is common in countries like Brazil, Columbia, Peru and Mexico, while being practically non-existent in Europe, the United States and Canada. For example, in Mexico all students at the UNAM, the country's most important university, are obliged to do social service consisting in internships in different settings such as prisons. In contrast, very few Spanish faculties of philosophy offer students in their final year internships.

The solution is not only to generate new discourses on the importance of poverty or animal ethics, but also to connect the subject with these realities. This has been put down to the metaphorical constraints of the logical-argumentative versus the experiential, which will not be repeated here.

This state of affairs has led philosophy to develop the external perspective with evident consequences: "Once a critical intellectual or theorist assumes such an external perspective, he or she will necessarily become a 'dispassionate stranger' or an 'estranged native' who is no longer able to decipher the normative force and moral richness of local understandings."[398]

Nihil novum sub sole, Horkheimer cautioned decades ago in reference to the ideological danger of this type of intellectual: "[…] a conception of the intelligentsia which claims to transcend party lines and is therefore abstract represents a view of problems that only hides the decisive questions."[399]

---

[398] Michael Walzer cited in Axel Honneth, *Disrespect*, 87.
[399] Max Horkheimer, *Critical Theory*, 223.

3.5. Dismantling Ideology and Social Exclusion in Philosophical Practice in Prisons and Outside Them

A criterion for unmasking a philosopher who voices his criticism is to gauge his capacity for deploying one of the first mechanisms of recognition: the smile. Honneth explains that the "smile"[400] is an invitation to the other, expressing that he is "loveable".[401] Additionally, this "welcoming gesture"[402] legitimizes the face of the other. It should be noted that these attitudes are not always inherent to philosophy professors or students, the latter being more interested in familiarizing themselves with the academic ins and outs for passing their exams, and the former in defending themselves against the smallest of slights or in becoming acquainted with the mechanisms for increasing their salary supplements. All in all, the emancipatory revolution does not only begin with listening to people at risk of social exclusion, but with a smile or a welcoming gesture, rather than with the dictate of truth per se, even though this takes the shape of the struggle for freedom against constituted power.

Furthermore, it is possible to discover a philosopher by analyzing his deeds, rather than his words. The processes of social exclusion are disarticulated in philosophical practices workshops. In the face of deverbalization, workshops can be organized in which groups and individuals are helped to put situations of injustice, which hitherto have been foreign to them, into words, so as to think about them and become aware of them. Likewise, they are trained to defend their positions with reasoned arguments. This is not performed in theoretical or general terms, but in a generally specific and related way with the questions of each individual or

---

[400] Axel Honneth and Avishai Margalit, "Recognition," *Proceedings of the Aristotelian Society*, Supplementary Volumes 75 (2001): 124.
[401] Idem.
[402] Ibid., 119.

group: one of the four characteristics of Lipmanian critical thinking is being sensitive to the context.[403]

Versus the "institutionalized repression of cultural traditions and the political learning processes of social resistance movements",[404] philosophical practice abandons the "arrogance of knowledge" of an all-powerful discourse that silences the other. Each context is approached with a smile or a welcoming gesture, abandoning the cave of the ideal world and developing specific sessions depending on the philosophical needs of each group. According to Beatriz Bixio, "the arrogance of knowledge appropriates any other and inhabits it as an object of knowledge. However, my personal experience has given me the conviction that they are particular subjects, students, youngsters and adults, each of them with their own name and biography. 'Strange' beings of whom we know very little."[405]

In prison, the arrogance of knowledge occurs when, instead of remaining in a listening position, the inmate becomes an "object of study", someone who is only expected to be obedient and who never deploys his own autonomy or creation on his own path:

> They [the inmates] are being constantly subjected to mechanisms of evaluation – also designed by academic institutions – which means that they can be evaluated according to parameters of sociability, dangerousness or social reintegration. It is what Larrosa (2000), on the basis of a profane pedagogy, would call "the arrogance of knowledge", which appropriates any other and inhabits it as an object of knowledge. However, my personal experience has given me the conviction that they are particular subjects, students, youngsters and adults, each of them with their own name and biography. "Strange" beings of whom we know very little; their desires, fears, lifestyles in prison, helplessness and violence, their abandonment are all great unknowns. This

---

[403] Matthew Lipman, *Thinking in Education*, 211–2.

[404] Axel Honneth, *Disrespect*, 137.

[405] Beatriz Bixio, "El enigma de las subjetividades," in *A pesar del encierro. Prácticas políticas, culturales y educativas en prisión*, eds. Mauricio Manchado, María Chiponi, and Rodrigo Castillo (Rosario: Espacio santafesino, 2017), 134.

strangeness is re-signified as soon as we begin to understand through open dialogue.[406]

The "us"/them dichotomy precludes the autonomy of prisoners, as "we" (the powerful), far from allowing them (those degraded to nothing) to formulate their own discourse, decide what they should think and do. When their action is heterodox versus ours, similar to what happens in a class or to the citizenry when they do not follow the dictates of a columnist legitimized by the editor of a newspaper, resources are compassionately employed to show them their mistake and the right path to their *reintegration*. Dialectics is akin to the imprisonment of a woman for disobeying her husband centuries ago,[407] giving electric shocks to people to cure homosexuality some decades ago and the sterilization of people with Down's syndrome some years ago.

Any chance of criticizing scholars has been left behind: "The experience of the other is not within our reach, but based on our own experience, filtered by academic knowledge. This is the reason why it is impossible to talk about 'them', their ways of being or living in prison. Rather, I opt for talking about an 'us'."[408]

If we do not want to make the same mistake, philosophical practice workshops should respect otherness, the existence of the different and the legitimacy of their discourse, which is coherent with their aural and non-auditing essence.

Philosophy workshops in prisons (and outside them) are framed in the body of educational activities. Their intention is not professional training (the objective of vocational training courses in prisons), but to generate humanity, autonomous beings. Likewise, these workshops are revolutionary with respect to the professional kind, for they do not follow the logic of the market (to create good workers), but that of critical humanization. Thus, the reflection

---

[406] Ibid., 133–4.

[407] Michel Foucault, *Madness and Civilization: A History of Insanity in the Age of Reason* (New York: Vintage Books, 1988).

[408] Beatriz Bixio, "El enigma de las subjetividades," 134.

orchestrated here can analyze how the logic that constructs prosumers, that is, producers and consumers, is the reason why many of them are in prison: due to their yearning to satisfy needs created by the ideology of the system. On the contrary, philosophical practice workshops pursue creative criticism for designing a rebel subjectivity in light of that perspective. This action deactivates many of the sources of crime by voiding the causes behind it. This is what we have discovered when some workshops have led to a reflection on the reason why many consumers of psychoactive substances have become addicted to them. The revelation that this was in the interests of the criminal ideology has buffeted their personal reality, causing them to reduce their consumption of these substances. Here is a way of breaking with the ideology of the system that neither Marx nor Horkheimer nor Adorno imagined. "For Bixio, the question revolves around the emancipatory capacity of cultural workshops and academic experiences in prison, indicating the differences between them but always stressing how important it is that these experiences should not annul otherness and that the pedagogical approach can enable the speech of the other and now not about him."[409]

In relation to the strategy that motivated individualism and the logic of performance, philosophical practice designs communities of inquiry (philosophy for/with children) that shape collective thought, oppose the fragmentation of the construction of knowledge (philosophy workshops) and open the democratic dimensions in participants (philosophy cafés).

As to the fact of "atrophying sociopolitical interests", the intention of philosophical practice and philosophy for/with children is to create responsible and critical citizens. Consequently, they end up recognizing that they cannot pledge their lives to the "material compensations" that society offers them to silence them.

---

[409] Mauricio Manchado, María Chiponi, and Rodrigo Castillo, "Presentación," in *A pesar del encierro*, eds. Mauricio Manchado, María Chiponi, and Rodrigo Castillo (Rosario: Espacio santafesino, 2017), 16.

Lastly, the conversion of the scholar into someone outside the system is countered because the philosopher does not make a judgment as an external observer, but fits into the discussion, facilitating dialogues, and senses the concerns and needs of the disrespected from the universe in which they are living.

Chapter 2
Broadening Academia through Philosophical Practice

1. Giving Voice to the Disrespected

If emancipation involves a rebellion against a reifying capitalism that does not take people into account, a possible form of liberation would involve carrying out activities without seeking financial gain or power, namely, avoiding strategic actions and implementing communication strategies. This is not always clear in philosophical practice or in philosophy for/with children, as can be intuited from the work of Stella Accorinti: "Us coordinators were pondering on something similar, on if philosophy for children were only of use to well-fed children, with family care and protection, with full rights, then sadly philosophy for children would be useless or all but useless."[410]

Although philosophical practice has a vocation for otherness, this does not necessarily mean that the other is excluded or at risk of social exclusion. Thus, it is essential to encourage counselors to pay heed to these aspects.

If free philosophy workshops were organized in education centers, great progress would be made towards liberation since they do not rely on any type of funding. However, there is a risk of not disengaging from the ideas of the capitalist system embedded in those centers (which can also ban activities of this type if they are incommensurate with their models). Moreover, there is a risk that those learning the lessons will instrumentally use them within the ideology of the system. This is more complicated if workshops are aimed at those excluded by society, since their ideas are outside its structures from the start.

---

[410] Stella Accorinti, *Introducción a la Filosofía para niños* (Buenos Aires: Manatial, 1999), 15–6.

Another frequent problem is doing a critical philosophy by and for philosophers: Inflammatory speeches are made on the importance of taking philosophy and critical thinking to the people, regrets are expressed about the manipulation and the zombie or remote-controlled status of society and analyses are performed on the best mechanisms for ensuring that the next generation will change. Regrettably, nothing more can be done, because going too far seems to be a cardinal sin that only serves to impoverish the purism of the major systems of thought. This begs a number of eloquent questions: what is the use of fostering critical thinking among those who need no convincing of its worth? What role does a philosophy that is only discussed and done by philosophers play? Is not this type of practice nothing more than another mechanism for silencing the other or of the arrogance of knowledge? Is there not a need for substituting speaking with listening?

It should be observed that this also occurs in some groups addressing the fundamentals of philosophical practice: people who meet to lay the foundations of the discipline, before putting them into practice. I have seen this not only 6,000 miles away from home, but also just a few yards away from where I live. Thus, we propose that studies of the fundamentals of philosophy should be performed on the basis of practice at research-action seminars, including field sessions and those of inquiry into theories and results. This has been the dynamic of the seminars that I have attempted to organize at my university in recent years.

The philosopher (practitioner) should avoid one of the basic mistakes of all paternalism with the inferior: to cease to talk *about* and *for* the other so as to do so *from* the other or, simply, to listen *to* the other and to help his discourse to take shape and to take flight. The philosopher should not be the spokesperson of anyone but, at best, an amplifier, a way of strengthening the discourse of the other by means of the aforementioned training in verbalizing and critical processes.

This implies a revolution in the field of research since not only the object of study is modified, but also the explanatory agent and the approaches made. This deserves further explanation. Traditional PhD theses tend to interpret an author or a theory: a different vision of the mind in Descartes, an interpretation of friendship in Aristotle or a comparison between Heidegger's *Being and Time*[411] and the reality of new technologies. The material and intellectual author of these hermeneutics has not varied for centuries: a Western, middle- or upper-class person pursuing the study of philosophy. A first step would be to modify the topics, namely, to put forward a thesis on the concept of visitor in the work of the German counselor Gerd Achenbach, on Lipman's category of careful thinking or on the creative citizen in Sátiro and its practical link to the Marfil group. Nevertheless, the proposal would be more revolutionary without the intellectual author having to change, that is, if a thesis on Sartre's concept of freedom were created in the minds of inmates who have been in prison for 20 years, a study of Rawls' communitarianism in a class of teenagers which has been employing Lipman's methodology for five years or a thesis on Adela Cortina's ethical obligations pertaining to the underprivileged world, authored by a community of adults who have been obliged to enter the world of drug trafficking to save their families from certain starvation.

Perhaps the reader is wondering whether or not we are proposing to punish these people with the writing of a PhD thesis. Albeit an interesting option, our proposal is different: we are suggesting that they be the intellectual, rather than the material, authors. Their voices can find a place in a PhD thesis through a student (material author) who acts as a (transparent) medium that gives shape to their discourses. The PhD student would assume their positions and would clear up any doubts in philosophy workshops. Resorting to a metaphor, the PhD student would act as the conductor of an

---

[411] Martin Heidegger, *Being and Time* (New York: State University of New York Press, 2010).

orchestra, although the music would be produced by all the performers.

The results of research of this kind would revamp academic content and would be in consonance with an adequate emancipation of the discourse forged by and for scholars. Likewise, this would broaden the horizons of philosophy not only in the sphere of content, but also in that of processes: it would lead to the introduction of new ways of thinking, conceptualizing, problematizing, arguing, etc. In short, it would displace the powerful subject from his central position in the creation of the discourse.

For those who consider that this utopia is more complicated to achieve than Thomas More's island, they should be reminded that it corresponds to the patterns of philosophy devised by women within a philosophy with masculine echoes; and to projects such as the Mexican indigenous universities which have already been approved by the Public Education Secretariat of the Mexican government.

What would the alternative be? To leave the amplifier in traditional hands, to wit, to continue to be beset by a dogmatic reductionism of Western and feudal philosophical content and ways of doing philosophy in which hierarchy and obedience to the powerful and the exclusion of the heterodox are maintained.

Lastly, would not those philosophers for whom philosophy is a Greek product be incurring in an ethnocentric model that ignores how Nezahualcoyotl and his Mexica companions offer an answer to the very metaphysical evanescence of the pre-Socratics, although through an aesthetic proposal involving the "flower and song" difrasismo?[412]

---

[412] Miguel León Portilla, "Flor y canto. Otra forma de percibir la realidad," in *Coordenadas 2050* (Ciudad de México: UNAM, 2016).

2. The Experiential Enhancement of Philosophy

Based on this call for new ways of doing philosophy, it would not be right to end without making a brief plea in favor of the experiential modes described throughout this work.

The Stoic world recognized philosophy as an art or life path. Learning did not depend on memorizing theories, but philosophy lived *through* those theories to bring about a transformation in life. It was just as important to be familiar with the theory of the oath, as cited by Seneca in Letter No. 37 to Lucilius,[413] as to exteriorize it as an existential way of coping with difficulties. As a criterion of validity philosophical practice proposes an analogous work in the field of education. If theoretical-practical philosophy promotes the learning of analytical, ethical or hermeneutic theories, philosophy workshops make it necessary to materialize the way of thinking of philosophers during them. As has been seen above, it is not exclusively a question of explaining the theory of Husserl, but to perform an exercise in which this is set in motion, like, for example, performing phenomenological reductions on a text or eidetic variation on a concept to discover its essence. Similarly, it is also possible to stage workshops mediated by exercises that help to "decipher the original sense" (as noted by Zambrano), like, for example, using her idea of the ways of looking at or relating to time. Last but not least, the Stoic exercises carried out in the framework of the BOECIO project are another example explained in the middle of this book. It is precisely in *The Complete Moral Letters to Lucilius* that this way of doing philosophy is defended, stressing that what is important are not the memorized lessons (the weights), but what is achieved with them (mastering one's passions and desires):

> Come now, show me what progress you're making in this regard. Suppose I were talking with an athlete and said, Show me your

---

[413] "You have promised to be a good man; you have enlisted under oath [...]", Lucio Anneo Seneca, *The Complete Moral Letters*, 100).

shoulders, and he were to reply, "Look at my jumping-weights." That's quite enough of you and your weights! What I want to see is what you've achieved by use of those jumping-weights. "Take the treatise *On Motivation* and see how thoroughly I've read it." That's not what I'm seeking to know, slave, but how you're exercising your motives to act or not to act, and how you're managing your desires and aversions, and how you're approaching all of this, and how you're applying yourself to it, and preparing for it, and whether in harmony with nature or out of harmony with it.[414]

This way of coping with the discipline does not only broaden it, but also converts it into a field of experimentation or experience: classes do not only serve to become acquainted with thinkers and their theories, but also to live the experience of thinking and living like them for a certain amount of time. Philosophies are proposed as existential events and, consequently, possibilities are opened up for a transformation that not only broadens its cognitive but also ontological horizons.

All this means that philosophical practice is more than an area of knowledge or sub-specialty of philosophy, as occurs with aesthetics, epistemology or the philosophy of technology. In addition, it should be understood as a transversal need in all sub-areas: it completes the theoretical modes in which it has habitually appeared. Accordingly, it would not be farfetched to claim that it should be included transversally as an action in all philosophy modules and in the training of all university professors who want to transcend theoretical reductionism on the basis of which they teach those modules (not to substitute them but to complete them).

As Walzer contends, this would undermine the dichotomy between philosophy and practice, as philosophers would not "adopt an external perspective", they would not be "impassive strangers" or be "alienated" from its content. On the contrary, students of ethics would have the chance to experiment with the potentialities and

---

[414] Epictetus, *Discourses, Fragments, Handbook* (Oxford: Oxford University Press, 2014), 11.

difficulties of veganism when studying animal ethics, while those of metaphysics would experience the tension of the being which is both evident and hidden, as has been seen in one of the workshops described above.

An exclusively theoretical training involves inconsistencies that Peter Raabe has addressed in the last book that he wrote just five years ago, expressing them in the following terms, which is a timely way of ending this work:

> It occurred to me that there must be a serious problem in the way we're teaching philosophy in our colleges and universities. I'm still not exactly sure yet what the problem is. It may be that students are being taught too much about how to win a philosophical argument and not enough about how to apply the philosophical skills they've learned to resolving real-life problems. Perhaps they're being taught philosophy at such an abstruse theoretical level that they can't see its practical application. Or it may be that they're led to believe that classroom philosophy learned from books is separate and distinct from everyday situations, and has nothing to do with real life.[415]

---

[415] Peter Raabe, *Philosophy's Role*, 250–1.

BIBLIOGRAPHY

Accorinti, Stella. *Introducción a la Filosofía para niños*. Buenos Aires: Manatial, 1999.

Adorno, Theodor. *Critical Models: Interventions and Catchwords*. New York: Columbia University Press, 2005.

Alonso, Ángel. "La soledad de las guerreras de Santa Martha." *Revista Internacional de Filosofía Aplicada HASER* 10 (2019): 13–25.

Amir, Lydia. *Rethinking Philosophers' Responsibility*. Cambridge: Cambridge Scholar Publishing, 2017.

Antón Pacheco, José Antonio. *El ser y los símbolos*. Madrid: Mandala, 2010.

Antoranz, Adriana Atencio. "El cuidado de sí desde la ética del psicoanálisis." PhD diss., Universidad Complutense, 2018.

Aranguren, José Luis. "La experiencia de la vida." In *Experiencia de la vida*, 23–50. Madrid: Alianza, 1969.

Arendt, Hannah. *Eichmann in Jerusalem: A Report on the Banality of Evil*. London: Penguin Classics, 2006.

Barrientos-Rastrojo, José. *Introducción al asesoramiento y la orientación filosófica*. Sevilla: X-XI, 2005.

Barrientos-Rastrojo, José. "Del pensar zambranista a la filosofía poiética en la consulta filosófica." In *Philosophers as Philosophical Counselors*, 207–221. Sevilla: X-XI, 2006.

Barrientos-Rastrojo, José. "Philosophical Counseling as Poietic Philosophy." *Philosophical Practice* 3 (2006): 17–27.

Barrientos-Rastrojo, José. "El atardecer del Pensamiento Crítico. Disquisiciones poético-zambranistas sobre el *Critical Thinking*." *Proyectos de Vida* 3 (2007): 22–7.

Barrientos-Rastrojo, José. *Vectores zambranianos para una teoría de la Filosofía Aplicada a la Persona*. Sevilla: Universidad de Sevilla, 2010.

Barrientos-Rastrojo, José. *Resolución de conflictos desde la*

Filosofía Aplicada y desde la Mediación. Lisboa-Madrid: Universidad Católica Portuguesa – Visión Libros, 2010.

Barrientos-Rastrojo, José. "La filosofía aplicada desde el pensamiento crítico y desde la racionalidad extendida. Del espíritu del cartesianismo y el hegelianismo al del unamunismo y el zambranismo." In *Temas de hoje. Temas de sempre. Educaçao, ética e filosofia prática*, coordinated by Eugénio Oliveira, 152–77. Braga: APEFP, 2012.

Barrientos-Rastrojo, José. "Fronteras analíticas de la racionalidad social contemporánea." *Sociología y tecnociencia* 3, no. 2 (2013): 71–88.

Barrientos-Rastrojo, José. "My involvement in Philosophical Practice." In *Philosophical Practice. Five Questions*, edited by Jeanette Bresson Ladegaard Knox and Jan Kyrre Olsen Friis, 15–32. Copenhagen: Automatic Press – Vince INC, 2013.

Barrientos-Rastrojo, José. "An *Experience* workshop with groups. Theory and practice." In *The Socratic Handbook*, edited by Michael Noah Weiss, 375–83. Zürich: Lit Verlag, 2015.

Barrientos-Rastrojo, José. "Experience and anagogic hermeneutic of symbol in Philosophical practice." *Journal of Humanities Therapy* 6, no. 1 (2015): 21–47.

Barrientos-Rastrojo, José. "L'orientamento esperienziale nella Filosofia Applicata como ampliamento della tendenza logico-argomentativa." *Rivista Italiana di Counseling Filosofico* 11 (2015): 9–31.

Barrientos-Rastrojo, José. "L'Educazione e la Filosofia Esperienziale Applicata come ricerca dell'originario. Da Maria Zambrano a Kitaro Nishida." In *La Pratica filosófica: una questione di dialogo. Teorie, proggeti ed esperienze*, edited by Elisabetta Zamarchi, Luca Nave, and Giancarlo Marinelli (Turin: Carta e Penna, 2016), 21–9.

Barrientos Rastrojo, José. "La Filosofía con Niños como experiencia transformadora. Una propuesta en organizaciones sin ánimo de lucro." *Childhood & Philosophy* 15, no. 32 (2019):

1–28.

Barrientos Rastrojo, José. "Philosophical practice as experience and travel." *Socium i vlast* 4, no. 78 (2019): 29–44.

Barrientos Rastrojo, José. *Hambre de filosofía*, Pamplona: Next Door Publishers, 2021

Barrientos, José, and Jesús Gómez. "Can wisdom be taught by philosophical practice? An Experimental Research." *Journal of Humanities Therapy* 10, no. 3 (2019): 35–61.

Bawer, Wolfgang. *Historia de la filosofía china.* Barcelona: Herder, 2009.

Benjamin, Walter. *Selected Writings/Walter Benjamin, Vol. 2, Part 2, 1927-1930.* Harvard: Harvard University Press, 2005.

Benjamin, Walter. *Radio Benjamin.* Tres Cantos: Akal, 2015.

Bernard of Clairvaux. *Obras completas de San Bernardo V. Sermones sobre el Cantar de los cantares.* Madrid: BAC, 1983.

Beuchot, Mauricio. *Las dos caras del símbolo: el ícono y el ídolo.* Puebla: BUAP, 2013.

Bixio, Beatriz. "El enigma de las subjetividades." In *A pesar del encierro. Prácticas políticas, culturales y educativas en prisión,* edited by Mauricio Manchado, María Chiponi, and Rodrigo Castillo (Rosario: Espacio santafesino, 2017), 133–42.

Brenifier, Óscar. *Filosofar como Sócrates.* Valencia: Diálogo, 2011.

Brenifier, Óscar. *La práctica de la filosofía en la escuela primaria.* Valencia: Diálogo, 2012.

Buber, Martín. *Yo y tú.* Madrid: Caparrós, 1995).

Bugossi, Tomaso. "La poética de la luz y de la razón creadora: Antonio Machado y María Zambrano." In *Actas III Congreso Internacional sobre la vida y obra de María Zambrano: María Zambrano y la "edad de Plata" de la cultura española* (Vélez-Málaga: Fundación María Zambrano, 2004), 46–55.

Camhy, Daniela G., and Gunter Iberer. "Philosophy for Children: A Research Project for further mental and personality development of primary and secondary school pupils." *Thinking*

7, no. 4 (1988): 18–25.

Carreras, Carla. "Filosofía para Niños: el desarrollo global de las habilidades de pensamiento." In *Filosofía para niños y capacitación democrática freiriana*, edited by José Barrientos Rastrojo (Madrid: Liber Factory, 2013), 91–113.

Cassirer, Ernst. *The Philosophy of Symbolic Forms, Volume 1: Language*. New Haven and London: Yale University Press, 1955.

Cassirer, Ernst. *An Essay on Man: An Introduction to a Philosophy of Human Culture*. New Haven and London: Yale University Press, 1977.

Caturelli, Alberto. *Historia de la filosofía en la Argentina 1600-2000*. Buenos Aires: Editorial de ciencia y cultura y Universidad del Salvador, 2001.

Charabati, Esther. "La filosofía de café: el primer café filosófico en México." *Revista Internacional de Filosofía Aplicada HASER* 11 (2020): 63–91.

Cirlot, Juan Eduardo. *Diccionario de símbolos*. Madrid: Siruela, 2018.

Cohen, Elliot D. *Philosophers at work. An Introduction to Issues and Practical Uses of Philosophy*. New York: Sanders College Publishers, 1989.

Comte-Sponville, André. *El amor. La soledad*. Barcelona: Paidós, 2000.

Curnow, Trevor. *Wisdom, Intuition and Ethics*. Hants: Ashgate, 1999.

Curnow, Trevor. *Wisdom in the Ancient World*. London: Duckworth, 2010.

Cruz, Raúl. "¿Habrá una filosofía p'urhépecha?" *Cultura P'urhépecha*, February 25, 2011, http://www.purepecha.mx/threads/4153-%C2%BFHabr%C3%A1-una-Filosof%C3%ADa-P-urh%C3%A9pecha.

D'Agostini, Franca. *Analíticos y continentales. Guía de la filosofía de los últimos treinta años*. Madrid: Cátedra, 2000.

de Haas, Leon. *Skeptical Interventions. A Critical View of Philosophical Practice*. Roermond: Platopraktijk, 2018.

Descartes, Rene. *The Discourse on the Method*. New York: The Liberal Arts Press, 1950.

Dewey, John. *Art as Experience*. New York: Capricorn Books, 1958.

Dewey, John. *How we think*. New York: Dover Publications, 2003.

Diestler, Sherry. *Becoming a Critical Thinker: A User-friendly Manual*. New York: MacMillan, 1994.

Dilthey, Wilhelm. *Gesammelte Schriften I*. Göttingen: Vandenhoeck & Ruprecht, 1973.

Dilthey, Wilhelm. *Introduction to the Human Sciences Volume 1*. Princeton, NJ: Princeton University Press, 1989.

Echeverría, Eugenio. *Filosofía para niños*. México DF: SM, 2006.

Ennis, Robert H. *Critical thinking*. New Jersey: Prentice Hall, 1996.

Epictetus. *The Discourses as Reported by Arrian, The Manual, and Fragments, Vol. I*. Cambridge, MA, London: Harvard University Press, William Heinemann Ltd., 1956.

Epictetus. *Enchiridion*. Mineola, NY: Dover Publications, Inc., 2004.

Epictetus. *Discourses, Fragments, Handbook*. Oxford: Oxford University Press, 2014.

Esquirol, Josep Maria. *La resistencia íntima. Ensayo para una filosofía de la proximidad*. Barcelona: Acantilado, 2015.

Feary, Vaughana. "Philosophical Practice in correctional facilities. Theory and practice." *Journal of Humanities Therapy* 4, no. 19 (2013).

Foucault, Michel. *Discipline and Punish: The Birth of the Prison*. New York: Vintage Books, 1979.

Foucault, Michel. *Madness and Civilization: A History of Insanity in the Age of Reason* (New York: Vintage Books, 1988).

Foucault, Michel. *The Hermeneutics of the Subject: Lectures at the*

Collège de France 1982-82. New York: Palgrave MacMillan, 1994.

Freire, Paulo. *Pedagogia do oprimido*. Rio de Janeiro: Paz e Terra, 1970.

Friedrich, Carl. *The Philosophy of Kant*. New York: Modern Library, 1949.

Gadamer, Hans-Georg. *Truth and Method*. New York: The Cross Road Publishing Company, 1982.

Gadamer, Hans-Georg. *The Relevance of the Beautiful and Other Essays*. Cambridge: Cambridge University Press, 1986.

Gadamer, Hans-Georg. "Gadamer's Philosophical Legacy." *Symposium* 6, no. 2 (2002): 115–34.

García Moriyón, Félix (coord.). *La estimulación de la inteligencia racional y la inteligencia emocional*. Madrid: Ediciones de la Torre, 2002.

García Moriyón, Félix, Roberto Colom, Santos Lora, María Rivas, and Vicente Traver. "Valoración de 'Filosofía para Niños': un programa de enseñar a pensar." *Psicothema* 12, no. 2 (2000): 207–11.

Gardner, Susan. "Participation in a Community of Inquiry Nourishes Participants' Perspective-taking Capacity: A Report of a Two Year Empirical Study. Philosophy for Children on Top of the World." *Educational and Child Psychology* 20, no. 2 (1999): 65–79.

Giner de los Ríos, Francisco. *Obras selectas*. Madrid: Espasa Calpe, 2004.

González Valles, Jesús. *Historia de la filosofía japonesa*. Madrid: Tecnos, 2002.

Gronke, Horst, and Uwe Nitsch. "Moving through Dialogue – Free Thinking in a Confined Space. Socratic Dialogue in Tegal Penal Institution," *Practical Philosophy* 5, no. 2 (2003): 13–25.

Gutteridge, Moira. *Constructive Critical Thinking*. Toronto: Hartcourt Brace, 1995.

Habermas, Jürgen. *Toward a Rational Society: Student Protest,*

Science and Politics. Boston, MA: Beacon Press, 1970.

Hadot, Pierre. *Philosophy as a Way of Life*. New Jersey: Blackwell, 1995.

Heidegger, Martin. *Vorträge und Aufsätze*. Stuttgart: Klett-Cotta Verlag, 2003.

Heidegger, Martin. *Was ist Metaphysik?* Frankfurt am Main: Verlag Vittorio Klostermann, 2006.

Heidegger, Martin. *Basic Writings*. New York: HarperCollins, 2008.

Heidegger, Martin. *Being and Time*. New York: State University of New York Press, 2010.

Hölderlin, Friedrich. *Hyperion, or the Hermit in Greece*. Cambridge, UK: Open Book Publishers, 2019.

Honneth, Axel. *Disrespect: The Normative Foundations of Critical Theory*. Cambridge & Malden, MA: Polity Press, 2007, Kindle.

Honneth, Axel. *The Struggle for Recognition: The Moral Grammar of Social Conflicts*. Cambridge, MA: Polity Press, 1995.

Honneth, Axel. *La sociedad del desprecio*. Madrid: Trotta, 2011.

Honneth, Axel. *Freedom's Right: The Social Foundations of Democratic Life*. New York: Polity Press, 2014.

Honneth, Axel, and Avishai Margalit. "Recognition." *Proceedings of the Aristotelian Society*, Supplementary Volumes 75 (2001): 111–39.

Horkheimer, Max. *Critical Theory: Selected Essays*. New York: Continuum, 2002.

Horkheimer, Max. *Critique of Instrumental Reason*. London & New York: Verso, 2012, Kindle.

Horkheimer, Max. *Eclipse of Reason*. Eastford (CT): Martino Fine Books, 2013, Kindle.

Horkheimer, Max, and Theodor Adorno. *Dialectic of Enlightenment: Philosophical Fragments*. Stanford: Stanford University Press, 2002.

Hume, David. *Essays Moral, Political and Literary*. London, Edinburgh, Glasgow, New York and Toronto: Henry Frowde,

1904.

Hume, David. *An Enquiry Concerning Human Understanding*. New York: The Liberal Arts Press, Inc., 1955 [1748].

Husserl, Edmund. *Experience and Judgment: Investigations in a Genealogy of Logic*. Evanston: Nothwestern University Press, 1973, Kindle.

Husserl, Edmund. *Ideas Pertaining to a Pure Phenomenology and to a Phenomenological Philosophy*. The Hague/Boston/Lancaster: Martinus Nijhoff Publishers, 1983.

James, William. *The Varieties of Religious Experience: A Study in Human Nature*. New York, London, Bombay, Calcutta and Madras: Longmans, Green & Co., 1917.

James, William. *Pragmatism*. New York: Dover Publications, Inc., 1995.

Jauss, Hans-Robert. *Pequeña apología de la experiencia estética*. Barcelona: Paidós, 2002.

Jeffries, Stuart. *Grand Hotel Abyss: The Lives of the Frankfurt School*. London and New York: Verso Books, 2016.

Johnson, Ralph H., and Anthony A. Blair. *Logical Self-defense*. Toronto: McGraw Hill, 1977.

Julien, François. *Un sabio no tiene ideas o el otro de la filosofía*. Madrid: Siruela, 2001.

Kandinsky, Wassily. *Concerning the Spiritual in Art*. New York: Dover Publications Inc., 1977.

Kopenawa, Davi, and Bruce Albert. *A queda do céu. Palavras dum xamã yanomami, A queda do ceu*. São Paulo: Schwarcz, 2015.

Kojcic, Zoran. "Socratic walk." *Revista Internacional de Filosofía Aplicada HASER* 8 (2017): 67–90.

Kojcic, Zoran. "Performance oriented method in philosophical counseling." PhD diss., University of Sofía, 2019.

Lao-Tse. *The Tao Teh King, or the Tao and Its Characteristics*. New York: The Project Gutenberg EBook, 2008.

Lago, Juan Carlos. *Redescribiendo la comunidad de investigación. Pensamiento complejo y exclusión* social. Madrid: Ediciones de la Torre, 2006.

Lahav, Ran. "Much More than Critical Thinking." Accessed January, 15, 2006. http://www.geocities.com/ranlahav/Reflection_4.html.

Lahav, Ran. *Stepping out of Plato's Cave. Philosophical Counseling, Philosophical Practice and Self-transformation.* Vermont: Lovey books, 2016.

Lahav, Ran. "The Philosophical Gardener: A New Paradigm for Philosophical Practice." In *New Frontiers in Philosophical Practice*, edited by Lydia Amir, 34–54. Cambridge, Cambridge Scholar Press, 2017.

Lahav, Ran. "Mexico ICPP 2018: The boundaries of philosophy." Accessed November 15, 2019. htttps://philopractice.org/web/blog/mexico-iccp-2018-the-boundaries-of-philosophy.

León Portilla, Miguel. *La filosofía nahual estudiada en sus fuentes.* México DF: Instituto Indigenista Interamericano, 1956.

León Portilla, Miguel. *Los antiguos mexicanos a través de sus crónicas y cantares*. México DF: Fondo de Cultura Económica, 1994.

León Portilla, Miguel. "Flor y canto. Otra forma de percibir la realidad." In *Coordenadas 2050*. Ciudad de México: UNAM, 2016.

Levinas, Emmanuel. *Humanismo del otro hombre*. Madrid: Caparrós Editores, 1993.

Lezama Lima, José, María Zambrano Alarcón, and María Luisa Bautista. *Correspondencia*. Espuela de Plata, Madrid, 2006.

Lipman, Matthew. *Thinking in Education*, Cambridge: Cambridge University Press, 2003.

Lipman, Matthew, Ann M. Sharp, and Fredrick S. Oscayan. *Philosophy in the Classroom*. Upper Montclair, N.J.: Institute for the Advancement of Philosophy for Children, Montclair State College, 1977.

Lipovetsky, Gilles. *El crepúsculo del deber. La ética indolora de los nuevos tiempos democráticos*. Barcelona: Anagrama, 1994.

Lohmar, Dieter. "The Phenomenological Method of Eidetic Intuition and Its Clarifications as Eidetic Variation." In *Husserl: German Perspectives*, edited by John J. Drummond and Otfried Höffe, 110–32. New York, Fordham University Press, 2019.

Machado, Antonio. *Proverbios y cantares*. Madrid: Ediciones El País, 2003.

Machado, Antonio. *Juan de Mairena*. Madrid: Cátedra, 2006.

Manchado, Mauricio, María Chiponi, and Rodrigo Castillo. "Presentación." In *A pesar del encierro*, edited by Mauricio Manchado, María Chiponi, and Rodrigo Castillo, 11–8. Rosario: Espacio santafesino, 2017.

Mannheim, Karl. *Ideology and Utopia: An Introduction to the Sociology of Knowledge*. New York: Harcourt, Brace & World, Inc., 1936.

Marcus Aurelius. *Complete Works of Marcus Aurelius*. Hastings: Delphi Classics, 2015.

Marías, Julián. "Un escorzo de la experiencia de la vida." In *La experiencia de la vida*, VV. AA., 101ff. Madrid, Alianza, 1969.

Marinoff, Lou. *Plato, Not Prozac!: Applying Eternal Wisdom to Everyday Problems*. New York: HarperCollins Publishers, Inc., 2000.

Marinoff, Lou. "Dada as Philosophical Practice, and Vice Versa: Reflections on the Centenary of the Cabaret Voltaire." In *New Frontiers in Philosophical Practice*, edited by Lydia Amir, 4–32. Cambridge: Cambridge Scholar Press, 2017.

Marinoff, Lou, and Daisaku Ikeda. *The Inner Philosopher: Conversations on Philosophy's Transformative Power*. Cambridge, MA: Ikeda Center for Peace, Learning, and Dialogue, 2012.

Marset, Juan Carlos. *María Zambrano. I. Los años de formación.* Fundación José Manuel Lara, Sevilla, 2004.

Martin, John F., and Mark L. Wenstein. "Thinking Skills and Philosophy for Children: The Bethlehem Program, 1982-1983." *Analytic Teaching* 5, no. 2 (1985): 28–31.

Marx, Karl. *Capital: A Critical Analysis of Capitalist Production.* London: Swan Sonnenschein, Lowrey, & Co., 1887.

Mendoça, Dina. *Brincar a pensar. Manual de filosofía para crianças.* Lisboa: Plátano, 2011.

Merleau-Ponty, M. *Phenomenology of Perception.* New York: The Humanities Press, 1962.

Moreno Márquez, César. "Tentativas Sobre el Rostro. Eidos y Punctum." *Er: Revista de Filosofía* 19, no. 19 (1995), 103–29.

Moreno Márquez, César. "Break/Freak: Fenómeno (Notas para una geneidética: Eidos y monstrum)." *Daimon. Revista de Filosofía* 32 (2004), 55–75.

Moreno Márquez, César. "Eidos y periferia. rutina y trascendencia in extremis en el horizonte de una humanidad proteica e híbrida," *Recerca* 12 (2012): 24.

Moreno Márquez, César. "De los objetos impelentes. ¿Quién iba a imaginarlos? Contribución a una fenomenología de la imaginación como configuración de escenas," *Anuario filosófico* 51, no. 2 (2018): 299–300.

Moreno Márquez, César. "De ida y por principio: no sin Fenomenología. Terapia filosófica y mundo de la vida." In *La Filosofía como terapia en la sociedad actual: desafíos filosóficos de nuestro tiempo*, edited by Juan José Garrido Periñán, Cristian de Bravo, and José Ordóñez. Sevilla: Fénix, 2016.

Mosterín, Jesús. *Racionalidad y acción humana.* Madrid: Alianza, 1987.

Nishida, Kitaro, *An Inquiry into the Good.* New Haven and London: Yale University Press, 1990.

Nomen, Jordi. *El niño filósofo y el arte, Cómo favorecer que los niños desarrollen el pensamiento creativo*. Barcelona: Arpa y Alfil Editores, 2019.

Nozick, Robert. *The Examined Life: Philosophical Meditations*. New York: Simon & Schuster, 1989.

Ortega, Juan Fernando. *Filosofía andaluza y filosofía en Andalucía. Delimitación conceptual* (Málaga: Universidad de Málaga, 2000.

Ortega, Juan Fernando. "Prologue." In *Filosofía y educación*, by María Zambrano. Málaga: Ágora, 2007.

Ortega y Gasset, Juan. *Obras completas 8*. Madrid: Alianza, 1994.

Ortega y Gasset, Juan. *Obras completas 2*. Madrid: Alianza, 1998.

Ortega y Gasset, Juan. *Historia como Sistema*. Madrid: Alianza, 1999.

Panikkar, Raimon. *Iconos del misterio. La experiencia de Dios*. Barcelona: Península, 1999.

Paredes, María del Carmen. "El concepto de 'sabiduría' en *Idiota de sapientia*." *Anuario filosófico* 28 (1995): 671–94.

Paul, Richard W., and Linda Elder. *Critical Thinking. Tools for Taking Charge of Your Professional and Personal Life*. New Jersey: Pearson FT Press, 2013.

Perelman, Chaïm, and Lucie Olbrechts-Tyteca. *Tratado de la Argumentación. La Nueva Retórica*. Madrid: Gredos, 1989.

Perniola, Mario. *Del Sentir*, Valencia: Pretextos, 2008.

Philips, Christopher, *Socrates Cafe: A Fresh Taste of Philosophy*. New York/London: W.W, Norton and Co., 2002.

Pogge, Thomas, and Luis Cabrera. "Académicos contra la pobreza: una idea para la que ha llegado su tiempo." *Revista Internacional de Filosofía Aplicada HASER* 3 (2012): 193–218.

Queraltó Moreno, Ramón. *La estrategia de Ulises o ética para una sociedad tecnológica*. Sevilla, DOSS, 2008.

Raabe, Peter. *Philosophical Counseling. Theory and Practice*. Westport: Praeger, 2001.

Raabe, Peter. *Philosophy's Role in Counseling and Psychotherapy*. Maryland: Rowan, 2014.

Reynolds, John, et al. *The Holy Bible, translated from the Latin Vulgate*. Douay: English College, 1609.

Rice, Eugene F. *The Renaissance Idea of Wisdom*. Boston: Harvard University Press, 1958.

Rickman, Hans Peter. *Wilhelm Dilthey: Pioneer of the Human Studies*. London: Paul Elek, 1979.

Ricoeur, Paul. *Hermeneutics & the Human Sciences*. Cambridge: Cambridge University Press, 1981.

Ricoeur, Paul. *Del texto a la acción*. México DF: Fondo de Cultura Económica, 2002.

Rilke, Rainer Maria. *Rilke's Book of Hours: Love Poems to God*. New York: Riverhead Books, 1996.

Rojas, Víctor (ed.) *Filosofía para niños: diálogos con menores infractores*. Bogotá: UNIMINUTO, 2015.

Romano, Claude. *Lo posible y el acontecimiento*. Santiago de Chile: Ediciones Universidad Alberto Hurtado, 2008.

Romano, Claude. *El acontecimiento y el mundo*. Salamanca: Sígueme, 2012.

Rorty, Richard. *Contingency, Irony and Solidarity*. Cambridge: Cambridge University Press, 1991.

Rorty, Richard. "Philosophy and the Future," in *Rorty & Pragmatism: The Philosopher Responds to his Critics*, edited by Herman J. Saatkamp, Jr., 197–206. Nashville & London: Vanderbilt University Press, 1995.

Ruiz Calvente, Martín. "Antonio Machado en María Zambrano." *El búho* (2007), 23–50.

Sartre, Jean-Paul. *Being and Nothingness: An Essay on Phenomenological Ontology*. New York: Philosophical Library, 1956.

Sátiro, Angélica. *Jugar a pensar. Recursos para aprender a pensar en educación infantil (4-5 años)*. Puebla: SEP, 2008.

Sátiro, Angélica. *La mariquita Juanita*, 2nd ed. Barcelona: Editorial Octaedro, 2017.

Scheleiermacher, Friedrich. *Los discursos sobre hermenéutica*. Navarra: Universidad de Navarra, 1991.

Schick, Frederic. *Making Choices: A Recasting of Decision Theory*. Cambridge: Cambridge University Press, 1997.

Seneca, Lucius Annaeus. *Minor Dialogues: Together with the Dialogue on Clemency*. London: George Bell and Sons, 1889.

Seneca, Lucius Annaeus. *The Complete Moral Letters to Lucilius*. Ottawa: Stoici Civitas Press, 2013.

Scheler, Max. *Ordo amoris*. Madrid: Caparrós, 1996.

Schuster, Shlomit. *Philosophy Practice: An Alternative to Counseling and Psychotherapy*. Westport: Praeger, 1999.

Shibles, Warren. "The philosophical practitioner and emotion." In *Thinking through Dialogue*, edited by Trevor Curnow, 50–7. Oxted: Practical Philosophy Press, 2001.

Singer, Peter. *The life you can save. Acting now to end world poverty*. New York, Picador, 2009.

Spranger, Eduard. *La experiencia de la vida*. Buenos Aires: Realidad, 1949.

Velasco, Juan Martín. *El fenómeno místico. Estudio comparado*. Madrid: Trotta, 2003.

VV. AA. *ETOR: Definición y metodología*. Sevilla: XXI, 2002.

VV. AA. "Why Are We Needed?" *Philosophy in Prison*. Accessed February 1, 2020. https://www.philosophyinprison.com/why-we-are-needed.

Yalom, Irvin D. *Quando Nietzsche chorou*. Parede: Saída de Emergencia Parede, 2007.

Zambrano, Blas. *Artículos, relatos y otros escritos*. Badajoz: Diputación de Badajoz, 1998.

Zambrano, María. *El sueño creador*. Madrid: Turner, 1986.

Zambrano, María. *Notas de un método*. Madrid: Editorial Mondadori, 1989.

Zambrano, María. *El pensamiento vivo de Séneca*. Madrid: Cátedra, 1992.

Zambrano, María. *La confesión: género literario*. Madrid: Siruela, 1995.

Zambrano, María. *Filosofía y poesía*. Mexico DF: Fondo de cultura económica, 2001.

Zambrano, María. *Cartas de la Pièce (correspondencia con Agustín Andreu)*. Valencia: Pretextos-Universidad Politécnica de Valencia, 2002.

Zambrano, María. *Hacia un saber sobre el alma*. Madrid: Alianza, 2004.

Zubiri, Xabier. "Sócrates y la sabiduría griega." *Escorial* 2 (1940): 189.